YAVANAPRIYA

YAVANAPRIYA

The Story of
Black Pepper and the

ARAMAIC
MALABARI

EASO VARGHESE

YAVANAPRIYA

Published by Happy Self Publishing
www.happyselfpublishing.com

For my dear wife Omana

Contents

Acknowledgements

I would like to thank my dear wife Omana - a postgraduate in history and a history teacher for twenty years. I thank her for her support in researching history for the book as an-inhouse consultant and giving me intellectual space to study and write. Without her unflinching support I would never have attempted a historical novel.

Minoo and Resina, my nephew and niece in-law, were a part of the project since its conceptualization. I thank them for encouraging me to shape the storyline with their valuable suggestions.

My daughter Tina helped me to acquire a substantial digital library to support my research with editions from overseas market which proved to be the backbone of the study. I also thank her for her critical reading of the manuscript and suggestions.

The map and the timeline accompanying the text is created by my son Anup and daughter-in-law Reena. The places and rulers in the story are better understood with their help. The manuscript was critically fact-checked by Reena. I thank them both for their help and suggestions in bringing clarity to the work.

I thank my editor Ms Sunaina Narang and the entire team at HSP for their support in showing the book light of the day with their professionalism in book publishing.

Not to Scale

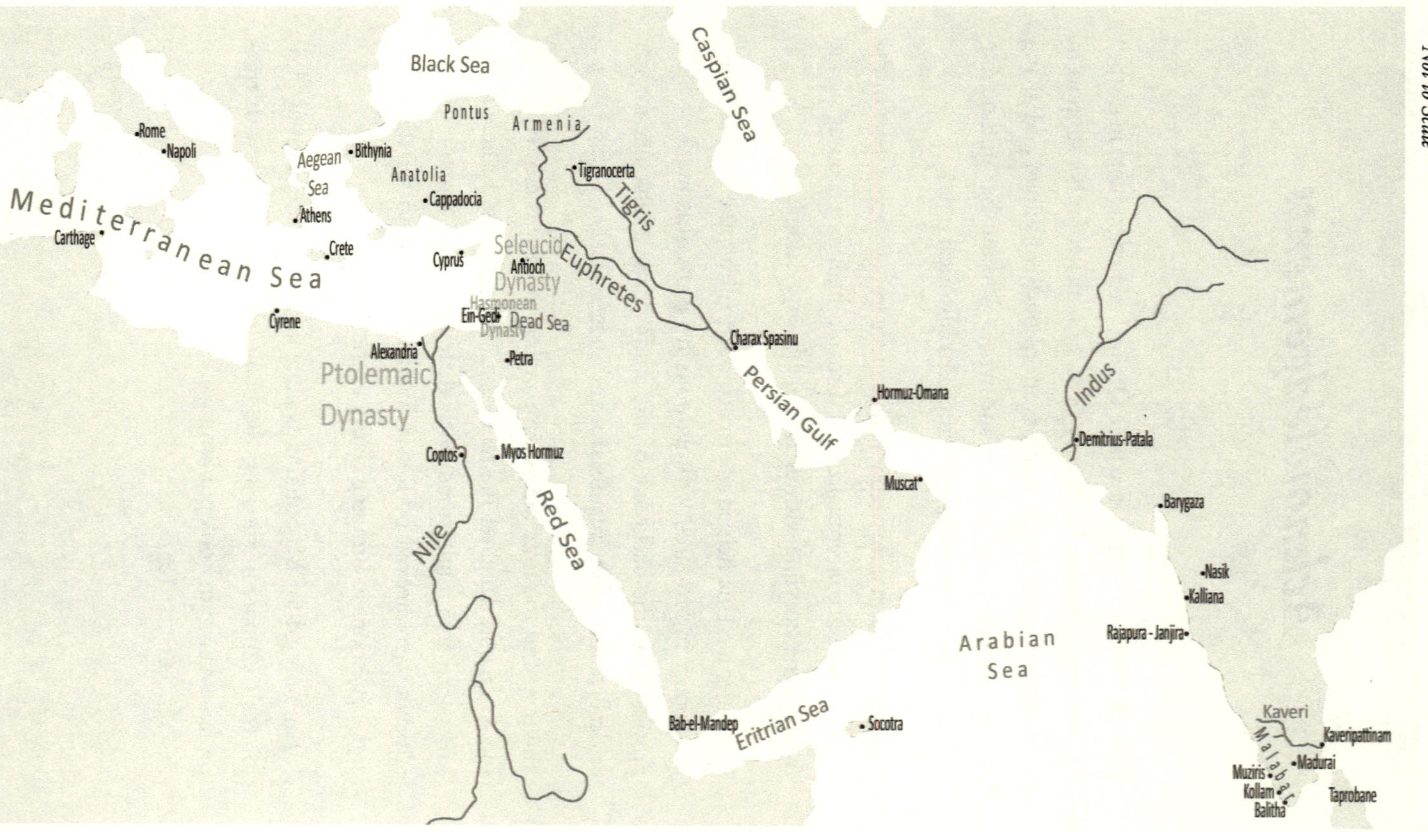
Mediterranean Sea
Black Sea
Pontus
Armenia
Caspian Sea
Rome
Napoli
Carthage
Aegean Sea
Bithynia
Anatolia
Athens
Crete
Cappadocia
Cyprus
Cyrene
Tigranocerta
Tigris
Seleucid Dynasty
Euphretes
Antioch
Dead Sea
Ein Gedi
Hasmonean Dynasty
Alexandria
Petra
Charax Spasinu
Persian Gulf
Hormuz-Omana
Ptolemaic Dynasty
Coptos
Myos Hormuz
Nile
Red Sea
Muscat
Indus
Demetrius-Patala
Barygaza
Bab-el-Mandep
Eritrian Sea
Socotra
Arabian Sea
Rajapura - Janjira
Nasik
Kalliana
Kaveri
Muziris
Kollam
Balitha
Madurai
Kaveripattinam
Taprobane

Timeline

Time	Ptolmeic Dynasty of Egypt	Selucid Dynasty of Syria	Hasmonaean Dynasty of Judea
170 BC		Antiochus IV Epiphanes	Mattathias Asamoneus
		Antiochus V Eupator	Judas Maccabeus
160 BC		Demetrius I Sorter	
150 BC	Ptolemy VIII Euergates II (Physcon)		Jonathan Apphus
	Married Cleopatra II and then Cleopatra III.	Alexander I Balas	
	163-145 B.C : A public rioting expelled him and recalled Ptolemy VI Philometor	Antiochus VI Epiphanes	
140 BC	*131-127 B.C. : Was Temporarily expelled from Alexandra by Cleopatra II and then recociled with her. In this period Cleopatra II Philometora Soteira ruled*	Demetrius II Nicator	Simon Matthes
		Antiochus VII Sidetes	
130 BC		Demetrius II Nicator	
		Antiochus VIII Grypus with Cleopatra I Thea (regent)	John Hyrcanus I
120 BC		Antiochus VIII Grypus	
110 BC	Cleopatra III Pilometor Soteria (Kokke) — Jointly with **Ptolemy IX**	Antiochus VIII Grypus / Antiochus IX Cyzenicus	
	Cleopatra III Pilometor Soteria (Kokke) — Jointly with **Ptolemy X**		Judah Aristobulus I
100 BC	Ptolemy X Alexander I	Seleucus VI Epiphanes	
		Demetrius III Eucaerus / Antiochus X Eusebes	Alexander Jannaeus
90 BC	Ptolemy IX Soter II (Lathyros)	Antiochus XII Dionysus	
80 BC	Berebike III Philopator with Ptolemy XI Alexander II	Cleopatra Selene (regent)	
		*83 B.C the syrians tired of selucid dynastic struggles offered **Tigranus the great** of Armenia the crown*	John II Hyrcanus and Alexandera Shlomziyyon
70 BC	Ptolemy XII Neos Dionysons (Auletes)	Antiochus XIII Asiaticus	Judah II Aristobulus
		Philip II Philoromaeus	
60 BC		< Roman Province >	John II Hyrcanus
50 BC	Cleopatra VII Thea Neotera — jointly with her brother **Ptolemy XIII**		
	Cleopatra VII Thea Neotera — jointly with her younger brother **Ptolemy XIV**		
40 BC	*(* This is the Cleopatra who as we know had children by Julius Caesar and by Marcus Antomius.. Around 30 B.C)* — jointly with her son **Ptolemy XV Caesarion**		Mattathias II Antigonus
			< Roman Province >
30 BC			

Author's Note

My father served in the 8th Indian division of the British army which saw action in Italy during WW II. As a child his military adventures fascinated me. His travel stories about boarding ship at Bombay voyaging the Persian Gulf and landing at Basra port and traversing the Syrian desert through towns of Kirkuk, Kermanshah, Damascus, and Aleppo remained with me. Then stories of his crossing the Mediterranean Sea to Italy to join the Allies in liberating Italy from fascist forces made him my childhood hero. The 'Monte Cassino' battle off Napoli and the Vesuvius volcano too were in his stories. He would also narrate his visit to the Holy Land and the Dead Sea basin. I remember him telling me how two-thousand-year-old scrolls were found by a shepherd boy in the Qumran hills near Ein-Gedi. My connection to these places widened as I grew.

A small berry, hot and spicy, belonging to Malabar in southern India, also made this wonderful journey to Rome two-thousand years ago. This is the story of black pepper or *Yavanapriya* meaning "passion of the Greeks."

Though the story incorporates historical events, this is a work of fiction, and the chronology of several events has been altered. Names, characters, places, and incidents either are products of my imagination or are used fictitiously. Any resemblance to actual events, or persons living or dead, is entirely coincidental.

Easo Varghese
9 February 2021

PART ONE

1

The Balsam of Judea

Yona remembered fondly the blessed land of Ein-Gedi while he climbed the steep hills of the Tamil country on the southern end of India. Ironically, Ein-Gedi was a large desert oasis in the Jericho plains about eight-hundred feet below mean sea level on the western banks of the Dead Sea. Whereas the Arayankav hills were a part of a tropical rainforest with peaks up to two-thousand five-hundred feet running all along the western shore of India.

There were many beautiful waterfalls in Ein-Gedi true to its meaning in Hebrew - the fountain of the goat kid. Nahal David was the biggest and his favorite. He would swim there to escape the heat of the desert with his friend Eber, or sometimes alone, watching the Ibex goats coming down to drink water. He would spend hours listening to the flute-like calls of the long-tailed birds and the pleasant birdsongs of bulbuls and sunbirds.

Here in southern India, he had found another waterfall like Nahal David called Palaruvi or milky river for its white-water flow. Like in Ein-Gedi the birds and animals were drawn to the water.

It was the month of Sivan (June, 65 BCE). Hebrew months of Sivan and Thammuz coincide with June and July which is the summertime in Judea. People slept out in the open or on housetops as the night temperatures rose.

"What a contrast!" Yona told the veteran soldier Nicanor, who was sitting next to him after a long climb to the first man-made black pepper orchard, handpicked and domesticated from the wild pepper plants growing in the thick, evergreen tropical rainforest. "It rains here constantly with short intervals of sunshine, but Judea is dry and hot," he further observed.

"The climate in Madurai is very hot too, though only a few stadia away," said Nicanor.

He had served as palace guard at Madurai palace for almost five years. Madurai was the capital of the Pandyan Empire of southern India and a major exporter of pearls and spices to the west through the Bactrian Greeks who ruled the Sindh and controlled the port of Demetrius-Patala at the mouth of the river Sindh. Five-hundred Yavana, or Greek guards, were employed by the king as palace guards at Madurai.

"Beyond the mountains towards Madurai it is dry weather during this part of the year, leave alone Ein-Gedi or Judea for that matter. Madurai gets rain like Judea in October," Nicanor explained.

"The mountains stop the rain clouds coming from the west to go further to Madurai beyond these hills. These winds blowing from the west during this time of year bring copious rain for the pepper crop.

The rain also brings the ships from the west. Almost three months of steady wind blowing from the west is our sailing force to the pepper country from ports of the Erythraean Sea," Nicanor continued.

Yona looked towards the western horizon. It was cloudy and dark with the rain clouds. He was expecting a ship from Myos Hormuz, the Red Sea port, with provisions and money. Maybe they are getting ready to sail, he thought.

As the rain grew stronger they took shelter in the watchtower. There were no enemy soldiers to watch out for, but animal life was abundant in the forest, and sometimes the wild boars and elephants destroyed the crops. They did not eat the pepper vines but trampled the trees or standards on which the pepper vines grew entwined.

Suddenly out of nowhere, an elephant calf not more than two months old appeared along with its mother. They were drawn to the pool of rainwater which had collected near the orchard. The calf was running and kicking water with its tiny legs and trunk enjoying the rain and, at short intervals, taking shelter between its mother's legs for protection.

The mother elephant looked up and saw Yona and the soldier sitting on the tree house watchtower and slowly withdrew into the forest.

"This place is also called the Elephant Country because of the elephant population, though smaller than the African breed, they seem bigger than the Seleucid war elephants brought from Pataliputra." Nicanor was unstoppable when the subject of war came up, and he often found ways of weaving it into a conversation.

"Yes, I have seen many of them standing beneath a huge mango tree picking fallen ripe mangoes. A small mango fruit in the wide mouth of an elephant may be insignificant but the sweet mangoes are aplenty for all mongers," said Yona. "The large fruit with a thorny rind, the jackfruit, is also unique to these forests and attract the elephants," Yona added. "It has a sticky latex, but the edible part is so soft and juicy. I am also a big fan."

"The Indian and African elephants, which fought face-to-face at the Battle of Raphia (217 BC), near Gaza for Seleucids King Antiochus III the Great and Ptolemy IV Philopator respectively, were not the same breed as we see here. The Indian Pataliputra elephants, maybe were progenies of the five-hundred elephants Seleucus I Nicator got from India as part of a war treaty. And the dwarf African variety called forest elephants from Nubia were brought to Egypt by the river Nile. Another breed called the African bush elephants are bigger than the ones we see here," Nicanor, the war specialist added.

The discussion turned to tigers which were also found in these forests.

"Tigers live still deeper into the forest and avoid human settlement." Nicanor had seen a couple of them. "People revere the tigers as companions to the hill gods. The monks meditating in the deep forests and living in caves called 'muniara' are believed to keep tamed tigers," Nicanor said.

Sitting on the watch-tower tree house Yona observed the pepper vine plantation. The vineyards of Jericho flashed in his mind which was the model on which this experiment succeeded. The supporting standards were fast-growing shrubs. These standards were pruned twice a year to regulate growth as a single stem and planted ten feet between rows and plants, which gave the look of a vineyard when viewed from a height. Pepper vines trailing on the standards were over two years old and inflorescences were seen on some plants already. This black pepper crop was domesticated from wild varieties of the nearby forests; the same way Jericho farmers domesticated the balsam shrubs. Yona had the agro-technical knowledge to replicate with black pepper what they had achieved with balsam in the Dead Sea basin. Bringing the wild plant to a vineyard-like infrastructure was the uniqueness of the experiment.

"Next year we will be able to include our crop in the shipment." Nicanor was confident.

"Not that fast. I feel the fifth year would give us a significant yield," said Yona.

The Ay kingdom was a small and friendly vassal nation to the Pandyan kings of Tamil country. Yona was glad of the prospect of having a good yield of pepper from the plantations he had established here. But more importantly he was glad to be freeing the people from the prophecy of the chief monk at the Qumran cave monastery. Its weight was a bondage he carried for the past fifty years.

People go to oracles and prophets to know their future but when your destiny is prophesized, one really is a burdened soul. Yona knew better.

● ● ●

Yonas' parents were members of an Israelite sect called Essenes. They lived in a settlement above the village of Ein-Gedi in the Dead Sea basin. Driven out of their homeland by Assyrian and Chaldean onslaughts, Israelites spread to the safest places they could find. When Assyrian servitude was over, the nation shrunk to tribes of Judah and Benjamin alone in size but some groups in the rest of the tribes of Israel also wanted to reunite and waited for their savior. The Essene sect taking steps for regrouping the tribes thus spread out, and his parents, hoping for such a reunion came back to their homeland over fifty years back. Believers of Messianic Judaism were growing in number in upper Galilee and Samaria.

Yona, being the eldest son of the family, was destined to be a monk in the Essene Order, for which his parents dedicated him. The first male child was offered to the monastery for training to be future monks and teachers. They would remain with the parents till about age eleven, under the supervision of the monks, getting trained in languages, the study of religious books and memorizing them with dedication. They would also listen to the talks given by elders at the monastery during festivals and special occasions. A large Essene community, which included Yona's parents, lived in Jericho and Ein-Gedi. Yona's parents had migrated from Ionia, a part of the Greek islands in the Ionian Sea, to join the Essene sect, selling their family business of spice trade. Yona had no memories of Ionia as they left it during his infancy, but his parents had several generations of standing there. His Hebrew name was Yannai, but people called him Yona because it sounded better with Yavana or Younan as the Ionians were called in the east.

The secret of Ein-Gedi was its balsam orchards. Most of the balsam shrubs plantation were in the hands of the ruling family now. Nobody could speak about them or even acknowledge the existence of such plants in Jericho, and it was kept as a royal secret from the outside world. It was believed that those who divulged the secret of the balsam to any outsider would be cursed. It was also believed that God would uproot him from under the heavens.

Balsam of Gilead, also known as Judean balsam was a unique crop which grew only around the Dead Sea basin and nowhere else in the world. Brought to Judea by Queen Sheba as a gift to King Solomon, the balsam was reputed for the aroma its resin produced. Balsam was sold at double its weight in gold and was the backbone of the Judean economy. It was strictly raised at the royal orchard alone and the crop was heavily guarded.

The agro-technical process of production and processing of the resin by the Judean farmers was a secret. The tree plantation would die if the agricultural practices were not done the way perfected by generations of Ein-Gedi farmers. They had the agro-technical monopoly which gave great value to the produce. They would not allow any outsider near the orchard. But during the harvesting of the resin and pruning of the trees, Essene settlers near the village were allowed. The Essenes, being pious and honest people who were poor by choice, who had no greed for wealth and never adorned any perfume, were the ideal choice. Balsam was a wild plant when it was brought to Judea now domesticated under expert hands. It was long extinct in its natural habitat.

Along the shores of the Dead Sea, further north of Nahal David were the Qumran caves. The caves were large enough to accommodate several hundred people at a time. Essene elders stayed and meditated there. Prayer meetings and conferences were also held there. Monks and scholars from other lands would arrive to impart sessions which were attended by Essene families like that of Yona's.

The Essene community, also known as Nazarenes, was made up of monks and lay persons. The monastic community led a communally organized ascetic life in their all but inaccessible caves in the Qumran. The lay members of the group lived in villages around Jericho, married and brought up children and strove to lead a pious and pure spiritual life. However, agriculture was their main occupation in Ein-Gedi. Since the cave monastery was close by, the villagers got a chance to listen to elders and teachers from lands like India, China, Athens, and Alexandria.

Yona always liked these gatherings and never missed one. As a child of twelve, he would show his friends how close he was to the elders. He liked to run errands for the visiting monks hailing from different parts of the world. He could converse in Greek, Aramaic, and Hebrew, which made him a favorite among the visitors.

Yona was eager to be with the cave community. Whenever he got there, he would stay for days together helping the cooks, the scribes or doing any odd job that was needed. Only adult men were qualified for joining the Qumran community. There was an initiation process of a one-year probation and two years of further training. One was eligible for "full table fellowship" upon the swearing of an oath of loyalty to the sect after the training process. Yona, at twelve years of age, would have to wait for several more years to be eligible for the initiation process.

Eber was a scribe in training. He also was a dedicated first-born like Yona, a few years older than him and his best friend. He would soon graduate to papyrus and goatskin to copy documents. Sitting on the mat with folded legs and the writing board on his lap Eber would hold that position for hours together under the supervision of senior monks copying documents. Papermaking was all done at the monastery. And Yona sometimes helped Eber in making pulp from the papyrus plants by passing the pulp through rollers to get thin sheets and then drying them. Senior scribes liked to use papyrus sheets brought from Mizraim (Egypt) because they were smoother and of a better quality and lasted longer.

A scribe was to be knowledgeable of everything. The training was long and hard. Languages, History, Religion, Mathematics, Astronomy, and grammar were all taught to make a scribe worthy of his profession. Aramaic, Hebrew, and Greek took many years to learn. All this knowledge was necessary to understand scripts before copying them.

Yona and Eber were good friends and had many things in common despite the age difference. During the long afternoons at the Nahal David when the elders were resting after their meal they would converse on different topics. Sometimes they would take short donkey rides to the edge of the royal orchards where their parents worked.

It was on one such ride that Eber told him about the curse of Jericho.

"The curse will come true in a few years' time. There are signs already and doom is imminent," Eber said, quoting the elders. "Joshua's curse will fall on the royal family anytime now!"

What is the curse of Joshua? Yona had no clue. He was a little hesitant to ask because Eber sounded as if everybody knew about it.

Eber prodded the donkey with the stick urging it to pick up speed. A donkey ride was always enjoyable for Yona though he was the pillion rider this time.

"What is the curse?" Yona gathered courage to ask.

They had come almost till the Wadi Qelt where the kings' highway to Jerusalem began. This was the location of the royal orchards where their parents were collecting dates for drying. Extended plantations of dates, grapes and balsam were now mostly owned by the royal family. They acquired the area cheaply, it being uncultivated dry lands. The soil was fertile, and the irrigation canals built by the king connecting the various springs and plantations made it prime agricultural property.

"All these agricultural developments are fine…The water from the springs have been diverted at first for irrigation, now they are planning to build palaces and bath houses here." Eber was in an all-knowing mood.

"But they already have the Doq Palace here," Yona quipped.

"That one is the king's son-in-law Ptolemy Abubus's palace," Eber said. "The present King John Hyrcanus I himself is planning winter palaces here and that is viewed by the chief monk as a sign of total annihilation."

"What is wrong with that? It is the king's property anyway." Yona was still puzzled and felt embarrassed to ask again.

"The curse goes back to over a thousand years after the destruction of the city of Jericho. When Prophet Joshua led the Israelites to the Canaan, he cursed the city of Jericho. After the great victory over Jericho, Joshua thanked Yahweh and praised him. Then he said, 'Cursed be the man who builds this city; with his first-born, he shall lay its foundations, and with the youngest shall he set up its gates. And a man accursed shall arise to be a fowler's snare to his people and be the cause of destruction of all his neighbors.'

"The Elders say the old city was right here where the plantation now stands. They are also suspicious about the influence of Romans in building the aqueducts and believe that the palaces also could be their idea. After the incident with King Antiochus IV Epiphanes, the Romans try to interfere in everything regarding Syria, Judea, and Egypt." Eber knew history very well and thought the elders' fear was political too.

Yona chuckled recollecting the incident of the circle the Roman general drew around King Antiochus Epiphanus threatening to attack if he didn't declare the withdrawal of his troops from Egypt before stepping out of the circle. "Those were the previous rulers of the Seleucid dynasty, but now our own people are ruling Judea," he chipped in.

"That is exactly why it is the problem of the land now. Our King John Hyrcanus I himself has prophetic gifts and he has prophesied that his sons will not live in the same peace and happiness as he had known in his last years.

"Do you see the long aqueduct starting from the heights of Wadi Qelt on the northern bank of the wadi?" Eber pointed. "That will bring water from all the springs to the western plains of the royal orchard which the king has recently acquired. They have already planted date palms and balsam shrubs there. Some yielding date palms may have been planted by earlier owners. Anyway, these orchards give regular employment to the lay Essene community living between Qumran hills and Ein-Gedi."

The watch towers built at the four corners of the orchard were large enough to accommodate several guards on duty and their living quarters in the upper level while the lower level was the processing area for date honey and perfume of balsam. The space also included a vine press.

"Your parents are here!" yelled a guard to Yona. The workers were leaving for the fields after the meal and some rest.

Yona's mother came out and gave him a handful of dates. "Take care and do not stroll far," she said, hurrying to join her co-workers.

They decided to head back to the monastery. Yona was worried about the doomsday prophecy and the destruction of all the peace and prosperity around.

When they approached the Doq Palace Eber stopped. "Do you know the story of this wretched palace? This was the venue of the multiple murders of King Simon Matthes and his two sons, by the kings' son-in-law Ptolemy Abubus who fortified the small palace and built a citadel to suit the pomp of the governor of Jericho that he was as appointed by King Simon himself. Ptolemy became very wealthy with the balsam of Judea and taxes on the trans-Jordan trade and wanted to be king himself. He plotted with the help of Seleucid Syrian King Antiochus VII Sidetes and looked for an opportunity. He invited King Simon Matthes for a banquet at the citadel and when everybody was under the influence of wine, his soldiers killed the king and his two sons, Matthes and Judas. He could not kill John because he was away at Gadara and had come to know of the murder before the soldiers reached him. He killed the traitors and was declared king and the high priest by the Jews. This is how the present king came into power taking name John Hyrcanus I."

"What happened to Ptolemy Abubus, the killer?" Eber asked.

"He withdrew to the Dagon Fort beyond Jericho with the mother and tortured her in front of John Hyrcanus I trying to bargain his escape. The siege continued till the sabbatical year when it was relaxed as per custom and Ptolemy escaped after killing the mother."

Yona began to understand the historical events and he was anxious to know what happened next and Eber continued.

"Antiochus VII Sidetes came with an army and sieged Jerusalem before the new king could settle down. He blocked all gates to the city and deprived the city of provisions and water. He built several towers along the city wall and started attacking the city with archers and fire canons. King John Hyrcanus I asked for peace for the Feast of Tabernacle and the hostility was stopped for seven days. A peace settlement was reached where the king would pay five-hundred talents (40,000 pounds) of silver and provide an army led by the king as an ally to fight the wars of King Antiochus VII Sidetes of Syria against Parthia. This is when King John Hyrcanus I opened the ancient sculpture of King David at the temple and removed three-thousand talents with which he paid the ransom and created a mercenary army to fight for King Antiochus VII Sidetes as a vassal king," said Eber.

"Maybe this is from where the money for the new palaces and estates at Jericho is coming," Yona interjected.

Some fear crept in Yona's mind. He did not like doomsday theories, but the prophecy of Joshua the Prophet, the king and the elders of Qumran monastery made him uncomfortable. The present rule was peaceful and prosperous. The only thing Yona didn't like about the kingdom was their breaking open the thousand-year-old sculpture of King David at the Jerusalem temple to avert a siege. They had taken three-thousand talents of silver at one time, and maybe many more, he thought.

The picture was falling in place but Yona still had some doubts about the rulers of Mizraim (Egypt). The Nabatean king whose lands bordered Jericho was in peace and Yona knew that they were the lords of caravans and controlled trade everywhere.

"The big power of the region is Mizraim and Ptolemies rule there," Yona murmured.

"Yes, the story of Egypt is also very interesting," Eber overheard what Yona said and caught up with the lead.

"Egypt is now ruled by Ptolemy VIII Euergates II nicknamed Physcon. So much has happened for the past thirty years in Egypt during his reign including a devastating civil war which crippled the country. Jews had great strength in Egypt, and they had resisted the accession of King Ptolemy Physcon with the help of Jewish commanders Onias and Dositheos at the behest of Cleopatra II, the widow of Ptolemy VI Philometor. King Ptolemy Physcon took brutal action as revenge against the Jews after his gaining power. He married Cleopatra II, his deceased brothers' wife and later married her daughter Cleopatra III who was his niece and stepdaughter. This made the mother and daughter fierce rivals. The enmity, at its peak, ended in setting fire to the royal palace which made the king flee to Cyprus and Cleopatra II became the queen. Her other daughter, Cleopatra Thea, was married to Syrian King Demetrius II whose brother Antiochus VII Sidetes was the Syrian king who sided with Ptolemy Abubus, the son-in-law of the Judean king, and laid siege on Jerusalem and got the ransom of five-hundred talents from our King John Hyrcanus I.

"Demetrius II and Cleopatra II jointly tried to prevent Ptolemy Physcon from gaining control over Alexandria from his exile but failed in doing so. This resulted in her fleeing to Syria and her involvement in the murder of Demitrius II. After Ptolemy Physcon regained control of Alexandria, to everyone's surprise, he reconciled with his wives Cleopatra II and Cleopatra III and made them co-rulers.

"Ptolemy Physcon then turned to trade. All western powers turned to the east with a design to capture its trade from the Arabs and the Jews, or for a direct trade with the east. The Romans also were big traders in Egypt by this time. Ptolemy Physcon relaxed his enmity towards the Jews as he took new direction. Slowly the Jewish, Roman and the Arab traders came back to Alexandria, and so did the intellectuals and the teachers from the world over.

"Eight-hundred pairs of tusks of Indian elephants along with large quantities of spices, pearls, gems, and animals were displayed at the triumph at Daphne by the Seleucid King Antiochus II (261-246 BC) which kindled the jealousy of many a king. The show outmatched the display of Ptolemy II (284-246 BC), in his triumph at Alexandria, several years ago. Ptolemy Physcon wanted desperately to steady his dwindling economy and to reestablish the connection his predecessor Ptolemy II had formed with Indian King Asoka even though ignorant about the political situation in India. The Egyptian government knew that the Jews and the Arabs kept a lot of secrets about the trade with the east from them. Ptolemy Physcon had the Nile and the Red Sea at his command, but the trade was taking place on land route from the east. Considering a tax at one fifth of the cargo, the wealth slipping out of Alexandria to the Arabs, the Jews and the Seleucids was enormous."

"Eber, can I ask you something? Why did the Jews go back to Mizraim again after all those years of toil in Mizraim under the pharaohs and the victories they enjoyed under Joshua and later years here in Judea?" asked Yona.

This was not a question Eber could easily answer. "Some people are destined to travel to all habitable lands. They find ways to prosper and rediscover Canaan in any land they reach."

Eber was older and Yona needed an answer. Years of training at the monastery had given him enough knowledge to find an answer to Yona's question.

"It all started with the conquering of our land and Egypt and all the east of Euphrates by Alexander the Great about two-hundred years ago. The Jews knew all the lands of Syria, Egypt, Mesopotamia, Assyria, and Susiana like the palm of their hands for obvious reasons because these nations had subjugated Israelites during various times. They took sweet revenge on all these countries by offering themselves as pilots and land guides to Alexander's army. Jerusalem also welcomed Alexander. The reward from Alexander for this help was the citizenship rights like that of Macedonians in Alexandria for the Jews and separate living quarters in Alexandria in keeping with their national customs.

"However, the reverse exodus to Egypt happened at the time of Ptolemy I Soter (305-282 BC) a few years after the death of Alexander. He lured them with the fertile Nile Valley. Not only people of Jerusalem but also of the countryside, and even those of the hills migrated to Egypt this time. The rich Nile delta produced much bigger yields of corn with less effort than the dry and rocky lands they had. This was also a getaway from their harsh rulers of the Antigonid dynasty which ruled Syria and Judea at that time," Eber concluded.

They finished the dates and found time for a quick dive in the Nahal David before reaching the monastery.

Yona couldn't sleep that night. Even though mentioned as a joke to Eber during the discussion, the incident of Antiochus IV Epiphanes and the Roman general and its gory aftermath kept him awake for a long while during the night.

He shuddered at the thought of those incidents which were often talked about at the monastery. They had shut down the Holy Temple and banned the religion altogether. There was bloodshed everywhere. Hasmoneans led the revolt against the Seleucids and won the war. Simon Matthes (Maccabee) laid the foundation of the Hasmonean dynasty, and the present King John Hyrcanus I was his son.

Could the fulfilment of the curse of Jericho be also as disastrous as the circle the Romans drew around the king? Yona pondered. He hated all wars and bloodshed.

● ● ●

Three Buddhist monks arrived at Qumran that day. They were on their way to Alexandria where a large group of Buddhist scholars and monks resided teaching Buddhist religion. It was the practice of many Buddhist and Jain monks from India to visit Qumran monastery on the way if they were not taking the Red Sea route to Alexandria.

From Charax Spasinu in the Persian Gulf, where the Euphrates and Tigris met the sea, they took the desert route to Petra and diverted to the Dead Sea and Tigris to reach Qumran. The route was difficult due to desert terrain, but frequent caravans of Nabataean merchants towards Petra were available on this route. The monks had an opportunity to sell pearls or precious stones they received as offerings in India. The proceeds were to be used for their stay in Alexandria.

The Essene community at Ein-Gedi was informed of the monks' visit from India and the scheduled prayer meeting at the Qumran cave monastery which the Indian monks would hold. Yona was thrilled at another chance to talk to the saffron-clad monks called Buddha Bhikkhu by the elders. Indian monks were always smiling radiating the true happiness of their body and mind. They recounted many stories and parables during their talk unlike the Greek scholars whose discourses were difficult to understand for a twelve-year-old, Yona thought.

There was a good gathering at the monastery eager to hear the Buddha Bhikkhus. The village community liked the simplicity and truthfulness in their message. The day's topic was on the greatness of giving and the achievement of heavenly bliss or Nirvana in the process.

"A humble act of giving, without being asked for, is called *daan* by the Buddhists. When somebody ask for alms, the act humbles him; but when you give to the needy without it being asked for, the giver is humbled. When a person can give away anything in *daan* including his wealth, prestige, family, and own self without any demand or second thought, he is able to reach the first level of Nirvana," the monk explained to the gathering.

"Therefore," he further explained, "it is difficult for the rich to attain Nirvana. Their possessions tie them down to their mortal sufferings."

He went on to recount the story of a rich man who wanted to attain Nirvana. The rich man led a pure life and did not harm anybody. But still the sorrows of the mortal soul haunted him. When the monks asked him to relieve himself of his wealth and possessions and live the life of a Bhikkhu living on alms and meditation, he turned away with a heavy heart. He loved his possessions, amassed with hard work and struggle, and therefore his sorrows also stayed with him.

"There are kings and wealthy merchants, back in India, giving away possessions and even kingdoms, to join the path of Buddhist teachings," he added.

Yona stayed at the monastery that day. He only wished he had an opportunity to personally meet the Indian monks. The next morning, there was a call from the elders. The head monk of the monastery, the righteous elder, wanted to meet him. This was very unusual and Yona quickly reached the chambers of the head monk.

"Yannai", the head monk called out his Hebrew name, in a very kind and soft voice. "I have an assignment for you," he said.

"Yes, master," Yona replied, looking at the monk. He was face-to-face for the first time with the head monk. The monk's eyes were deep blue, and his silky golden hair was parted in the middle and spilled over to his shoulders. The white garment he was wearing gave him an angelic look. Three other Buddhist monks were also present in the chamber smiling sweetly at Yona in their saffron robes and closely shaven heads.

"You will accompany the Buddhist monks to Alexandria and be there till they want you there. You will have the opportunity to study from them and understand the world around you."

"Yes, master," Yona replied, his heart thumping in excitement.

The head monk blessed Yona and placed his hand on his head and prayed.

Then he prophesied, "This community at Qumran will be destroyed. The congregation will be dispersed to the four corners of the world. The royal support Qumran monastery is receiving from the kingdom of Judea will end and brothers will fight for the kingdom as the sons of Solomon did, bringing disaster to everyone. The holy of the holies will be desecrated. However, the righteous will prevail, grow, and prosper. I am sending you to Egypt. As our forefather Joseph, you will one day, be the deliverer of the community."

All present at the chamber said Amen.

Destiny had a greater role for him rather than being a member of an ascetic group. He was to become their savior. He was destined to show the way, and deliverance to Nazarenes in a new country, thousands of stadia away from their homeland.

● ● ●

Yona pondered over the prophecy after fifty long years, (now in 65 BC) standing among the pepper orchard he raised reminiscing how the black pepper overtook balsam as a synonym of prosperity to the lay Essenes people who lived in the desert oasis of Ein-Gedi.

The prophecy came true after the death of John Hyrcanus I in Judea, his widow died of starvation being imprisoned by her sons. Aristobulus and Antigonus, the king's two sons died mysterious deaths at Jericho palace. Several years later, the civil wars for the crown eventually helped the Romans who annexed Judea and all of Syria as a Roman province and the man accursed as prophesied by prophet Joshua turned out to be John Hyrcanus I, the builder of Jericho.

And somewhere in the process, the Qumran community fled to safer havens, maybe as a reward for their righteous living, Malabar being one such abode.

2

Alexandria and the North Star Dhruva

Yona, as a twelve-year-old, was elated to know that his friend Eber was also allowed to travel with the monks up to Beer Sheba, halfway to the port city of Gaza, from where they would board a ship to Alexandria. Eber was to discuss astronomy with the monks on the way to learn their view of the sun calendar as practiced by the Tamil Indians. The Essenes had a special place for the sun in their astronomical studies and followed the sun calendar unlike the moon calendar followed in rest of Judea. The Essenes thanked God every day in their early morning prayer facing the sun which was believed to brighten lives.

The monks were scholars of astronomy. It was natural for religious leaders to promote the study of astronomy or the heavens – the final abode of humans as taught by them. Indian traditions of astronomy were in scholastic debate at Alexandria as various versions of the solar calendar were gaining popularity in the west.

The chief monk was Jayasena, dark-eyed and over fifty years old with a well-built body for a monk. Nirathasena was tall and lanky and Somadutta was the youngest in his early thirties and handsome. His smile radiated a universal love which drew Yona's attention.

The travel plan was finalized, and a camel caravan organized for their journey across the Judean hills to Beer Sheba. The monks would ride on camelback and the boys would be on their donkeys. The caravan captain and his assistants would attend to the animals and the security for three days travel to Beer Sheba, the land of the wells. The onward journey with trader caravans coming from Petra or Rekhem towards the port of Gaza was already arranged by the monks before coming to Qumran monastery.

Eber had been to Beer Sheba before. The only travel Yona had undertaken away from Ein-Gedi was to Jerusalem which was a steep climb, travelling on top of the mountain ridges and steep hills which they completed in one long day. Now they would travel along the shore of the Dead Sea plains and the hills of Judean desert where the soil was more copper-brown than the off-white limestone hills of Jerusalem. The journey was going to take almost three days.

Yona and Eber had leather water bags resting on their shoulders. Dried dates and figs added to their personal luggage. New sandalims with straps tying up the calf was the new footwear Yona got along with a handcrafted sudarim or head gear from his mother. His father gave him a fine Jewish upper garment called tallith. The whole attire transformed Yona into a very serious-looking Jew sans the beard, but only he knew that the girdle belt was doing the magic of holding them together. One is considered an adult and ready to face the world at twelve years of age in their community and with the added weight of the prophecy, Yona looked a celebrity in the eyes of his mother.

Forage for the donkey was packed like a cushion on which Yona was sitting. There was a small bag filled with corn tied to the donkey's face just below the eyes for the donkey to munch on along the way. Both the donkeys were familiar to their riders and ready, and already munching corn.

They set out early in the morning. The air was cool, and the climb was on a slow gradient hill till they reached the southern end of the Dead Sea, and the party took a western turn circumnavigating the Judean hills where the path opened to dry open desert scattered with rocky hills at many points. The leading camel was tied to the other camel to prevent it from taking a different direction. The caravan was small with only five camels and two donkeys. They had come from Rechem or Petra with the Buddhist monks and would go back to Petra after the party reached Beer Sheba, their destination.

The caravan captain was an elderly man with a half-grown beard. Being fully covered with cloth, his face and hands were the only visible parts. He held the rope halter of the leading camel. The camels were tethered from head to tail in a line which made them move in a single file. The two caravan assistants did all the running about and the boys also helped in whatever way they could, and they made friends with the boys instantly.

"Do not walk very close to the camel when it is disturbed, it may bite," said the elderly caravan captain.

Yona looked at the camel's pale white color and remembered it was the one which made a lot of violent noise and hauling while loading. The captain had balanced the weight on both sides and the camel had grown quiet. Even though a rebel, it was the handsomest camel in the pack. Yona gave a few dates to the animal and it seemed to love the gift.

"You are a good man." The captain was watching. "One can win the heart of a camel with dates."

Eber however was not pleased at wasting dates on the camel. "Tell us about the caravan we are to join at Beer Sheba." He turned to the assistant.

That was sufficient to kindle the Nabataean pride at being the lords of the desert caravans.

"Thousands of camels with loads of frankincense and myrrh owned by several Nabataean traders join the caravan to Petra from Charax Spasinu, at the mouth of the river Euphrates. No other trader group than the Nabataeans join this desert caravan because of its harsh trail. Availability of water is top-secret, and the wells are mostly hidden or guarded by the Nabataean community. There is another route touching Palmira and Damascus to Petra with better caravanserais, mainly used for trade intended for Lebanon ports and Tyre while our caravan is catering to Egyptian ports.

"A camel travels about 250 stadia (thirty miles) a day and the caravans reach Petra in a month where many traders sell their products to other traders dealing with Egypt, alternatively hold the stocks for better price at the store houses of Petra, sell animals to herders and start preparation for the next trading cycle, and the story goes on."

"Tell us about the invasion of Petra by the Greeks and their repulsion by the Nabataeans. It is often told to ridicule the Seleucids." Eber knew something about the Nabataean warriors, even though the invasion had taken place two centuries ago, the story still ran in Jericho.

"It was Antigonus the one-eyed general of Alexander the Great who attacked Petra to capture the Nabataean trade to Egypt thereby weakening his arch-rival Ptolemy. His friend Athanaeus with four-thousand infantry solders and six-hundred cavalry men organized an army and attacked Petra at night while most of the Nabataean men were away at a nearby market leaving women and children at the mountain refuge. The Greeks killed many and looted six-hundred talents (50000 pounds in weight) of silver and large quantities of frankincense taking women and children as prisoners. Within an hour the men returned to find the loss and embarked on a hot pursuit of the attackers. The Greeks did not envisage it to happen so soon and were not well guarded. The Nabataeans killed all the infantry including the leader and recovered all their belongings and loved ones. Only a few cavalry men could escape.

"He made a second attempt. This time Demetrious son of Antigonus led the attack. They could not locate the Petra abode even after wandering for three days in the desert because the entrance was well camouflaged. Nabataeans sent ambassadors to the king to reveal the reality of the Nabataean people. 'King Demetrious, we live in the desert where there is nothing you desire like water, grain or wine. We do not want to live as slaves and have therefore chosen to live in the desert. We cause you no harm and request you to accept our present and consider Nabataeans as friends.'

"This incident gave Nabataeans some respect as a tribe which would not cow down easily." The caravan assistant concluded with an air of pride at belonging to the same tribe.

By noon they stopped for rest under the shade of a juniper bush. The camels had sensed water and were attempting to break the tethers. There was a water source in a gorge nearby sufficient for the camels.

"Prophet Elijah sat under the juniper tree running away from queen Jezebel for fear of his life." Eber told Yona recollecting the scripture. "He must have travelled the same route as ours to Beer Sheba."

Yona looked around realizing juniper was the only vegetation to be seen. He was familiar with the juniper trees as they grew in Jericho hills too. They had lovely flowers with a pleasant fragrance. Though the flowering season had almost ended, a few flowers could still be seen. Juniper trees drew water from deep below the desert topsoil and made excellent firewood which burned with a typical loud crackling sound. Charcoal made from juniper wood was much sought after in every kitchen.

The caravan captain collected some juniper leaves and started squeezing its juice out by crushing it. Then he applied it to his knees, ankles, and calf muscles. "This is good medicine for joint pain and fatigue from long walks but poisonous if ingested."

The monks and the caravan assistants applied some juice from the plant on their tired limbs, but the boys were happier with munching the dates and aiming the pits at some target.

The next phase of the journey was very interesting for the boys. The captain asked all to hop onto the animals as they slowly descended a deep canyon which looked like a never-ending open tunnel. The rainy season was over but there were water pools with shallow water at intervals.

"Watch out for *tzefa* vipers and scorpions! They hide beneath loose rocks and come out when provoked." The captain's voice was loud and resonating in the canyon.

It was cooler and there was no worry of the camels going astray. In no time the captain was sleeping on the camel's back ignoring the push forward action of the camel impacting him. The camels proceeded onwards till the sun came down and formed a ball of cold fire.

The caravan climbed up the crater and they looked for a place to camp for the night. Yona noticed the juniper trees gave way to eshel or tamarisk trees which were taller and had a wider canopy. The nightfall was very quick like blowing off a lamp in the room. Luckily for the assistants who were being scolded by the captain for their slow work, the tents were made, and the campfire lit before it was dark, with active support from the boys and the monks. The only food they cooked was a cup of tea made from some herbs the captain carried which helped to wash down the hard bread they had for dinner. The captain and the assistants shared a hookah and went into deep sleep almost instantly. The monk observed the quizzical look on Yona's face and told him they were smoking a hallucinating Indian herb.

Eber found the opportune moment to broach the subject of the sun calendar with the monks and jumped straight in.

"The Qumran monastery is following an ancient method of measuring time and the calendar recons a solar day unlike the rabbis of Jerusalem who use a lunar day to calculate the calendar year. This gives a basic error of 364 days in the solar year as against 354 days of the lunar year, and therefore the Mosaic festivals and the holy days differ widely in these calendars. The Qumran solar calendar divides 364 days into four seasons of three months each with thirteen weeks to a season. Each month has thirty days with one day added at the last month of each of the four seasons. With fifty-two weeks in a year, the festivals and the holy days recur at the same point each year." Eber looked a bit nervous but sounded confident. "I understand the Tamils of southern India also follow the sun calendar and would like to know the similarities with that of the Qumran calendar."

"How is the first day of the year pitched?" the youngest monk asked.

"The calendar begins on the first Sunday in the constellation of Aries." The answer came promptly.

The monk then explained, "We are aware of the controversy over solar and lunar calendars here. The Egyptian calendar is also solar in nature using as a fixed point the reappearance of the dog star Sirius in the eastern sky. The Romans are also in the process of revising their calendar, but they want to pitch it on the equinox, the point at which the orbit crosses the celestial equator. We will be discussing these matters in detail at Alexandria. Tamil calendar is also solar in nature and draws from ancient astronomical data called *Thirukkanida Panchanga* which contains a calculation of over three-hundred- million years," the monk added.

"The time taken for one revolution of the earth around the sun or the time taken by the sun to return to the same position relative to the background of the fixed stars in the sky is taken as a year in the Tamil calendar. The system resembles the Qumran calendar by pitching on the fixed stars of the constellation for accuracy, thereby eliminating the shortcomings of the lunar calendar as you mentioned in the beginning."

Yona was admiring the clear sky with the bright stars, the discussion Eber was having with the monk faded as he slipped into a deep slumber.

When Yona woke it was still dark, but the camels were already tethered and were ready for the day. He hopped on the donkey half asleep.

There were frequent oases on the way indicating the availability of groundwater and therefore the journey was less tiring for the animals and the caravan moved faster than anticipated, reaching Beer Sheba by nightfall. Yona witnessed high-pitched international trade activity for the first time, and of course, his first stay in a caravanserai. It was an entirely different world.

The caravanserai was a long two-story building built on three sides of a large square area leaving one side protected by a gated boundary wall. Hundreds of animals were resting in the open ground. Goods were being bought and sold in the open hall of the ground floor, while resting rooms for the traders and locker rooms were on the upper floor. They all had meals together and the caravan captain and the assistants went to the lower floor. The noise and the excitement of the new environment kept Yona awake.

The next morning, they went to Beer Sheba city. Near the entrance was the governors' office where they sought information about the caravan going to Gaza port and met its representative.

"The caravan will leave in two days' time and we will fetch you from the caravanserai early in the morning. The chief merchant has arranged a horse cart for the Indian monks and sent his respects too." The representative was very caring and respectful.

The chief monk thanked and blessed him, and he turned to the other monks. "There is enough time before we travel to Gaza and we will visit the city in the meantime. Arrangements for Eber's return journey to Ein-Gedi will also have to be made."

"I have come to Beer Sheba before and I can find some group travelling to the Dead Sea basin and join them for the return." Eber was confident.

Beer Sheba was built on a hill, for that matter all cities in Judea were built on hills, to get a good view of the surroundings for security reasons.

The main gate was guarded and opened onto a square. Men of different skin colors and attire were bustling in and out. Wealthy merchants and high-ranking officials were riding well-groomed Arabian horses making elegant tapping sounds on the paved road.

The roads were laid out as interconnected streets which was new to Yona who was used to beaten paths which always climbed a steep hill or came down to a valley. The streets demarcated areas for administrative, commercial, military, and residential use. The caravan captain dressed in a Nabataean tunic with golden collar and kufiya, the colored headgear, came with them to show them around. The captain said the city had a huge underground water storage system carved out of rock which provided water for the whole year. The wadi overflowed during the winter rains and water was collected in the storage underground.

The main square opened to a small square with triple inner gates with guard rooms on the side. The inner square opened to parallel streets touching the outer boundary street, thus connecting every part of the town. The middle of the town had an observation tower giving a strategic view of all surroundings, several stadia outside the city wall.

The best part of the town was the store houses built in a row next to the gate. Amphoras filled with wine, oil and other precious goods were stored under strict guard. Merchants could use it as a warehouse awaiting settlement of trade contracts. The captain said large amounts of money were collected as tax by the governor for this facility. Goods going to Egypt through Gaza or to Rome through Jaffa were bought and sold here by intermediaries.

Yona admired the governor's palace with its large reception area on the side of the gate while leaving the town after the tour. A quick visit to the well of patriarch Abraham was also made before heading back. The sun was almost setting when they reached the caravanserai. People were turning heads to look at the rare sight of three saffron-clad Buddhist monks, two Jewish boys in tallith and three Arabs in tunic and head dress making a colorful company, melting the cultural boundaries.

As they were walking back Eber made a mental note to visit the well the angels had shown to Hagar, the mother of Ismael, the first-born of patriarch Abraham.

"Eber, patriarch Abraham's well was dug again by his son Isaac but he was prevented from using it by the shepherds of Gerar. Is there any other well in the name of Isaac?" Yona asked.

"Actually, Isaac came to Beer Sheba from Gerar and there was no quarrel over the wells he dug in Beer Sheba," said Eber.

"Do you remember the story from the scripture about patriarch Jacob going out to the east from Beer Sheba when he was fleeing Esau?" asked Yona. Now it was a game on Beer Sheba.

"Not only that, when Jacob went out to meet Joseph in Egypt, he halted in Beer Sheba," countered Eber.

"I know another instance. Prophet Samuel's sons, Joel and Abiah, ruled in Beer Sheba as judges. They were corrupt judges and Israel got their first King Saul after their dismissal." Yona had the upper hand now.

"Prophet Elijah, running away from Queen Jezebel, sat under the shade of the juniper tree in Beer Sheba." Eber wouldn't let him win easily and Yona could not remember any more instances in the scriptures about Beer Sheba, ending the game reluctantly.

After dinner everybody went up on the rooftop and spread sheets. The Buddhist monks went into their evening prayer and so did the boys.

The Beer Sheba sky was clear and glowed with the infinite number of stars. Yona could not believe his eyes. "I have never seen such a brightly lit sky!" He could not hide his excitement.

"Beer Sheba sky is special," the monk said. "It is clear, stunning, and mostly cloudless. That is why we came up on the rooftop, to assess the planetary position in the horizon in comparison to the Indian sky."

Eber, with his trained eye started identifying Mars, Venus and Saturn – Earth's closest neighbors.

"*Kimah…Kimah…Kimah*!" shouted Eber looking at the Seven Sisters, the Hebrew word for the star cluster known as Pleiades in the Greek world.

"In India 'the Seven Sisters' are called the star of fire, Krttika and are associated with anger and stubbornness. It refers to six wives of the six sages who fell in love with fire and was called 'star of fire'. The seventh who stayed apart was called Arundhati, the wife of another sage, and she is a part of the Ursa Major star cluster," the youngest monk who was closest to Yona whispered.

The monk showed Andromeda galaxy to the boys. "If you are lucky, you can witness a meteor shower which is special to these skies."

Yona was suddenly interested in the stories of the stars. "Tell us more stories," he urged the monk.

"Can you identify the North Star?" asked the monk.

Yona pointed to the bright star with the help of Eber.

"In India, we call it the Dhruva Star. There is a story behind the star positioned there as per Indian folklore. There are other stories about its origin in different countries too," he added.

"There was a king called Uttamapada who had two wives called Suniti and Suruchi. Queen Suniti had a son called Dhruva and Queen Suruchi had a son named Uttama. Suruchi was the favorite wife and therefore Uttama had more freedom with the king. One day, Dhruva tried to sit on the king's lap along with Uttama which Queen Suruchi did not like and scolded Dhruva telling him that he did not deserve to sit on his father's lap nor rule the kingdom when he came of age.

"Dhruva was only five years old and was deeply pained. He complained to his mother who consoled the child and told him that a sincere prayer to God alone could reverse his predicament. Dhruva accepted his mother's words and went into a deep forest, sitting on a rock he started chanting his prayers to God.

"Although Dhruva began his prayers with a desire to win his father's love and affection, as his prayers progressed, he lost all material desires. He realized the body was composed of perishable elements but the soul which dwelt inside the body was not susceptible to either birth or death.

"Finally, God appeared before Dhruva and asked him for his desires, but Dhruva no longer had any desire for the material world. He just asked for the Lord's grace. The Lord said that he would become the Pole Star in the sky living forever reminding mankind of his glory and love for the Lord."

Yona gazed at the Pole Star with respect now. If all the people travelling by sea and the desert took guidance from the Pole Star for direction, he thought, it sure was a life well lived.

Eber found company to leave for Ein-Gedi the next morning.

"Yona, you have the responsibility of a prophecy on you and the future of the community will depend on the wise decisions you make, as foreseen by the chief monk. Lead the life of a monk yourself and remember you were a monk right from the day your parents dedicated you to the monastery. My responsibility is on scribing and copying the scriptures and documents for a larger audience but yours may involve saving the community from extinction."

Yona did not say anything as he was watching a moving caravan with loads of precious merchandise carried by animals big and small destined to unknown lands.

They hugged and promised to meet again as Eber was leaving. Yona saw tears in his eyes but felt dumb and emotionless himself.

● ● ●

The journey to Gaza port was faster with the comfort of a horse cart and well-laid roads. They were on the coastal highway connecting Ezion-Geber, Gaza, Ashkelon, Jaffa and up to Ptolemais. One long day took them to the port city at the designated caravanserai.

The vast Mediterranean was altogether a different world for Yona, the boy from the Dead Sea basin. The sea smelled sweet and less salty and the activity was overwhelming.

The Nabataean settlement of Gaza was on the south of port Gaza and was called Gerar. Large store houses with an amphorae of oil and aloe juice stacked for western market destined to Rhodes, Athens and Rome took most of the storage area. The goods meant for the Egyptian market were small in quantity but were much more valuable. Most of the frankincense, myrrh and balsam went to Alexandria. There was a large population of Jews also in Gerar trading along with the Nabataeans connecting the Cyrene market with Gaza and Alexandria.

As part of the custom procedure the names of passengers and the purpose of visit to Alexandria was given to the captain when they arrived at the port to board the ship. Yona looked at the ship they were to travel in. It was smaller in comparison and had a triangular sail while the bigger ships had square sails.

The captain looked at the boy with the puzzled look. "She may be small, but she will fly past these big bellies with her triangular sail."

Yona, smiled at the captain, noticing most of the ships had square sails unlike the one they were about to sail on. The desert boy had seen boats in the Dead Sea harvesting bitumen and that was all he knew about ships.

Yona noticed there were ten oarsmen and the captain's assistant. There was a secure hold for the valuable goods and some hammocks for the merchants to rest but everyone preferred the deck. It was cool on the deck by the time they set sail in the afternoon. The oarsmen got the ship into the open sea and adjusted the sail windward as per the captain's instructions.

The Buddhist monk Nirathasena had a tired look and asked how Yona was feeling. "It is like the donkey ride with the constant rocking of the floating boat."

"Some people feel uneasy when suddenly moving from firm ground to water because the brain needs to adjust to the shaky ground. Your frequent donkey rides made the brain adjust to the new environment quickly," the monk reasoned.

Late into the night Yona and the younger monk played a game of identifying the stars, especially the North Star and its relation to the Big Pan or the Pleiades. Yona learned another trick to locate true north by looking at the North Star and the Pleiades, and he could tell the direction they were heading.

"You are very good at learning," the monk said in appreciation. "This information will give you the right direction wherever destiny will take you."

It was still dark when Yona woke up and suddenly realized he was on the deck and the monk had protectively placed his hand under Yona's head. He was a bit ashamed to see that his saliva had trickled onto the monk's hand from his open mouth. Yona looked up and saw fatherly love in the monk's eyes.

"Wake up and look at the lighthouse of Alexandria. It is already visible," the monk said. Yona watched the burning light almost at level with the ship and growing in height as they got nearer.

The custom officials boarded the vessel as soon as they docked and started taking details of the cargo for valuation and tax calculation. The merchants were carrying valuable goods and therefore the inventory was taking a long time. A money lender was arranged to pay the tax and loans were to be secured by the sale proceeds of the goods. Necessary documentation was also done in the ship before the passengers could land.

Names of passengers, their purpose of visit and the local address were collected for the minister's office. The officials treated the monks respectfully. Their admiration was visible when they learned that the monks were also astronomers from India and would be conducting teaching sessions at the academy. Buddhist monks from the local monastery or the Vihara were waiting to receive the monks from India.

For a desert village boy, the sights of Alexandria were ethereal. Yona clutched the youngest monk Somadutta's hand tightly as they walked on the causeway towards the Buddha Vihara near the Jewish quarters. The ruling Ptolemaic descendants, the Greeks, the Jews, Syrians and the local population, lived in different quarters or sections of the city.

Yona looked back at the port at which they had landed and at its amazing lighthouse. The light glowing from the furnace lit on top of the lighthouse gave way to the rising sun in the great sea making the port glow with golden rays. The brass plates of the royal naval ships mirrored the light like a thousand flashlights.

The harbor of Alexandria was like an island connected to the mainland by a mole. This causeway also served as a marina for the many small ships and dhows for docking. Yona looked towards the large ships, several times larger than the one he had travelled in, docked in the harbor. Those were the grain ships he was told, transporting wheat and other grains from Egypt to Athens and Rome. Yona remembered the story of Joseph in the Holy Book. Abandoned and sold by his brothers in his youth, he rose to power in Egypt and sent grains to his father, during the times of famine in Judea. Joseph could do that because he was the chosen one; Yona could now imagine the struggle he must have undergone in his mind as a boy leaving his kith and kin to enter the unknown world, abandoned. The prophecy of the Essene chief monk resounded in his ears, he feared that something terrible was going to happen to him.

The sights at the harbor brought him back to reality. The Egyptian war ships with two and three lines of oarsmen were elegant to watch. The royal ships with purple sails seemed fully covered with bronze plates as they glittered in the sun. The harbor had a festive look and was buzzing with activity. Yona liked the place and felt good surrounded by the sea and the ships rather than the desert country he had left behind with its caravans dotting the horizon. Here, water doubled for sand and the dots were replaced with incoming ships, showing up with their top sails first in the horizon. The sea also smelled sweet here, different from the Dead Sea with its pungent aroma.

They settled down at the Buddhist Vihara. The lecture sessions were to begin the next day. Yona was to be present at the academy to lend a helping hand to the monks and he also could listen to the discussions on eastern astronomy. Monk Somadutta promised to take Yona to the city center and the museum of science and technology when he visited the grand library of Alexandria.

The royal Greek quarter where the rich and the royal families lived had magnificent palaces and villas. The Vihara where Yona was staying with the monks was on the north-east part of the city. The main attractions in Alexandria were Alexander's mausoleum and the museum which held the famous library and theatre. The main street was very wide and ended at the moon gate at one end of the mole.

The lecture sessions were held in the conference rooms of the library. As it was already an announced event the hall was full and overflowing.

Greek, Hebrew, and Aramaic were the most used languages at Alexandria beside the local dialect, and Yona was familiar with all three. At the academy, Jayasena, the chief monk was giving a discourse. He was talking about the measurement of time according to the lunar calendar, a technique explained in the ancient Indian text *Adharva Veda*. The sky was divided into twenty-eight divisions with each *Nakshatra* (or star) ruling a division. Keeping Ujjain in India as a starting point longitudinal positions could be arrived at for any point on the earth. Yona listened carefully because the monks would ask him what transpired at the academy when he got home.

Jayasena took out a chart and showed how to calculate the position of the ruling star any day of the year, backward or forward. A very attentive crowd was taking notes; among them Yona recognized the official who had taken down their names when they landed at the harbor.

The next day, the young monk Somadutta was leading the session. He recounted the story of Dhruva which Yona already knew. People in the audience also knew about the star Dhruva which they called Polaris.

When he narrated the story of the Sapta Rishi or the seven stars with which one could identify Dhruva, the audience responded with Ursa Major a name which the astronomers in the west used.

The government official seemed interested in the topic and asked questions about the Indian methods to find directions in the open sea. The monks had details of all stars directly overhead India for all days of the year. The theory explained that if someone set sail after finding the star in his horizon, he could direct his course with this lead corrected to the tilt of the earth and reach his destination safely.

There was one problem. The celestial sphere would continue to turn after one set off on journey. So, the position of the star on each day, in relation to Dhruva, which does not move, was to be calculated. The answer seemed to half satisfy the official.

A few days later, when the talk was over for the day, the government official who introduced himself as Kleomenes, came with a summon for all the three monks from Hierax, the minister of state, to appear before him. They were escorted to the palace by two guards. Yona also went along as the chief monk kept him close.

The minister was being updated about the lecture of the monks from India by Kleomenes. The minister Hierax was feared by all because he ran the government due to the ill health of King Ptolemy Physcon.

3

The Discovery of India

Somadutta, the younger monk was reading aloud from a papyrus roll and the two other monks from India and several local monks present were closely attending as Yona entered the room. Someone waved at Yona to sit down.

"King Ptolemaios and Queen Cleopatra, the sister, and Queen Cleopatra, the wife, proclaim an amnesty to all the subjects for errors, crimes, accusations, condemnations and charges of all kinds up to the 9th of Pharmouthi of the 52nd year, except to persons guilty of willful murder or sacrilege. And they have decreed that persons who have gone into hiding because they were guilty of theft or subject to other charges shall return to their own homes and resume their former occupations, and their remaining property shall not be sold. And they remit to all persons the arrears up to the same period in respect of both rents in grain and money taxes, except to hereditary lessees who have given surety."

Somadutta stopped reading. "There are more to the scroll explaining the rulers' bent towards lenience and encouragement of agriculture and shipping, both being the highest tax gainers for the country."

"Ptolemy Physcon cannot be blamed entirely for the cruelty in the first place," one of the local monks vented his views.

"Cleopatra II grabbed the crown away from him twice and he killed his stepson and own son both brought forth by her, at two different incidents to stay afloat. When both of her schemes failed, she handed over the country to her son-in-law, the Syrian Seleucid King Demetrius II. The resultant political game took the life of the Syrian king and planting a ruler of the Egyptian king's favor in his place, who later became his son-in-law. Thus, he clipped her wings and then made her the co-ruler. I think he only acted out of necessity. The worst hit was the intellectual community. The past twenty years have been a dark period as far as they are concerned. Many went away and started an academy in Cyrene, Athens, Antioch, and Rome. Now the tone is mild, and several teachers are back, and the library is active with conferences and presentations."

"True, the Jews and the Greeks who supported her faced the brunt," added another monk. "Ptolemy Physcon placed the entire army including the Greek soldiers and officers under the command of an Egyptian for the first time as an outcome of the revolts to counter the Jews and Greeks. He even promoted Egyptian Paos to be the Epistrategos as well as honoring him with the highest court rank of blood relative. Thus, the cult of Alexander the Great was diluted in authority in Egypt."

The conversation died suddenly as Eliazer, the Jewish officer attending Cleopatra II, the sister, was ushered in. After the formal welcome he sat next to the chief monk.

"There is nothing to worry. The king actually wants to improve relations with every race now. Maybe he is looking forward to a friendly relationship with India too." The Jewish official with the Egyptian army and a sympathizer of Buddhist monks affirmed sensing the grim mood in the room. "All the three rulers are in one voice when it comes to strengthening the treasury and improving tax gains," he added.

Everyone knew that he was a spy. He made sure the new monks from India were present and then departed.

Legal matters were settled in the court by a band of magistrates called Ekklesia in Alexandria while there was a special court of magistrates headed by the minister, which took up cases under classified matters and reported directly to the king. The local Buddhist monks were concerned when the summons came from the special court of Episrategos or the minister.

King Ptolomy Physcon was also known as "pot belly" for his enormous physical appearance. Unlike the Greeks he would wear a dress made of gauze covering his entire blown-out body in a worse than naked debauch appearance. His excesses and lavish grants to the Egyptian temples, together with the never-ending battles with the Greeks and the Jews, hit the trade most and the income generating activity slowed down emptying the treasury.

Hierax, Paos, Lochus, all were very skillful ministers and during each one's tenure the policies aimed at improving the treasury took prime place. The wise measures made up, in part, for the vices of his master. After the current announcement of the amnesty and tax relaxations trade was slowly coming back to normal. Cinnamon, frankincense, and other spices used in various temple worship was in short supply and the enquiry of its origin for import led to the present court enquiry.

When the monks were ushered into the court room there were a few others also present. The Exegates or the royal official in charge of the city and the knight general were in discussion with the minister. Elegantly dressed in naval captain's attire, Eudoxes of Cyzicus, a voyager and explorer from the Ionian island of Cyzicus was seated on a bench. There was also a sailor, dressed like a familiar Nabatean caravan trader, with a headgear like that of an Indian or an Arabian, seated on the bench. Yona was extremely nervous. The official surrounding was unfamiliar to him. The silence of the court room and the armed guards made him weak in the knees.

The minister opened the court session. "Traditionally, the cinnamon, frankincense and other spices were supplied by the Arab traders for various uses of the temples. Punt, at the edge of the Eritrean Sea was thought to be the source of these spices. Now the Arabs are asking a higher price and they claim short supply of spices as a reason. The king asked me to find out the truth about the origin of spices which is one of the objectives of this session.

"The second objective is to find out the truth about the Indian sailor sitting here. He was picked up half dead in the Red Sea. Having lost his crew and knowing only Indian language he was kept under supervision till he could pick up enough Greek to communicate. The story he recounts is contrary to all our knowledge about India and its products. He portrays India as a land with a great wealth of precious stones, spices, aromatics, and ivory. The amazing thing about his statement is that he claims India is accessible by sailing east across the Eritrean Sea. He also tells of favorable season for such travel."

It was clear that the intention of the Ptolemaic government was to break the monopoly of Parthians and Arabs in trade with India. It was common knowledge that ships plied between Barygaza (present day Bharuch in Gujarat) in India and Charax Spasinu in the Persian Gulf only with the permission of the Parthians. Arabs prevented Indians to trade in the Red Sea keeping the monopoly of trade with the east.

The minister called the Arab to give his testimony. His name was Al-Nakab.

"Where do you get the cinnamon from? Do not tell us the story of the giant birds and the ox meat which we know is a bluff."

Al-Nakab was completely shaken. It was said that giant birds made nests with cinnamon quills on lofty hilltops and the harvester would keep huge pieces of ox meat as bait which the birds would carry to the nest. The nest would break at the weight of the meat and the harvester would collect the cinnamon quills which fell to the ground.

"My Lord, we collect cinnamon and incense from Petra, and we understand that it comes from Saana in southern Arabia and is brought up by the desert caravans," said Al-Nakab.

"Have you ever travelled to Saana yourself? And if yes, have you ever seen a cinnamon tree?" asked the minister.

"My Lord, I have travelled to Saana several times, but I have not seen a cinnamon tree," answered Al-Nakab, a bit relaxed now.

"Introduce yourself, Indian!" The knight general called out.

Bowing with folded palms to everyone present, the Indian said, "My name is Kannan. I am the subject of Pandyan King Yenathy of southern India. We sail on small boats to Sukhadaradiva catching the westerly winds from our coast with cinnamon and pearls. We stay there for a few months and return when the wind reverses."

"Sukhadaradiva (now Socotra island) is an island off Eudemon Arabia," the city chief intervened.

"Now what does the Indian sailor say?" the minister asked. "Have you seen a cinnamon tree?"

The Indian held both palms together and bowed again as a mark of respect.

"Cinnamon trees grow in the southern part of India and Taprobane Islands (Sri Lanka) adjoining India. It grows to a height of five men on top of another. The small branches are cut, and the bark is removed and dried. This dried bark is sold as cinnamon quills here. I have seen the tree myself. My ship had a consignment of cinnamon. This time we sailed further into the Red Sea for better market but were attacked by pirates in the Red Sea and everything was lost," said the Indian.

"At Alexandria cinnamon sells at five measures of silver for a measure of cinnamon but one can get five measures of cinnamon for a silver denarius in India." The Indian sounded confident.

The magistrate turned to the saffron-clad monks.

"Do you agree with the statement the Indian sailor made?" the minister asked.

"Yes, my Lord," the chief monk said, "Cinnamon is a product of India and is brought to the Sukhadaradiva or Socotra as it is known here, in small boats."

"Tell me about your voyage," commanded the magistrate to the Indian sailor.

The Indian sailor started to narrate the story he had been repeating from the day of his rescue. At first it was mostly action with his hands and face because nobody understood his language. After a few months in the custody of the Ptolemy administration he was able to present his story with decipherable clarity with the help of an interpreter.

"We set sail from Taprobane, the southern end of India in December-January in small boats with square sails. Eight to ten men accompanied us with the merchandise of cinnamon and pearls which were lightweight. There was steady wind blowing towards Socotra during this time. We took water from Lakshadiva islands and kept a steady west course to reach Socotra in about fifteen days. The Arab merchants from Saana bought the goods from us. There are many Indians in Socotra island and we stayed there for about six months waiting for the wind to reverse. I had heard about markets in Myos Hormos and Alexandria, but the Arabs did not let us travel in the Red Sea."

"How did you find your way in the night?" asked Eudoxes, the Greek captain.

"We sailed with the help of Dhruva (The North Star) and the Saptharshi (The Big Dipper) stars at night. During the day we took direction from the sun. From the Indian coast, after Lakshadiva islands we turned left towards west and kept west until we reached Socotra island. There was also a steady wind blowing towards the west and we took direction from the wind also."

Eudoxes was convinced that there was truth to the Indian's narrative. The minister also seemed to approve the veracity of the argument.

"What is the difference between the stars' position in Alexandria and India? How can we find direction in the Indian Sea?" the minister asked, pointing towards Jayasena, the monk.

The monk was much relaxed now. He explained the Indian thoughts on astronomy in *Adharva Veda*, an ancient text.

"The pattern of the stars in the sky remain constant everywhere. Stars are fixed in positions relative to each other, but they are not stationary relative to the horizon. Therefore, it appears as if the stars rise in the east and set in the west. Dhruva is the star in the North Pole, known as Polaris in the Greek world. This star keeps true north and therefore finding direction in relation to the North Star is practicable in Indian seas also. Saptarishi are stars in the Ursa Major constellation of the Greek world which is shaped like a pan (Big Dipper). These stars are used to locate the North Star.

"In the Indian concept twenty-seven stars are identified according to their appearance on different longitudes. The rising and setting of these stars help in finding time and date because the night sky is different on each day. Taking the center point as Ujjain in India we can find our celestial position after ascertaining the star position of the day. With corresponding changes in position, this can be replicated for any part of the world."

The minister declared his verdict. "I will apprise the king of the matter and till we hear his decree all the witnesses will stay in the palace quarters, under guard."

Palace quarters were a wonderful place. Yona admired the picturesque mosaic flooring, colonnade porch and the marble benches. Inside a bath house with running water was another wonder for Yona. But the fear of the armed soldiers and the cruel stories about the king made him so nervous that he could not enjoy the luxuries. They would be presented before the king tomorrow, the guard at the palace quarters had announced.

The monks woke up early, bathed and sat for morning prayers. Kannan, the Indian also got ready. Nakab and Yona were the last, but before sunrise everybody was ready in their best dress. The guards accompanied them to the waiting hall for the visitors.

After a while, the chief usher to their majesties came to the hall.

"You shall follow me to the audience chamber now. Bow low to show your respect as you enter and as I introduce you by calling your name, you bow again to all their majesties and crown princes."

He took them to the captain of the guards who took down their names and purpose of visit. The chief monk explained to the official that Yona was his student and personal valet.

The chief usher in his cultivated voice yelled, "The delegation of sailors and astronomers from India is presented to their majesties. He named each one of them with a title and then turned towards the group. The last name to be announced was that of Yona. "Presenting astronomy student with the Indian monks, Yona son of Michael of Jericho on the Dead Sea."

Yona bowed low.

"Gentlemen, I present you to the Divine Majesty, Ptolemaios Euergetes, the King of Egypt, Cyrene, Cyprus and other possession; Her Divine Majesty, Queen Cleopatra, the Sister; Her Divine Majesty, Queen Cleopatra, the wife; and the Divine Children: Prince Ptolemaios Philometer, Prince Ptolemaios Alexandros, and Prince Ptolemaios Apion."

The group entered a big hall behind the usher as directed, bowing most humbly, walked a distance and halted. Yona looked around. There were soldiers along the wall fully armed and glittering in their brass metal plates as sunrays filtered through the glass ventilators. There were desks for clerks who sat alert with pens in hand to take down the utterings of the crown. Other servants stood at attention ready with wine, napkins, and fruits. Incense was burning and the nostalgic smell of Judean balsam made Yona happy.

The royal contingent sat on a golden throne.

"Wow, the boy is from Jericho, I want to own that country one day for those lovely balsam orchards," Queen, the wife, was the first to address the group.

Yona realized the source of the sweet smell of balsam but kept silent.

Queen, the sister, looked at Yona, the Jew, with some fondness as all the support she had in the kingdom was from the Jews and the Greeks of Egypt, though she was not keen on the balsam.

"Do you grow jadamanasi also there?" enquired Queen, the sister. "The Arabs bring it here along with the balsam."

Kannan, the Indian was quick to reply. "Her Majesty, jadamanasi is a product of India. The oil is extracted from a plant called spikenard in these lands. It is aromatic and a valued medicine at the same time. I had some of it on my ship which I lost to the pirates."

Now that the queens had enough reason to support the Indian contingent, the minister took courage and introduced the story of the Indian and his voyage into the Red Sea.

The minister proceeded, "The cinnamon and the frankincense for the temples, black pepper for embalming, various aromatics, ivory, and pearls are all the product of India. They produce exquisite hard wood for sculpture and other art forms. Currently, we buy all these at exorbitant prices from the Arabs. If we can buy them from India directly this would mean a lot of savings to the treasury. We have clear proof by way of submissions made by the Arabs here that the stories spread by the Arabs about the Indian wares were false and misleading.

"The Indian is ready to guide our ships to the new route to India without touching the ports of the Parthians. The monks vouched for the story of the Indian as they are also from India. They are astronomy teachers at the academy and are capable of finding direction with the help of the stars.

"Lastly, captain Eudoxes of Cyzicus has already paid his respects to their majesty at the games and festival held by their majesty in the honor of Persepnone, the goddess. He was with the delegation from Cyzicus and at the formal announcements of their festival in the honor of the goddess. After learning about the Indian sailor, he has approached us for permission for a royal exploration voyage to India which he wishes to captain. He already has authored his success as exploration voyager in his book *Description of the Euxine Sea*. The estimate for such a voyage is also made for their majesty's perusal."

The minister bowed and submitted documents.

Ptolemy Physcon was a cruel king but a clever one too. He had been a pupil of Aristobulus, a learned Jew, and Aristachus the grammarian. He had a love of letters and authored himself a few works. He took a liking to Eudoxes and gave his decree.

"We permit you to take up the voyage. Our military posts along the Red Sea will give you assistance. The Indian sailor, the monks, the Arab and the boy will be your prisoners in the ship, and you will be free to deal with them. You will return with sufficient stock of aromatic and other goods as mentioned by the queens. You have our gracious leave to withdraw. Be in good health."

The group bowed and walked backwards to the entrance as directed by the chief usher.

A great surprise was waiting outside in the lounge for Eudoxes.

"Hey, Eudoxes, what are you doing here with the circus of easterners?" Arillus asked, looking at the multi-racial gang, clad in tunics of maroon and white accompanying Eudoxes. Lucius Marcus Arillus was a Roman businessman whose ships plied the Mediterranean Sea transporting grains to Rome and Athens from Egypt. He was waiting in the lounge for an audience scheduled with their majesty.

Eudoxes shook hands with him. "My friend, what brings you here? For me, we are planning an India voyage, sponsored by the Ptolemais."

"That is wonderful, my shipping company is getting some extra payload by way of a four-hundred tonner grain ship. I have come here to get the blessing of the divine majesties for the launch," said Arillus.

"Yes, I heard about the ship but did not realize it is your company owning her," responded Eudoxes.

"How about your trip? Is there a merchant consortium or you are on your own in this venture?" asked Arillus.

"No... No. There is no consortium. The royals control the full stake," said Eudoxes.

"Ok I will put in some money and would like to buy some pearls for the elite in Rome. I need to keep some high-ups in good humor there. A few oriental pearls can do the magic. The current trend in Rome among the ladies is pearls. You know, the grain trade is extremely competitive these days," said Arillus.

"Yes. I also know of your ways to cut competition too. You are welcome for the contribution. Draw up an agreement and I will collect the money from the financiers," responded Eudoxes.

Little did Eudoxes know that he was tying a noose for himself with the agreement.

The chief usher came for Arillus and he bid farewell to Eudoxes and walked inside.

Egyptians traders had little knowledge of the geography beyond their own coasts. The trade was carried on by buying goods from their nearest neighbor on one side and selling them to those on the other side. Long voyages were wholly unknown. Although Egyptian traders had grown wealthy from carrying the merchandise of India and Arabia from ports on the Red Sea to the ports on the Mediterranean, the Egyptians gathered no knowledge of countries from where the goods came.

India was known to the Greeks as a country to be reached by sea via Euphrates and the Persian Gulf. In the times of Ptolemy nobody thought India could be reached by sea from Egypt, as all voyages hitherto were undertaken by crossing the coastlines of many nations.

King, Ptolemy Physcon ordered a vessel to be given to Eudoxes of Cyzicus's command for his exploration voyage to India. The crew was also picked from among able Syrian prisoners from Phonicia serving terms in Egypt with a promise to set them free after a successful voyage. The captain was free to choose his personal guards and pilots.

The problem Eudoxes faced was insufficient funds for the purchase of goods as Indian products were costly. The royal treasury had its limitations. Financiers were reluctant, partly because they did not want to do business with the rude King Ptolemy Physcon who was sponsoring the voyage and because of the risk involved in financing merchandise of an exploration voyage. Arillus, however, paid for some of the expenses.

Eudoxes zeroed in on a ship with a square sail, a merchantman, as the sea going merchant ships are called. It was a twentyer, a name of ships with similar number of sailors. He decided to keep the oars and the sails hearing the stories from the Indian about the dangerous shallows of the Indian Ocean. Eudoxes got a lateen sail fitted on the aft for speed and maneuverability in unknown wind conditions.

The hull had two compartments for storing fresh water and another for live fish. There was a two-months' supply of grains and dried food which were packed and ready. The ship was well built and was part of the transport ships of the royal navy, though used for short voyages in the Red Sea between Arabian and Egyptian shores.

His twenty sailors were king's men who could take up arms in case of need. This posed a great danger of mutiny in adverse situations making the captain's position precarious. His hunger for exploration made him ignore the negatives. Eudoxes recruited ten more men as his personal team to work as bodyguards, carpenters and lookouts.

● ● ●

Eudoxes set sail from Myos Hormos to India in the beginning of the month of July. The monks, the Arab trader and the Indian sailor were on board, under guard. The monks' party included Yona too. The captain was pleased to know that Yona's parents were from Ionia, which was his homeland also. He gave Yona enough freedom to observe and learn seafaring techniques.

The Red Sea was familiar to Eudoxes and they reached Arabia Eudemon (Aden) in about twenty days. They docked there, took water and provisions, and waited for the Indian pilot to give signal to sail at favorable wind. Eudoxes made sure that no one saw the Indian, the Arab or the monks during their stay at the port. He announced his course to be coasting towards India to mislead any suspicious enquiry.

It was in the beginning of the month of August when the wind was favorable according to Kannan, the Indian. After locating the Dhruva star in the northern horizon, he pointed one hand to the North Star, and he pointed the other hand at ninety degrees to the east. This direction, according to him, would take them to India.

The monks were also convinced of the direction. They worked with the captain to locate the constellations of Andromeda, Cassiopeia, and Cepheus as they were known in the Greek world and advised Eudoxes that these stars would be visible over India in August and September months, and the direction could be corrected with their location in relation to the position of the North Star.

The wind was steady and Eudoxes was amazed at the discovery of the constant speed and direction of the wind. It rained heavily every day. The intervals in between two spells of rain presented a clear sky in the night and sunshine during the daytime. It was a boon to identify the direction. The piloting was perfect, and they saw landfall at Kalliana, south of Barygaza in about thirty days.

Two small fishing boats manned by two fishermen approached the ship. Seeing the Buddhist monks they shouted in the local tongue.

"Do not land at Kalliana. There are navy boats from Barygaza arresting people on the ships and taking them to their port to pay taxes. You may find yourself in jail," they warned.

Jayasena, the monk, talked to the fishermen at length. The battle for the port of Kalliana between the Sythians and the Andhra kings of Satvahana kingdom made it difficult to land in Kalliana. Ships from Barygaza were patrolling the sea for any merchant vessel taking to the open sea without touching their port thus depriving them of the taxes. More and more vessels were taking to the open sea route to the southern ports these days.

According to the fisherman the Satvahana kingdom was supportive to the Buddhist religion and therefore the monks would be safe to land in a port under their control.

"We have a war-like situation at Kalliana port," the monk Jayasena told the council called to assess the situation. All the sailors and the guards were present.

"The Sythians or Sakas who were driven out of Parthia have entered the Indian peninsula and have taken over some of the Greek controlled area in Sourashtrene province like Patalene. Now they are pushing further south and want to capture access to the sea." Everybody was intently following every word being uttered.

"Barygaza is still with the Greeks and they fear losing all the trade with the east in due course and have intensified the coastal operations to capture and tax ships avoiding Barygaza port. There is threat from the Greeks, Sakas and Satvahanas at Kalliana. The fishermen are suggesting we land at Rajapura, a Satkarni stronghold, about eight-hundred stadia (100 miles) down south," he added.

Taking the advice Eudoxes sailed down further south and chose the sea inlet of Rajapura to land. The monks had knowledge of the area and the Buddha Vihara up the hill. The lateen sail and the rowers came handy in the coastal sail to Rajapura.

"This is a wonderful place to land!" Eudoxes exclaimed at the sight of the sea inlet.

But things were not so easy. There was a military base of the Satvahana king. The captain and the monk took the ship's boat to go ashore and met the Gaulmika, the head of the military regiment, for permission to land.

The military regiment was placed to keep peace and order at the village considering its strategic importance. The regiment had nine chariots, nine elephants, twenty-five horses and forty-five-foot soldiers.

Matters were easy with the presence of the monks. Many soldiers were Buddhists though Sri Satkarni I, the king was a Brahman, the priestly class, as was the Gaulmika.

They were allowed to berth on a small island-like harbor across the village within the sea inlet.

"You can put up tents in the island till the wind reverses for your return journey and sell your wares. Dhows going up to Barygaza with aromatic and other goods sometime stop here for water. There is a sweet water well in the island which you can use too. The Arab sailors call this island Janjira." The Gaulmika was respectful towards the monks.

Eudoxes was a happy man now. The voyage was a grand success. He sat down and completed the scroll. Maybe for another book once I reach home, he thought.

Kannan, the Indian's homeland was further south, and he hoped to be free to go as the voyage was successful. He promised to arrange for goods at a bargain and to talk to the buyers about the wine they had brought along.

The ship's council decided to set the prisoners free, but Al-Nakab wished to stay with the ship and joined the carpenters engaged in repairs of the ship.

The monks wished to go to the Bedse cave monastery which was about a day's journey from Rajapura. Horses were hired from the village for the monks to cross the forest track along the road to the monastery. The monks rode the horses and Yona was pillion riding. From the seashore it was a steep climb of over one-thousand cubits (1500 ft) to the monastery, most part of the road was forest of shrubs and trees of less than ten cubits (15 ft) high.

Yona had a strange reminiscent feeling of climbing the mountain ridge road to Jerusalem from Jericho. The only difference was the bushes here. By evening they reached the Bedse monastery. Surprise of all surprises, the monastery was almost like Qumran with its cave prayer hall, the veranda, and the hermit caves. Yona realized why the Buddhist monks visited Qumran often; they were similar in many ways. The monks were dressed in the same way, but for the color of their clothing – white for the Qumran monks and maroon for the Buddhists. Yona felt a strange feeling of homecoming.

Monks from Alexandria were most welcome at the monastery. Their story was heard with such enthusiasm that the whole monastery was in attendance. The Essene Yona was the darling of them all. He also felt one among them with his vegetarian habits and prayers.

"Buddhism is convenient to the traders too, who help in construction of large rock cut monasteries like this one as an offering," the local monk joined in the conversation. "We have facilities for safe-keeping of the valuables and money when the traders are visiting distant markets. We provide them with food and stay during the rainy season and, to some extent, protection from wild animals and robbers too. The construction of this facility is going on with artisans from Jordan Valley who made the Nabataean Petra helping the local stone workers with the art of columns and arches. I have visited the Petra tombs and the Qumran cave monastery during my visit to Alexandria." He looked at Yona and smiled.

"Yona is our responsibility now. He had come with us to Alexandria and had to make this strange voyage under compulsion. We have to see that he is safely returned to Alexandria with assured welfare till he is capable of independent living," the chief monk Jayasena said.

Everyone bowed in agreement.

The travelling monks had plans to visit other monasteries and therefore Yona stayed back at Bedse monastery.

Bedse caves had lovely surroundings. From the hilltop the view reached the horizon. The rainy season had turned the greenery into a dark shade of green. The tender leaves were still yellowish green, and it cooled the mind. Many local monks returned to the monastery for the rainy season, meditating most of the time.

Yona sat on the granite bench overlooking the plains for the whole morning. Deserts of Negev and tropical rainforests of coastal India were poles apart but the Buddhists here and the Essenes in Jericho had something strange in common, he thought. Both communities were searching for the attainment of reunion with the Almighty by simple living, prayer, and meditation. He also realized that money separated the pure from the practical here too into Mahayana and Hinayana sects as it did with the Pharisees, Sadducees, and the Essenes, back home.

"Have you started meditating yourself, you little monk?" A local monk came up to Yona with a supervisor of stone workers. "Meet Korah, the supervisor of cave construction from your land. And this is Yona, the Essene monk." He called Yona a monk half teasingly.

"He is not old enough to be a monk of the Essene order; I am from Jericho myself." Korah greeted Yona with a countryman's embrace.

The stories were exchanged. Korah was brought in by the Buddhist monks from Petra for supervising the stonework here. They made good friends, talking Aramaic.

"These several rock cut monasteries flourished during the reign of King Satvahana Sri Satkarni who gifted these hills and villages to the monks. Traders from the west also donated towards the construction. We are on the trade route going to southern India from Kallyana, the port your ship tried to land. My job here is to design secret lockers to hold the valuables of the traders for safe keeping while they visit markets – a service these monasteries offer in return for the hefty donations," Korah said.

Together they walked to the site to see rock being hewn to make a large prayer hall with a long line of columns cut from the rock.

"In the west, we place pieces of chiseled rock on top of another to make a column but here we just hew it in situ standing." Korah explained the difference.

Days passed by. Repair and maintenance of the ship was done, the torn sail was replaced, and everybody waited for the appropriate time to sail back. Eudoxes sold his wine amphorae and procured aromatics. Al-Nakab was a great help in identifying and quality testing the purchases and in bargaining the Arab way as money was scarce for Eudoxes.

Pearl merchants came with Kannan and Eudoxes was brought to his spending limits cursing the stingy Ptolemy Physcon. Some pearls for Arillus were procured. The opportunity to make a great fortune was lost due to a lack of funds.

The three monks from Alexandria gave a purse of pearls to Eudoxes to secure the future of Yona and his welfare till he made independent earning.

Favorable wind towards the west would start soon, Eudoxes charted and documented the voyage plan and the favorable season for travel to and fro with the help of the Buddhist monks. Experienced voyager as he was, Eudoxes collected sufficient information to take the voyage on his own. Kalliana and Barygaza had a large group of Greek businessmen, some of whom he met doing business with the west, helped him to chart a return voyage plan. Eudoxes was convinced that open sea traffic would kill the coasting business and Egypt would gain enormously by opening the Red Sea route.

Westerly wind grew strong by November and they set sail for home. The voyage was uneventful till they reached the Arabian shore. Yona found the captain upset once they set sail from Bab-el-Mandap, the port at the tip of the Arabian Peninsula, and entered the Red Sea. The wind was not favorable, and it seemed to be blowing from all sides. The rollers kept the vessel dancing. Yona suspected something had gone terribly wrong with the mood in the ship. Unlike the voyage to India when everybody was happy at the thought of exploring the unknown and getting rich with the Indian wares.

It all started when two sailors of the Egyptian crew overstayed their leave at Bab-el-Mandap. The captain questioned them about the delay in joining the ship but the issue did not go any further. They had brought in some hemp and were smoking it with friends in the hold. Yona half asleep in the hammock overheard some conversation in Greek alluding to the arrest of the captain which he promptly communicated to Eudoxes.

The two sailors were summoned the next day.

"Did you buy any pearls from India with the advance money I gave you?" asked the captain. Unwittingly they said yes, and the captain demanded them to show him the pearls. They had nothing to show as they had sold them at Bab-el-Mandap.

Eudoxes was infuriated. No one had seen him in such a rage. His right hand gripped his sword.

"I have information that you are traitors and have given out information about the ship and the cargo to the spies. Before I count to three you better tell me the truth or face the charge of mutiny!"

The sailors were quivering. "We did not say anything against the captain or the ship. King Ptolemy's men said all the goods including personal purchases belonged to the king and would be confiscated at the port. They agreed to pass the sale proceeds of the pearls to our family in exchange for the information they wanted about the voyage."

The other sailor interfered. "Captain, he is the spy of the king and I have the blessings of the queen, the sister. Our job was to report on the voyage. The cargo was fully financed by the royal treasury and involvement of the Roman businessman was our concern."

This turn of events gave the other sailor courage, and his voice was firm. "Captain, you have joined with the Romans letting them conquer our nation. After long years of suppression, we have now some recognition as ethnic Egyptians in the kingdom of His Holiness Ptolemy Euergates. I am ready to give my life to protect my freedom." His name was Akar and he sounded rebellious. Everyone was stunned.

"Then why did you sell your pearls and send the money to your family knowing well that our pearls would be confiscated at the port? You are a traitor, and you deserve to die." The Greek sailor stabbed his knife through Akar's heart and with one swift move overthrew his lifeless body.

Eudoxes drew his sword and asked everyone to calm down. But the other Egyptian also quickly jumped overboard. Nobody tried to rescue him.

"Go and sit in my cabin and do not come out till I order you to do so." Eudoxes pointed the sword at Yona and he promptly obeyed. Yona did not hear anymore arguments. It was quiet very soon, and the captain came into the cabin and shut the door.

"Boy, take off your clothes." Quivering, Yona did not hesitate. The captain took out two string of pearls concealed in ribbon from his pocket and tied it to Yona's waist and said, "Now listen, the big ribbon is meant for Arillus, the Roman, and the smaller one is for your welfare given by the monks in India. If there is any question from the customs authorities, show them the letter addressed to the Buddha Vihara in Alexandria about your welfare, and tell them the pearls are a gift from the Indian monks. If they do not arrest you, go to the Buddhist monks and tell them the whole story." The captain looked at Yona and raised his voice. "Do I have to tell you to get dressed now?" He opened the door and moved to the deck.

Eudoxes was not surprised to see a small group of Egyptian soldiers at the dock when they berthed at the Red Sea port of Myos Hormus. The cargo was moved to the waiting caravan of animals under the soldiers' supervision. The captain and the sailors were taken into custody. Despite such a disastrous end to the expedition, the seamen were content with the good food and water the soldiers gave them making their taste buds come alive after almost eight months of their departure for India. Coptos, the river port of the river Nile was their destination which was seven days journey from Myos Hormus.

Exceptionally large sail boats plied the river Nile. The sailors relaxed, even though chained, forgetting the perils of the ocean. There was confusion in the city when they reached the port of Alexandria. The king was on his deathbed and power mongers were plotting for supremacy, so Eudoxes's expedition took back-stage. A group of Buddhist monks were at the port hearing the news of the returning Indian expedition. At the port, Eudoxes and the sailors were taken to prison and they handed the saffron-clad boy to the waiting monks.

The monks at Alexandria decided to send Yona to Cyrene for safety as they suspected the soldiers would want to arrest Yona too for interrogation.

4

Silphium of Kurena

It was still dark when Yona and the young monk Padasena of the Alexandrian Buddhist monastery walked past the mausoleum of Alexander the Great and the library hall towards the port. The bright flames from the furnace of the lighthouse served as a guiding star.

There was unusual military movement in the city. The guards were everywhere. The saffron-clad Buddhist monks were the only peaceful group in the city. The Greeks, the Romans, the Egyptians and the Jews were all tense as King Ptolemy Physcon was on his deathbed and a power struggle among the aspirants to the throne was imminent.

"I had gone inside the palace through this gate and the building to the left is where we were kept before the voyage to India with captain Eudoxes," said Padasena.

The subject of India was very popular at the monastery. The local monks wanted to know about the cave monasteries, the grand

Viharas donated by rich merchants, and the wealth donated by local kings to the monasteries.

Padasena looked through the gate of the palace. The minister seemed to be having a meeting of the senior officials of the royal navy as several armed guards in naval uniform were guarding the palace besides the palace guards.

"Because of the naval ships berthed all over the port and along the causeway, our ship is anchored in the northern side of the port. We may have to take a boat to board her." Padasena was a little annoyed.

As they reached the end of the mole, a boatman was calling passengers going to Cyrenaica on the Apollonia. The guard at the gate was checking every passenger but looking at the two monks he smiled and shook his head for them to pass. Yona and Padasena climbed on the boat. Yona's hand felt the belt with the pearls with comfort of freedom. Even Padasena was not aware that Yona had with him pearls and precious stones worth a fortune sewn onto his belt.

Once on the deck of the Apollonia Yona looked back. The furnace on the lighthouse was put off. The mirrors reflected the sunlight sharing its position with the ships passing by or approaching the harbor. The glittering brass plates on the naval ships shone gold. What a blissful scene of the morning sun for an Essene monk to be. He kneeled in prayer.

"The 250 cubits (380 ft) lighthouse called Pharos is the highest structure on earth." Padasena was a student of history and an interesting storyteller. Yona enjoyed his company.

"Look at the construction: It is square on the lower portion, octagonal in the middle section and circular at the top. It took twelve years to be built," he added.

The ship was moving away from the port. The sun was rising. Cool wind of the Mediterranean blew over the deck and the morning sun was pleasing. Padasena started recounting the story of Kurena or Cyrene, the city of the Egyptian province of Cyrenaica (present day Libya).

"Kyrene was a princess and daughter of King Hypseus of the Lapiths. She was a great huntress and guarded her father's herds on Mount Pelion. Her bronze tipped javelin and sword slayed wild beasts and lions. God Apollo saw her fighting a lion bare-handedly and fell in love. He married her and brought her to north Africa. Apollo founded the city of Cyrene in her name and made her the ruler.

"Greeks settled in Cyrene over four-hundred years before Alexander's invasion of Egypt established themselves as the upper class due to their trading relationship with Athens and Rome. Cyrenaica is also called Pentapolis because of the five cities on the coast, namely Berenice (modern Benghazi), Arsinoe, Ptolemais and Apollonia which was the original port of Cyrenaica. Obviously, these cities were renamed by the Ptolemaic rulers. Cyrene remained the capital city.

"Coastal Mediterranean is separated from the arid zone of the African desert by peaks about 1500 cubits (2100 ft) and have a hot dry summer and a mild rainy winter. Forests and woodlands and the most valuable silphium grow wild here. Abundant crops of wheat and barley grow here due to the numerous springs emerging from the highland. Cattle, sheep and horse breeding flourish in the pasturelands. Olives and figs are also in plenty making it a blessed country. The jewel of Cyrene is silphium. A condiment, a medicine and an aphrodisiac, it grows only on the coastal tract of Cyrene.

"As an intellectual and artistic center of the Greek world, Cyrenaic thinkers expounded the doctrine of moral cheerfulness that defined happiness. The Buddhist doctrine found a match here. The monastery founded by the Indian monks sent by King Asoka is the one we are going to."

Yona was keenly listening. "Qumran monastery also teaches love and happiness," Yona chipped in. He did not realize the depths of Greek intellectual thought and that of Buddhism and Judaism in the light of Essenic teachings. It was still to mature in him in the years to come.

"You will have great teachers in Cyrene in all spheres of philosophical thought and religion," said Padasena. "It will be up to you to make good use of it."

Yona was still interested in the history part. "What happened after Alexander's invasion?"

Padasena looked at Yona's anxious eyes. The storyteller is thrilled when the audience has fire in the eyes for more. He began to live the story.

"Magas of Cyrene ruled Cyrenaica after Alexander and his father Philip's short rule who served as military officer in the service of the king. He fought as commander of one division of the phalanx in Alexanders' wars. Philip was an independent ruler of Cyrene, but he died early. Ptolemy became pharaoh and the religious head of all Egyptian temples and the people. He developed Alexandria to be a cultural and commercial capital of the world, as dreamt by Alexander."

"What was Alexander's dream?" Yona knew it was a stupid question to ask but he had to fill the gaps before going further.

"Don't break the thread… Now that you have asked Alexander had a great vision of bringing together the eastern and western world together. The wisdom, wealth and culture of a combined world was his vision, at least after visiting the great university of Taxila in India. Now let us go back to Cyrene," Padasena insisted.

"After the death of Philip, Magas's mother took him and his siblings to Egypt to visit Euridice, the wife of Ptolemy I Soter and the founder of Ptolemaic dynasty. The visit turned out to be disastrous for Euridice because Ptolemy fell in love with the beautiful Berenice, mother of Magas and divorced Euridice to marry her. Thus, Berenice became the Egyptian queen and queen mother of the Ptolemaic dynasty.

"This is how Magas of Cyrene became the stepson of Ptolemy and an Egyptian prince; with the result Cyrenaica was added to the Ptolemaic rule as a province. But Magas longed for his country and was sent as governor of Cyrenaica when he was twenty-one years of age. He loved to call himself Magas, son of Philip, rather than add the title Ptolemy to his name."

"Magas turned rebel at the death of Ptolemy Soter, his stepfather, and crowned himself King of Cyrene…"

"For family men, the elders' advice was to rejoice only with the wife of your youth and not to go astray with other women, to quote King Solomon." Yona could not resist interfering with a verse from the scripture.

"Yona, you were paraded before the Ptolemies before your India voyage, right?" asked Padasena.

"Yes. King Ptolemy Physcon, Queen Cleopatra, the mother, Queen Cleopatra, the wife, Prince Ptolemy Lathyros, Prince Ptolemy Alexander and Prince Ptolemy Apion were there," replied Yona.

"Did you know Cleopatra, the mother, was the king's brother's wife? And Cleopatra, the wife, was his wife's daughter with his brother; and Ptolemy Apion was son of a Cyrenaic concubine born to the king? Marital relationships in Ptolemaic Egypt were quite different from Solomon's teachings. The result of such relationship was disastrous too...

"We were discussing Magas. He married from the rival camp of Ptolemy, the Seleucids of Syria. His wife was Apama, the daughter of Seleucid King Antiochus I. With the help of his father-in-law, he attacked Egypt but failed to make any progress. However, he kept his independence till his death, at the price of a marriage alliance for his daughter Berenice II with Ptolemy III. After the death of Magas Ptolemy attached Cyrene as a province of Egypt.

"Magas helped to establish Buddhism in Cyrene. During his rule, Indian King Asoka sent a mission to the west. The monastery at Cyrene has a copy of the edict of Asoka which says: 'The conquest of *dharma* has been won here, on the borders, and even six-hundred *yojanas* (6000 miles) away, where the Greek King Antiochus rules. *Dharma* has also won beyond his kingdom where four kings named Ptolemy, Antigonus, Magas and Alexander rule, and likewise in the south among the Cholas, the Pandyas, and as far as Tamraparni (Sri Lanka). Asoka also claims that he encouraged the development of herbal medicine for men and animals, in the territories of the Hellenistic kings," explained Padasena.

Yona was quiet for a moment. Then he remembered the medicine men called therapeutics of Qumran monastery. "I have seen Indian herbs brought to Judea from the east by the therapeutics. I remember there was a great market for the herbal medicine from India at Socotra island which we visited on our way to India. When you said Pandya kings of India, I remember having seen teak timber from Pandya country transported to distant harbors while we were in India."

"You seem to have now visited both ends of the territory where Asoka claims to have spread Buddhism. It really is an envious achievement for your age." Padasena could not suppress his envy.

Port of Apollonia had a fine temple with a pure white marble colonnade. Right next to the temple was a large gathering. The king's minister of trade, the stratego, was presiding over the weighment of silphium for export. Tax collection for consignment of silphium was the major source of income for the exchequer. They both watched the proceedings as Padasena explained that this happened only a few times in a year.

"What is silphium?" asked Yona.

Padasena expected this question from the ever-questioning Yona.

"Silphium is the lifeblood of Cyrene." Padasene took a deep breath like an athlete. He loved sharing the knowledge he had acquired by long hours of study at the Alexandrian library. Callimachus, the chief librarian gave him permission to stay late and had given him access to ancient papyrus rolls, as a recognition for his zeal. Padasena thought it would be failing on his part not to pass on the ancient wisdom. People sometimes thought he was taking it too far.

"Silphium primarily is a medicinal plant, producing a resin called laser which has multiple uses. It is found only in Cyrene and called the 'gift of Apollo' in Cyrenaica. There is a great demand for silphium from Greece and Rome where it is sold in its weight at the same rate as silver."

Yona looked at the sack-loads of silphium being weighed and wondered at the amount of silver it would generate in value. "How is the resin harvested? Is it collected like frankincense? I have seen gum oozing out of frankincense tree in Jericho."

"You will see silphium plants in the hills closer to the shore," Padasena explained. "It is a fennel with sweet smelling flowers and thick stalks. The resin is extracted from the cuts made on the stalk above the roots. Resin oozes from the wound and solidifies when exposed to the air. It is then harvested. Silphium is in great demand in Greece and Rome for its use as a condiment, a food preservative, gum resin. It is an edible vegetable when the stalks are used in food, and medicine. Silphium is also grated over meat and cabbage for flavor. As a drug, it is close to panacea, prescribed for fever, cough, deceases of the eye, muscle and joint pains and toothache. It helps to dissolve blood clots and eliminate worms, and a best antidote against scorpion bite. But its use is most prevalent in an entirely different field. Greek goddess Aphrodite blessed silphium to be an aid to enhance sexual pleasure. The royals and the rich everywhere grab the drug at asking price. It is also widely used as an abortifacient drug making it most sought after.

"For the farmers, it is a fodder with benefits of enhanced milk production and vitality of animals. Shepherds over-graze the wild fennel almost to extinction. It will be a wonder if the plant will still exist in a few decades. The golden goose is always short-lived," he added.

Both Yona and Padasena were monks, even though of different religions, they were destined to practice celibacy and could not really understand the mad rush for silphium by the royals and the rich.

● ● ●

The city of Cyrene was about eighteen stadia (18 miles) from the port city of Apollonia. Horse carts took passengers to and fro and they hopped on the one calling for passengers. Some fellow passengers smiled at the young saffron-clad monks which gave Yona confidence in an alien country.

As they were passing the necropolis of the Cyrene a passenger asked curiously, "Are you new to the city?"

Padasena replied affirmatively. "Yes, we are here for the first time visiting the Buddhist monastery at Cyrene."

"Oh, Yes. The monastery on the hilltop on the northeast." The passenger knew the place. "You enter by the southern gate and pass the temple of Zeus and the Hippodrome to reach the hill temple. I am going to the horse breeding farm nearby and I will show you the way. I am Danios." He introduced himself.

"Thank you very much. We greatly appreciate your help," replied Padasena.

The horse cart dropped them at the gate. The credentials and the purpose of the visit were verified by the guards at the gate. The paved roads of Cyrene welcomed Yona. Little did he know that a large part of his youth was going to be spent on this soil.

"On your right is the temple of the sun god Zeus. This is the largest temple in Cyrene. The temple of Apollo in the north-western end is also big. But people say this temple is the largest in the world dedicated to Zeus. I will make a quick offering to God before we proceed further." The heavily bearded person Yona befriended first in Cyrene hurried to the temple.

The Hippodrome was large. There was some horse-racing training session underway and a small crowd was watching.

"They are such lovely animals, aren't they?" said Danios in admiration as he rejoined the group.

"We have vast meadows here best suited for horse breeding. We also feed them silphium for strength. Our horses are in great demand throughout the Mediterranean rim," he boasted, sotto voce.

"From here you turn left, and the hilltop temple will be visible after a short walk." Danios pointed towards the Hippodrome.

As they climbed the hill, tall fennels with large yellow flowers dotted the road.

"These are the silphium plants," Padasena made a calculated guess in identifying the plant which he had not seen before. "I remember seeing its drawing in the library hall," he added.

Yona looked at the plants with curiosity and told himself that this was silver growing on the hills.

● ● ●

Buddha Vihara or the monastery in Cyrene was a small setup. It had the royal backing during the time of King Magas, the first Greek king of Cyrene, when the first Buddhist mission from India visited Cyrene. But in the later years, Cyrene monastery took a supporting stand to the Alexandrian Buddhist community which grew to a thirty-thousand strong.

Padasena and Yona washed their feet and entered the veranda. Along the outer wall, around the building, prayer wheels were placed. They rolled each wheel while Padasena, chanting a prayer, took one full round before entering the main hall of the building.

They were taken to the chief monk. Padasena introduced himself and Yona handed over the letter from the chief monk of the Alexandrian monastery.

The chief monk was a Greek who had taken the Buddhist name Ananda. He was a bit overweight for a monk but with a welcoming smile and a pleasing demeanor. His head was bald. Maybe he never needed a head shave was the first thought that came to Yona's mind.

The chief monk smiled at Yona. "So, we have a celebrity here, an India returned monk!"

"Yona has not joined the Buddhist sect yet. He is dedicated to being a monk in the Essene order of Qumran monastery. The saffron robe is a camouflage," interjected Padasena.

"Here you will be one of the students learning the chants and rituals of Buddhism." Ananda was stern.

"The rule of His Highness Ptolemy Physcon is not kind to other religions and the worship of Egyptian gods is encouraged and therefore a camouflage will not work," he added.

"There is another letter from captain Eudoxes with me." Yona excused himself, went to a corner and removed the belt with the pearls and the letter.

Chief monk Ananda read the address on the roll. "This is addressed to the Roman businessman Lucius Marcus Arillus. The other one is from the Indian monastery about the welfare of Yona. There are two purses also along with it. We will keep the letters and the purses in the safety vault here and wait for the addressee to collect it." He turned to Yona. "You need to be careful about the letter. Captain Eudoxes has angered the Ptolemies and they might look for you if they get to know about the purse. Spies are everywhere especially since King Ptolemy Physcon lived and ruled Cyrene, the land of his exile for so many years before recapturing the rule of Egypt. You continue your camouflage strictly to avoid anything untoward happening," advised the chief monk.

Padasena left the next day, a bit annoyed about Yona not disclosing the secret of the letters to him during the journey, despite Yona repeatedly telling him that he had promised the captain not to disclose anything because it could cost him his life.

● ● ●

On 21st of June 116 (BC) Ptolemy Physcon died. Cleopatra II, the sister, also died by the end of the same year. Ptolemy Physcon, though brutal, was the cleverest king of the Ptolemaic dynasty. In his will, he left Egypt to be jointly ruled by Cleopatra III, the wife, and any one of his sons of her choice. The other son, the crown prince was to rule Cyprus, the island-province of Egypt, as desired in his will.

He willed Cyrenaica to be ruled by Ptolemy Apion, his son with the concubine Irene, also called Ithaca, from Cyrene. But there was a catch. The king had already willed the country of Cyrenaica and his ancestral royal estates there to the rule of the Roman republic, to ensure protection and to regain his rule over Egypt, while on exile at Cyrene. But this would happen after the time of Ptolemy Apion.

Ptolemy Apion was to be crowned as king of Cyrene in the days to come. The news made the Roman businessmen of Alexandria very happy. Cyrenaica would be a Roman province eventually, the silphium and the wealth it commanded would pass through them now.

Lucius Marcus Arillus was informed of Yona's whereabouts but he delayed meeting Yona for political reasons. Once the political horizon was clear in both Egypt and in Cyrenaica, and the rulers of

Egypt were ready for another trade mission to India, he visited Yona at the monastery.

Yona membered the toga-clad Roman businessman in discussion with captain Eudoxes at the palace when they were taken to the court of King Ptolemy Physcon before the voyage to India.

"Do you remember me?" asked Arillus. He was sitting with the chief monk. The letters and the purses were on the table.

"Yes, I do. I remember you with the captain at the palace," Yona replied. In the same breath he continued, visibly worried about the captain's fate, "Have you met captain Eudoxes? He was worried about the king's wrath when we parted."

"He is fine and is preparing for another expedition to India. I have read the letters and have received the purses you entrusted with the chief monk. I was waiting for you to come before I opened the purse sent by the Indian monks for your welfare," assured Arillus.

"By Jupiter!" exclaimed Arillus as he opened the purse. "These jewels are valued more than those I acquired through Eudoxes. This will ensure your welfare anywhere in the world and I will be more than ready to take you as a partner in the business with this treasure as your investment."

He turned to the chief monk, "Let the boy be here till he is able to take up things individually and I will provide for his welfare. I will come again after the new king's accession to the throne. I have plans to expand activities here and to buy some property in Cyrene." Arillus left after making a handsome donation to the monastery.

● ● ●

There were other teenagers in the monastery. Some of them were adopted by the monastery as orphaned children but there were others sent by parents to learn the Buddhist ways, mostly from Alexandria. Yona joined the group. His fluency in Greek, Aramaic and Hebrew languages helped him to make friends among the students quickly at the monastery.

Before sunrise, bathed and dressed, everybody was to be present at the prayer hall. Chanting the prayer *Om mani padme hum* which continued for almost an hour. This chant was written on the prayer wheels too which was rotated by all while walking the veranda.

Yona would praise Yahweh for the morning sun in the Essene way, as taught by the monks at the Qumran monastery before the prayer hall gathering. The boys helped old monks in many ways; they took up tidying the place and assisted in the kitchen. There were teaching sessions after breakfast and after lunch. The evening prayer was attended by all the senior monks presided over by the chief monk. He gave a talk on matters of faith and learning.

The chief monk Ananda was a learned teacher of Greek and Vedic Indian knowledge. Yona found his talks very revealing as he quoted stories from both faiths while explaining the Buddhist vision. Yona visualized another dimension considering the Judaic and Essenic ways he was familiar with.

Yona was fascinated by the story of creation the chief monk explained one day during one of his sessions. Vedic Indians and many eastern cultures followed the composition of the five elements that ruled the universe.

"The basic five elements which make up the universe are earth, water, temperature, air and the soul. These elements change form but never get destroyed. Also, these are the five elements that form the foundation of the human body, or any living organism.

"Firstly, the earth is an element found in various forms. It also forms part of a living body because all living beings die back to the earth. The minute living organisms on earth keep taking shape in different forms. A disintegrating mountain or a human body undergoes this change. Similarly, water is another universal element which takes various forms like the earth. Be it a river or sea water flows like blood in the veins. Here too the minute form takes different shapes. The third element is air which reaches the minutest part of every living body as breath; it is also seen in different form in the universe. The fourth element is fire. The nature of fire is to create heat. We see the fire of the earth, fire of the sky, and the fire of the stomach or the digestive power; the minute form is eternal in the universe. The fifth and the most important is the soul. The essence of life within all forms of life. It is the element of God in everything we see around us. Buddhist Nirvana is the process to elevate the soul in us to the ultimate source or God.

"We see similar views in Greek thoughts too. The four elements of earth, water, air and fire were the essence of life, as proposed by Empedocles. The *Akasa* of the Indian thought, not the sky which the word *Akasa* originally means, but the eternal soul was left out in the Greek thought process till Aristotle added the fifth element, ether, another way of expressing the soul," explained the chief monk Ananda.

Yona enthusiastically raised his hand to ask a question. The chief monk Ananda smiled and asked Yona to stand up. Pre-empting his question, the monk said, "I know you have the Jewish creation story in your mind. God created man in his own image is what the Jewish Bible says. I would add that the likeness of God in man is the soul which is a part of God himself. The likeness to God need not be confused as a physical likeness."

Yona was satisfied with the answer even before the question was asked. He smiled and sat down.

● ● ●

As years passed, Yona gradually picked up the essentials of the Buddhist teaching. He lived in Cyrene almost twenty years before he left for Jerusalem.

One morning chief monk Ananda spoke about pleasure during one of his sessions. "Cyrene has a tradition of philosophical teachings from the times of Socrates through his disciple Aristippus. He taught the ethics of pleasure. He held the idea that pleasure was the highest good. His advice was to avoid pain by abundantly enjoying the momentary sensation of pleasure. Sex, food and wine were prime pleasure-givers to him. His thoughts were mellowed by the followers of the Cyrenaica school during the past two-hundred-and-fifty odd years.

"Buddha taught the opposite. Pursuit of pleasure is in fact the very root of suffering. Even when we experience them, we are not content, we crave for more. Therefore, these short pleasurable vibrations never satisfy us completely. The satisfaction of cravings results in further suffering. The way out is to free oneself of these cravings and the mad pursuit of its fulfilment."

The talk went on explaining the ways to be free from the craving of pleasure, as the great teacher Buddha taught, to free oneself from suffering by understanding the "truth of suffering", "the truth of the cause of sufferings", "the truth of the end of suffering" and "the truth of the path that leads to the end of suffering."

"The commandments to be practiced in order to achieve these goals are, he again quoted Lord Buddha, 'do not kill', 'do not steal', 'do not commit adultery', 'do not offer false testimony' and 'do not corrupt your mind'. The Buddha said, 'We are shaped by our thoughts. We become what we think. When the mind is pure, joy follows like a shadow that never leaves'," the chief monk concluded.

Yona recollected the prohibition of *lo tachmod* (do not covet), the last of the Ten Commandments that God instructed the Jews from Mount Sinai. Coveting leads to robbery, adultery, leading to murder too. The essence of Buddhist teaching he found in the Ten Commandments, learned by heart during his childhood days.

Ptolemy Apion became the ruler of Cyrene enthroned as per the will of Ptolemy Physcon. Rome's intervention was required for the transfer of power from the unwilling stepbrothers in Egypt. The Roman navy and army took up the protection of Cyrene, as Apion did not have the resources to build a force that could defend its territory and the ports from civil unrest and pirates. It was a welcome arrangement for Rome whose people were made the legal heirs of the country after the rule of Ptolemy Apion, by an earlier will of the dead king.

Arillus visited the monastery again, this time with a bearded man. "This is Danios, the caretaker of the hippodrome just down the hill from here," he said.

"Oh, I know him. He was the co-passenger on the cart I took from the port of Apollonia. Actually, he showed this place to us." Yona beamed.

"Our consortium has purchased the hippodrome and the surrounding property from the royal estates and being partner you will from now on oversee our Cyrene operations of the consortium. Danios will assist you and continue to be the caretaker." Arillus sounded relieved to see Yona now as a grown young man and learned too.

"We are in the process of building a villa here to which you can move once completed," said Arillus.

The monks and his friends at the monastery were sad that Yona was to leave. "He is not going far away. We can meet him whenever we want. He has the responsibility of a Roman businessman now as he is a partner to the establishment he represents. It will be good for us to have Roman friends now that the transfer of Cyrene to Roman hands is around the corner." The chief monk was proud of Yona's new position.

The construction of the villa took a couple of years to complete. Yona visited the property and the construction site frequently. This gave him an opportunity to listen to the Cyrenaic Greek philosophers too.

The Cyrenaic school of philosophy had a long standing since the time of Socrates. The Aristippus pleasure theory had mellowed by the prominent current thinkers who followed Epicurus who proclaimed that the highest pleasure was obtained from knowledge, friendship and living a virtuous life. However, he was against the idea of divine intervention, freedom from fear and absence of bodily pain through knowing the limits of one's desire. Too much food or sex would lead to dissatisfaction. He called for a wise and just (neither to harm or to be harmed) life to attain pleasure and contentment.

Another line of thought which originated from Athens was also popular in Cyrene. These teachers were talking to smaller groups like the stoic philosopher and mathematician Zeno who taught from his stoa or porch of his Athens home. This was accessible and therefore

Yona could attend several discourses of the stoic teachers. The Essene way of life had many similarities to stoic teachings.

The stoics taught that the universe itself is God and the laws of nature is fate. The goal of life was to live according to nature. The philosophy propagated that all people are manifestations of the universal spirit and therefore should live in brotherly love.

Yona listened intently as the teacher explained the views of stoics on pain. "One should endure pain or hardship without display of feelings of complaint. Accept your fate and be indifferent to pleasure, pain or fortune."

Yona wondered how similar the thought related to the Essenes of Qumran community. They were poor farmers and artisans like potters and carpenters, wholeheartedly accepting the situation and praised God for nature and all things in the universe. Universal brotherhood was the guiding light. There is happiness in leading a virtuous simple life, he thought.

The teacher said, "Virtue is the highest good. Satisfaction can be achieved by following the road of virtue."

Yona discussed the teachings of the stoics with chief monk Ananda of the Buddhist monastery.

"The stoics do not believe in Nirvana or the link with the ultimate spirit. Buddhism and the Vedic religion believe in the spirit, which is godliness in man, though there are many similarities between stoicism and Buddhism."

● ● ●

Beyond the royal property, a part of which was now with Arillus, there were many Jewish farm owners. They were not citizens of the city of Cyrene but had property rights conferred on them by the earlier Ptolemaic regime being war veterans of the Egyptian army. There were Jewish synagogues outside the city limits. They had constant communication with the Jewish community in Jerusalem and would send tithe and other offerings to the temple at Jerusalem periodically. Yona was eager to know the situation in Jericho and made visits to the synagogue to meet the Jewish brethren there. Jason of Cyrene was a Jewish historian whose talks at the synagogue Yona attended.

The situation in Judea was grim with war on all sides. Judea was now ruled by Alexander Janneus, the Hasmonaean king. The weak Seleucid dynasty in Syria was beset by a power struggle between half-brothers Antiochus Gryphus and Antiochus Cyzicus. In Egypt, Cleopatra III, the cunning queen, became all powerful after weaning Ptolemy Alexander to Cyprus and Ptolemy Apion to Cyrenaica. She ruled with her puppet younger son, Ptolemy Soter II nicknamed Lathyros as co-ruler.

Cyrene Jews were threatened by the eventual takeover of their properties by Rome on the one hand, and prying Egyptian rulers igniting wars on Seleucid kingdom and Judea for takeover of Judean territories, on the other. This unrest helped to build Jewish youth joining militant groups like the Sicarii a militant Jewish group which opposed the Romans. They carried a weapon sicae, or small draggers, concealed in their cloaks.

Yona was tense about the increasing possibility of destruction of the Essenes of Judea and his prophesied role as their savior. My hour has not yet come, Yona thought to himself.

● ● ●

Villa Romana Arillii was completed in two years. Villas of Cyrene hitherto were of Greek design but this one had the Roman touch to it. Situated on a hill slope facing the Mediterranean Sea and overlooking the vast pasture lands, it gave a panoramic view of the valley, the hippodrome in particular.

The villa was built around a wide courtyard with a distinct arrival complex with large drawing rooms, bedroom complex and kitchen complex. Bath houses, dining rooms and the library complex took the elite position of opening onto the courtyard. A well-stocked cellar with large wine storage vats and amphorae running underground had easy access to the upper level.

The colonnaded veranda connected the complexes with mosaic floors and floral edges. The atrium was the formal room where guests were received. On each side of the atrium there were small rooms called cubicula which were used for private meetings. The atrium opened onto different wings. The center of the atrium had a small pool too.

The peristylium, or the garden area, had sculptures and busts of ancestors. The gods of the Arillii household were in a small shrine along the portico. And the bust of King Ptolemy Apion was placed in a prominent place in the atrium.

The venue for formal entertaining and lavish dinners was off the peristyle gardens in an area called the exedra with its exquisite triclinium couches. The walls were beautifully painted with wall décor, the elaborate mosaic floors with large graphics added radiance, beauty and elegance.

A grand housewarming party was organized with lavish feasts and celebrations lasting a week. King Ptolemy Apion made a visit to the first Roman villa in Cyrene and unveiled the sculpture of the king.

Arillus made a strange request to Yona that day. "I would like you to wear a toga, the Roman way while I introduce the partners of the consortium to the king."

"A toga? I am not a Roman citizen. How will your Roman friends tolerate my wearing the toga?" Yona protested.

"There is no bar for wearing a toga. I have seen many including freed men in Rome wearing toga. After all, this country is destined to be a Roman province in a few years, and you will have the right to become a Roman citizen. I have decided to sponsor you for the citizenship on the grounds of your being a partner of the consortium."

Yona accepted the request. The only mismatch was Yona's shaved head in Roman attire.

Yona was introduced to the king with reference to the Indian voyage.

"I remember a Jewish boy and some saffron-clad monks with captain Eudoxes. Nice to meet you again," said the king.

"I am destined to be a monk myself in the order of the Essene sect of the Jews. I was sent to Alexandria for learning from the great teachers there. Also, I am blessed with the opportunity to learn from eminent teachers at the Cyrene academy here. I am a businessman by chance and at heart am still a monk," Yona replied.

"Come to the palace someday. I am interested in many things Indian, including the philosophy of the saffron-clad monks."

"Yes, your highness." Yona bowed.

Arillus was immensely pleased with the opportunity for closer ties with the ruler. He knew well how to create wealth with connections.

Nostalgia overtook Yona. The arena of the rich was not where he wanted to be. Life of a monk with frugal food habits and totally vegetarian diet made him feel like a fish out of water at the villa. His people at Jericho were poor by choice and abhorred luxury. They chose the better wisdom which could not be taken away. There was war and bloodshed in Judea, and he wanted to be with his people in the days of distress.

● ● ●

As the years passed, silphium became near extinct in Cyrene due to over exploitation and grazing. Smuggling and piracy added oil to fire. The Arillus consortium had the monopoly of silphium export now but demand from overseas market could not be met on many occasions. Arillus came down to Cyrene to sort things out.

"We need more protection for our fennels, and we will bring in mercenaries who can stand against these smugglers and thieves. We will place a veteran centurion of the Roman army here to improve the situation. At any cost, we will have to keep our royal customers supplied with enough silphium." Arillus told Yona.

Yona had been in search of an alternative to the silphium and came across another fennel with similar culinary properties widely used in the east called asafoetida.

"I would like to explore the scope of asafoetida, a fennel of the east, for our use," Yona said. I may have to travel east of Euphrates for that. Maybe I will get to know more about our aloe farms in the island of Socotra too," said Yona.

"That suits well for the current situation too. You can oversee the Socotra operations. The Red Sea trade also needs a shot in the arm. The east is becoming more important now and ways to bypass the

Parthians will decide the future of trade with India." Arillus was content with the turn of discussion.

"Very well, you prepare for your journey." He added, "In the meantime, I will send official communications to Socotra about your arrival and taking charge there." He paved the way for a coveted reunion with the Jericho community for Yona.

5

Asafoetida and Charax Spasinu

Yona visited the Cyrene synagogue outside the city gates. Besides the sabbath day worship he had two other reasons for the visit. He knew that the historian Jason of Cyrene was there who could be consulted to understand the present situation in Judea, Syria and Egypt in detail. After the death of Ptolemy Physcon, these countries were in conflict for one reason or the other. It was a peaceful time when Yona left for Alexandria but now the war-killing mounted in all these countries making travel and life difficult. The other reason was to find out if any delegation was going to the Jerusalem temple with whom he also could travel. These well-guarded delegations periodically travelled to the temple to submit the tithe collected and other religious matters connected to the Jews in Cyrene.

Yona was in luck. Jason was free and was in a mood to talk. Also, a delegation was in preparation to travel shortly and they could take

Yona too. Villa Arillii and the partner of the Roman consortium had acquired some recognition already.

"The new rulers of Egypt, vicious Cleopatra III also known as Kokke, her two puppet sons and three daughters together made life miserable to one and all." Jason was sarcastic and his voice hard. "The Jewish generals Cherkias and Ananias of Egypt prevented her from attacking Judea. These generals are the sons of Onias IV. When the high priest Onias III of Jerusalem temple was deposed, his son Onias IV travelled with a large following to Egypt (162 BC). They were received by the then Ptolemy Philometer and settled in Leontopolis delta to erect a temple to Yehweh," explained Jason.

"I've heard about the uproar it created in Judea," Yona said. "A temple to Yehweh outside Jerusalem was unthinkable. It was made more complicated when the Holy Book was translated into Greek at the temple, at the insistence of the king."

"The Egyptian Jews were rich with trade and the rulers were on their side. Therefore, nobody could prevent it from happening. Moreover, who can prevent the prophesies of prophet Isaiah from being fulfilled which says, 'in that day shall there be an alter to the Lord in the midst of the land of Egypt and a pillar to the boarder thereof to the Lord'." Jason took over.

"Cleopatra IV, the elder daughter of the deceased King Ptolemy Physcon was married to her brother Ptolemy Lathyros, the current co-ruler with his mother, Cleopatra III. The mother made him divorce Cleopatra IV and marry his younger sister Selene, to be known as Cleopatra V. The divorced daughter changed sides to the Syrian kingdom with the intention to marry the Seleucid contender to the Syrian kingdom Antiochus Cyzicanus who was at war with his half-brother and ruler Antiochus Gryphus. This move, she made with evil intentions because her eldest sister Tryphania was married to Antiochus Gryphus of Syria and she hated her. She wanted to win Seleucid queenship with the marriage when she was deposed from the queenship of Egypt." Jason explained the political situation in detail.

"Cyzicanus was defeated in the war that followed and he fled to Cyprus," he continued. "Gryphus did not want the victory marred by the murder of his wife's sister. Cleopatra IV took shelter in the temple at Ptolemias where she clung to the deity. Her hands were severed at the orders of Tryphania, her own sister. It did not take more than a year for Cyzicanus to take revenge for the death of his wife to-be by killing queen Tryphania brutally.

"What a turn of events in Egypt after the death of Ptolemy Physcon!" Jason exclaimed. "Judea also had a turbulent time. The then king John Hyrcanus I of Judea sided with Antiochus Gryphos against Antiochus Cyzicanus which brought in Ptolemy Lathyros to the scene in support of Cyzicanus. He gave an army of six-thousand men to Cyzicanus which plundered the domain of the Judean king. Peasants and villagers were attacked mercilessly.

"Present Judean king, Alexander Janneus, started his reign with slaughter." As Jason turned to the situation in Judea, Yona listened eagerly. "He found the civil war in Syria had weakened the country and it was the best time to capture Syrian cities and led an army to the city of Ptolemais. The result was disastrous. With the help of Ptolemy Lathyrus reigning in Cyprus, not only was the attempt thwarted, but it gave Ptolemy Lathyrus a reason to invade Judea and take the city of Asochis in Galilee. The battle on the banks of Jordan ended in a loss of thirty-thousand men and another ten-thousand Jews were taken captive to Ptolemy Lathyros, king of Cyprus. Alexander Janneus had no option other than calling for help from Cleopatra III, Queen of Egypt, who never wanted her deposed son getting powerful and readily helped to prevent the advance of Ptolemy Lathyros. The Jews of Alexandria were on the side of the queen and her two generals were Jews. This action however made Judea a war zone for all the neighboring kings and the suffering of the poor villagers multiplied," Jason continued. "Cleopatra III's army captured Ptolemais and Alexander Janneus submitted to her humbly. Ptolemy Lathyrus pushed back to Gaza, a coastal town for wintering, indicating that there was more to come. Cleopatra III was advised to annex Judea to Egypt. But for the dissuasion of Anannias, one of her chief generals alleging that it would be unfair to attach the domain of a king seeking friendship, a great tragedy was averted. Cleopatra agreed to the alliance with Judea and returned.

"Alexander Janneus' hurt ego made him cross the Jordan and attack Gadera with success. He then marched to Amathus, the fort which held large treasures and took it all. The war zone now extended to the banks of the Jordan river too along with the Syrian borders with the Antiochus brothers and Palestine with Ptolemy Lathyros. Theodotus of Amathus did not rest till he confronted Alexander Janneus and killed ten thousand of his men. He took back what was looted from his city and much more. Alexander Janneus reached Jerusalem empty handed and gave enough reasons for the Pharisees, his enemy among his own men, to mock him to their hearts' content.

The setbacks would not stop the war like Alexander Janneus. The people of Gaza had invited Ptolemy Lathyrus against his wishes and that was enough reason to start a war with Gaza. Ptolemy Lathyros had long gone to Cyprus but the grudge burned inside King Alexander Janneus. Gazans tried to get help from the Nabatean King Artias without success.

"We are amidst this war now," Jason came to the present situation there. Last year he besieged the town of Raphia and Anthedon, cities close to Gaza and this year he attacked Gaza itself. There was a massacre at Gaza. The city of Gaza was laid waste, a heap of ruin. He made some successful advance against the city of Tyre and Emath before getting back to Jerusalem. But the opposition of the Pharisees in Judea is growing from bad to worse." Jason concluded on the situation in Jerusalem.

"Joppa is safe. We can take the road to Jerusalem from there," the local rabbi said, pointing to the delegation getting ready to go to the Jerusalem temple.

Yona bid adieu to his friends at the Buddhist monastery and at the hippodrome. The gentle horses at the breeding station which he saw growing up from birth responded to his silent farewell caress. When he had first walked the road to the monastery from the hippodrome, there were silphium blooms on both sides and now there were none. There is never enough for greed, he thought. When the Roman market found the use of silphium as a contraceptive medicine it did not take more than a decade to wipe the plant to almost extinction. Villa Arillii was now getting ready for the new boss, a retired centurion of the Roman army with pride, half happy in getting rid of the vegan monk who prayed five times a day and wore white wraparounds.

"Maybe, the centurion will save the remaining silphium from the poachers and smugglers," Yona exclaimed.

It was one of Arillus' consortium ship which was taking the party to Joppa. Besides friends from the synagogue there were also guards present in the party. They were called Sicarii because they were armed with daggers, the swift use of which made them fearless warriors. The ship was going to Cyprus and was shoring because of bad weather.

The ship's captain was a Greek known to Yona. He was fascinated by the voyage Yona made to India with captain Eudoxes. "His success made open sea voyage to India fast and profitable because it avoids taxes of several ports. Now ships return in the same year with spices and aromatics. A new minister and administrative officer for the Red Sea operations will arrange for escort ships till Bab el-Mandap."

"I do not know much about the further adventures of captain Eudoxes." Yona was apologetic for the lack of information.

"King Ptolemy Physcon was angry and wanted to put him in prison for making trade arrangements with the Roman consortium on a ship fully sponsored by the king. He was saved by Cleopatra, the sister, and went in hiding. After the death of the king, when she assumed the crown, she sent him on another voyage to India. This trip was very successful, and he made his money too. The political situation was changing rapidly in Egypt and there was no more India trip by Eudoxes. The next voyage he made was to circumnavigate Africa to reach India without crossing the Red Sea and the desert but unfortunately nobody survived the shipwreck in the African coast. Some say the crew was eaten by the cannibalistic tribes," the captain explained.

"He was a father figure to me. He made sure that I was safe before the Egyptian authorities arrested him. It was not only me, he made life easier for all his crew by allowing them to trade in some pearls," said Yona.

He went silent with thoughts about captain Eudoxes.

As they sighted land and the Joppa harbor was getting closer, the captain, in order to cheer Yona up, recounted the story of the Greek Joppa.

"Do you see the rocks on the eastern side of the harbor? Like the one about Cyrene, there is a legend about the rocks of Joppa harbor. Cepheus and Cassiopeia, king and queen of the country, boasted of their daughter Andromeda's beauty and discredited that of the daughters of Nereids the sea god. Poseidon, the girls' companion and brother to Zeus and the sea god decided to punish queen Cassiopeia and sent the sea monster Cetus to ravage the coast and the kingdom. The desperate king consulted the oracle of Apollo who announced that no repose would be found until the king sacrificed his daughter Andromeda to the monster. Stripped naked, she was chained to the rock on the coast for the monster Cetus. The story came to a happy end when Perseus killed the sea monster and married Andromeda."

"I have seen a marble sculpture of naked Andromeda chained to the rocks at the Apollonia temple," Yona remembered.

The berthing ship brought Yona to the present and the sufferings of his people. He again went silent.

"Yona is back on the shores of Joppa." His friends from Cyrene mocked Yona, recollecting the Jewish Bible story of prophet Yona. "Nineveh, your prophet is coming." Yona did not smile. His heart was heavy like the real prophet Yona, after whom he was named, at the thought of the people he was prophesied to rescue. This time it is not Nineveh, it is from the heart of Judea, Jericho itself, he thought. He looked back at the ship and wondered if it looked more like the sea monster Cetus or the monster fish that vomited prophet Yona to the dry shore.

"We are taking the same route to Jerusalem taken by the Phoenicians who brought cedars for the temple as desired by King Solomon," the elder of the group said.

The loaded mules and the men on horses were seasoned pilgrims with dynamic strength. The plains of Joppa were beautiful. Several rivulets provided water for the orchards and the cereals growing in the fields. Lydda was the first walled town they came across.

"Hadid and seven-hundred and twenty-five members of the Lod clan were settled in Lydda after the return from Babylon with Zerubbabel. The house was also called 'Shephelah.' It is called the valley of craftsmen because cloth, leather, wood and metal all requisites for a journey are traded there." The elder explained to Yona because all others were familiar with the town. The road to Jerusalem intercepted the main highway between Babylon and Egypt at Lydda, which gave swift business to the town's craftsmen.

They crossed many cold flowing rivulets. Skillful riders were needed to cross the tract of Mount Carmel called Sharon. At Emmaus, the party reached the Kiriat Yearim ridge road to Jerusalem. "These forests are blessed because the Arc of the Covenant was kept here for twenty long years before being taken to the Jerusalem temple." The elder exclaimed with reverence.

The party stopped at Emmaus and rested the animals. From out of nowhere, a group of armed men appeared.

The leader dismounted his horse and pointed his sword at the pilgrims indicating for them to move away from the luggage they encircled while resting. The guard of the Cyrene pilgrims got up and reasoned with them. "We are not traders and do not have anything of use to you. We are going to the temple for our festival of Tabernacle."

"Do what I say!" He shouted but nobody moved.

Then suddenly, the guard swiftly grabbed a sword and jumped on the leader and stabbed him. The short sword was tainted with blood.

Yona looked at the leader who made a strange sound in his attempt to breathe and a stream of blood sprang from his throat before he fell on the ground face down. Without a word, the rest of the bandits disappeared into the bushes.

The guard wiped the blade of his sword and concealed it back in his robe. And then sat down as if nothing had happened.

The journey to Jerusalem was short but it was a good idea to rest the men and the animals before entering the holy city of Jerusalem. Cyrene pilgrims had a lodge in Jerusalem, built and run by the Jews of Kurena as they were called there.

Yona found himself burning inside with anxiety at the thought of his people at Jericho and stayed awake most of the night while others of the party were sound asleep with fatigue from the journey.

The delegation from Cyrene reached the temple before sunrise. There was already a large crowd rushing to the counters. The offerings counters and the money exchanges were already open. The Cyrene delegation went directly to the treasurer's office. Yona did not go with them; after all he was an Essene.

The feast of Tabernacle approached. Pilgrims from different parts of the country formed groups with their elders in the center and discussed matters of politics and religion. Yona sat with a group to listen. They were Sadducee supporters and traders of eastern goods from Damascus.

"King Alexander Janneaus is doing the right thing." A member of the group said with assertive hand gestures. "This is the opportune time to take control of the cities on the trade routes. The amount of wealth these cities have created in the recent past is enormous.

Both Syria and Egypt have a civil war like situation and if we stand together, we can bring back the times of glory."

"But we are also in a kind of civil war. The Pharisees do not see this opportunity, they are going against the king blindly. The head of the Pharisees, Simon ben Shetah is none other than the brother of Queen Salome Alexandra. When the king's brother-in-law, who is a frequent visitor of the palace, is the leader of the opposition, it is no wonder they have such following among the common people. She is thirteen years older than the king and since she put the diadem on his head when her earlier husband King Aristobulus died, it seems the king listens to her. Moreover, he is never sober at home with his heavy bouts of drinking." Another member responded.

"But think of the trade! We have all the cities on the Mediterranean rim under our control from Gaza to Ptolemais. Any trade crossing the sea will pay tax to us which will bring the prosperity of King Solomon's time back again." A member of the group shouted louder to make his point.

"Yes, it is true. The Nabatean's access to Gaza from Petra and from the Red Sea port Ezion Gaber in the gulf of Aquba are blocked, so is the access of the Syrian routes from Parthia and Mesopotamia to the Phoenician ports of Tier and Sidon. Nobody realizes the value of the great victories of the king. The common people are only interested in the nitty grittiness of the religion," said another.

Yona remembered the talk by Jason at the Cyrene synagogue. He saw the pattern of the king's stratagem. It was port of Ptolemais first. The golden sea port which the Silk Road from China and the spice road from India had access to. Unfortunately, the attack brought the king of Cyprus, Ptolemy Lathyrus the bitter enemy of his mother Cleopatra IV of Egypt, into the mainland for the first time, and

Cleopatra herself later. This made the situation complicated and the king had to meekly put up with them. This situation he reversed with the recent campaigns.

Sukkot, the feast of Tabernacle was under way. The king was back in Jerusalem. Yona decided to stay on for the festival. Twenty years had passed since Yona left Ein-Gedi for Alexandria. The main difference between the times, Yona thought, was that people had become very secretive. Groups gathered and talked in hushed voices. There was a sense of general distrust while looking into the eyes of strangers. The air was not becoming of a happy harvest festival where people prayed, ate and stayed together thanking God for blessing them during the past year and for more blessings in the coming years.

It was the fifteenth day of the month of Tisheri in the Jewish calendar. On the first day, the Lulav and Etrog, the prayer for blessing, was recited continuously through the week-long festival. Yona remembered making the bouquet of lulav with the youngest leaves of the date palm, hadass or myrtle plant and aravah or willow plant. The prayer involved holding the lulav along with the etrog or the citron and waving it on all sides touching the chest with every wave and praying for blessings.

At the Holy Temple, every burnt offering and peace offering sacrificed on the alter was accompanied by a flour offering and by pouring of a prescribed amount of wine on the alter. During the seven days of the festival of Sukkot water too was poured on the alter as libation accompanying the daily morning sacrifice. Water libation was a contested practice by Sadducees because it was not explicitly mentioned in the Tora received by Moses at Sinai, though accepted as a law.

The crowd was getting stronger and since King Alexander Janneaus was to officiate as high priest in one of the morning sacrifices, the security was tightened by increasing the number of soldiers in the temple compound. It was strange that soldiers from Judea and Syria were not allowed because the king did not trust them. After the day's prayer was over Yona decided to proceed to Jericho.

Jericho was only a quarter of the distance away from Jerusalem as opposed to Joppa. The descent was less tiring but fraught with danger. The villagers preferred the beaten tracks to the laid roads and therefore there were no paved roads there. Moreover, the ridge road was so steep on both sides that one could only trust his own footing than that of an animal. While coming up the hill to Jerusalem, mules and donkeys were used mostly to carry the load but on return people preferred to descend on their own.

Early in the morning, Yona made a quick visit to the temple to bid his Cyrene friends farewell as they had more business to do there. As he passed the city gates, there were large groups of people entering the city for the festival. Citron lemon was in season; the trees were full of beautiful yellow fruits. Almost everybody was holding one in preparation of the lulav.

"Why are you going to Jericho now when everybody strives to be here during the festival?" One companion from Cyrene asked.

"My prayer is for the welfare of the poor Essene villagers unwittingly placed in the thick of hostilities between Antiochus brothers of Syria, Ptolemy Lathyrus of Cyprus and his Egyptian mercenary army plundering the villages of Judea, Cleopatra and her son Alexander of Egypt. And our own King Alexander Jannaeus who divided the people by killing his own subjects for reasons best known to him."

Yona was confused and bitter. "I would prefer to be with the peasants of Jericho than being part of this tug of war of ethical doctrines!"

Yona bid farewell to the friends of Cyrene and thanked them for their help in getting to Jerusalem. As he walked down the ridge road to one of the deepest landmasses from sea level, the climate also started changing drastically from a cool misty morning to a hot and dry desert air. The off-white limestone turned red as he reached ground level. To his surprise, there were aqueducts bringing water to the royal orchards where the date palm trees had grown tall and looked pretty. He went straight to the village where he stayed with his parents.

Night was falling but the beaten path was still visible, perhaps because it was so familiar or because the moon was already up and shining. There was no light in any of the houses in the village. Weeds have grown tall on the path and the backyards were in a state of abandonment. Half collapsed walls and roofs made the picture complete. He found his house. The walls made of sandstone rubble were standing roofless. Yona went inside. Broken pots and abandoned cooking vessels were on the floor. Yona cleaned a part of the floor with a piece of cloth he found, took a large drink of water from his sheepskin sack and lay down resting his head on a stone waiting for daybreak.

The prophecy of the chief monk of the Qumran monastery resonated in his ears even more loudly in the silent and confused night as Yona looked at the open sky through his roofless house. Is this the moment of truth? he asked himself. But how? Events from the day of his departure to Alexandria with the monks almost twenty years back flashed in his mind frame by frame as he slipped into a deep sleep.

He dreamt of his parents pruning grapevines in the royal orchard almost bare after the harvest. His father removed every branch that bore no fruit and every fruit-bearing branch he pruned to make it bear more fruit. The main stem remained strong and healthy. Then the vine produced fresh and healthy branches, each one sprouting from the strong stem and started to flower profusely. The dry branches were still burning piled up in a heap.

Yona woke up to the sound of chirping birds. The familiar soothing calls of the birds brought him back to reality. He had to find out what happened to his parents and the villagers. Yona decided to go to the monastery immediately. He remembered the dream. Somehow it was soothing. Yona headed to Qumran before dawn. Essene villages along the road were in an abandoned state. At Nahal David, the waterfall he frequented during his childhood, he rested.

"Why are these villages abandoned?" Yona asked the first person he met.

"They are the Essenes." The man taking a dip in the water replied in a raised voice louder than the flowing water. "They have all gone to Pella beyond Jordan. When King Jannaeus started herding villagers from Judea as laborers for the siege of cities in war zone, whole villages around Ein-Gedi left. It's been several years now." He came out of the water and invited Yona to break bread with him. "I am a potter. I supply urns to the monastery. I have no idea why they need so many urns. They do not drink wine or eat meat. God only knows what they store in them. It is war everywhere and the people are starving. At least I can feed a few mouths with the money." He suddenly went mum as if he had broken a secret and looked suspiciously at Yona.

Yona thanked him for the food and they parted ways. Yona could picture the events better now. He had heard about the independent city of Pella in Transjordan. Pella in Macedonia was the birthplace of Alexander the Great. The Macedonians gave the name Pella to many towns which reminded them of their great leader Alexander. There was a large colony of Greeks in this Pella of Transjordan, right from the days of Alexander, maybe because of the medicinal hot water springs in this region. The city was also famous for its glass products.

Yona, almost thirty-three years old now, wise and strong, was visiting the monastery after twenty years. He asked for his friend Eber, the scribe. Their embrace was tighter and longer and without words, but it told a long story of despair and loss.

"Where are my parents? I had been to the village to find only abandoned houses. The same is the case of other villages too."

"The past few years had been like hell from the shores of the Mediterranean to the sea of Galilee and beyond with wars waged by our King Janneaus, Ptolemy Latherus of Cyprus, Cleopatra and her other son Alexander, and to top it all, between the Antiochus brothers. People were herded from villages as slaves for siege works and war labors. Thousands of soldiers and villagers were killed. Those within the walled cities had some recourse but our community living peacefully in villages had no protection by way of walls or arms. Many perished to the sword of the plundering soldiers. Many fled east looking for a peaceful land. Transjordan towns and those along the Euphrates welcomed some. We also encouraged the villagers to leave for Pella, a Transjordan town with a large Greek population, from where they could find a haven. I am happy to see you now and am convinced that the prophecy about your role in the rescue of the community will be fulfilled." Eber recollected the day Yona departed to Alexandria with the Buddhist monks.

Yona did not respond. Can a messiah cry? Yona wondered. It tortured him to think that he had been absent when they had needed him the most. He who was prophesied to be their deliverer.

They sat down at Eber's office; he was the chief scribe now. A large team of scribes with boards in their lap were busy copying documents. "It is much busier now than the old days," Yona murmured. Another group was waterproofing large urns with bitumen from the Dead Sea. It was like the mummification process he had witnessed in Alexandria.

"What is all this?" Yona asked. "You seem to be very busy."

"The days of the community are numbered. The teacher of righteousness has prophesied that the days of apocalypse have come. We already have experienced massive earthquake damage at the monastery. It will not withstand another one like that. We are taking measures to prepare against the annihilation prophesied." Eber sounded anxious. Yona could relate the scene to that of Prophet Noah busy building the boat the Lord had instructed him to make, explained with dramatic actions at the synagogue for the children by the rabbi.

"What are the urns for?" Yona could not hold himself back anymore.

"We have decided to make several copies of the scriptures and the documents and store them in the sealed urns so that they survive the destruction."

"Our king, Alexander Jannaeus, swore to help the monastery and consulted our righteous teacher Judas on all matters. This has changed recently, and he has become a wicked king and a wicked priest!" Eber said, emphatically.

"I had seen elaborate arrangements for the king's visit to the temple for the Sukkot ceremony," Yona said. "There were more soldiers than pilgrims at the temple."

"There is bad news from Jerusalem," a messenger on horseback announced. "There are massive killings in the temple and several thousands are put to sword by the soldiers."

"Why? What happened?" A big roar arose as the messenger was taken to the chief monk.

"The Pharisees abused the king, calling him son of a fallen woman, recalling her being prisoner of the Syrian King Antiochus. They claimed the king is not fit to be the high priest while he was performing water libation at the altar. In his anger, he poured the blessed water on his feet instead of the alter on the offerings and the commotion started. People started throwing citrons held with lulav towards the king and the soldiers on guard started the massacre at the orders of the king. I ran out of the temple complex before they closed it from inside." The messenger was still shivering with excitement.

"The pilgrims from Cyrene started throwing the citrons first, and all of them were put to death immediately," the messenger continued.

"Bloodshed in the temple by our own king is unheard of. We had heathen kings doing it before, but this definitely is the end of times as prophesied." Eber hurriedly escorted the messenger to the chief monk. Yona followed.

"Is our righteous teacher safe?" the monk asked.

"Yes, I saw him retiring to his chamber at the temple complex."

Yona was introduced to the chief monk. On hearing the story of the past years and the present assignment to Socotra the monk was pleased.

"Take in as many people at Socotra. It is a blissful place. The Essene families who have already fled to the east can also be rescued with this arrangement. They will not be fugitives anymore. Put them to farming and trade. They can also work with the Therapeutae who are already there with the Jewish community on the mainland. God has chosen you for the welfare of the righteous people."

"Amen. The prophecy of his being the savior of the community is fulfilled. While he was leaving for Alexandria with the Buddhist monks, this prophecy was uttered by our beloved previous chief monk," Eber said.

Yona wept like a child and prostrated before the chief monk praising God aloud.

After dinner, Yona and Eber spread mats on the roof.

"Remember Beer Sheba sky?" Eber asked Yona looking at the clear blue sky recollecting the caravan journey they had undertaken with the Buddhist monks almost twenty years ago.

"Yes, I do. There are very few places on earth with such a magnificent view of the night sky." They both had much more important subjects to discuss than the stars now but where to start, both wondered.

"Why do you think the king is in such a bad mood?" Yona opened the current topic first.

"He was brought up in Galilee away from the sight of his father John Hyrcanus who disliked him. His association with the rich Sadducee merchant community taught him about the trade from the east passing through the upper Galilean and Syrian cities making them rich progressively. Most importantly, his childhood companion was none other than our teacher of righteousness. His ascension to the throne was prophesied and he was called to rule the country by the name of truth.

"The problem was his uncle, the queens' brother, the leader of Pharisees, who wanted to influence the rule. Alexander Janneaus wanted to make Judea great like during King Solomon's time with his expansionistic policies to attract maximum tax from the trade passing through his domain, while the rituals and rules of the religion was important to the other party. He ignored them but took to heavy drinking which made him a cruel king killing his own people too without any mercy."

Eber somehow collected his wits to tell Yona about his parents and other members of the village.

"Your parents' village was robbed by the mercenary army of the Syrian king once supplied by Ptolemy Lathyrus, mostly of Egyptians. They killed many, set fire to houses and robbed the people and took slaves. Our king gave a fitting reply to this assault later, but the loss cannot be repaired."

Yona did not speak for a while. The silence told him the story of their disappearance. Then he got up and looked straight into the eyes of Eber and announced, "I must reach Charax Spasinu on the mouth of River Tigris on the Persian Gulf at the earliest to find estranged Essenes and from there I will catch a vessel to Socotra, my destination."

"I am quite relieved by the words of the chief monk and my directions are clear now. I have put down the bondage of the prophecy on me and I feel free now." Yona was calm but determined to fulfil the prophecy of being the savior of his community.

● ● ●

Obodas I was ruling the Nabataeans. His success in ambushing King Alexander Jannaeus of Judea at Gadara gave him confidence to reciprocate even though his access to Mediterranean ports was blocked. The Judeans were now preparing to block the highway to Damascus from Petra which would, if succeeded, be fatal for the caravan trade. Therefore, Obodas I supported all efforts to destabilize Judea by befriending groups rebelling against the Judean king within the country. A delegation was sent to King Obodas I by the chief monk of the Qumran monastery and he welcomed the delegation of Essene monks from Ein-Gedi with interest.

"There is war on all sides at Judea and the defenseless villagers of our sect are planning to flee the country to the more peaceful east. We have come to request your kindness to use the desert route to Charax Spasinu for our people." The delegation from Qumran monastery made their submission to the king.

"Where do you want to go? India?" Was the first reaction of the king.

"No. We have our people living along the gulf, descendants of the people deported by the Mesopotamian king, centuries back. We hope to find peace there," the monks replied.

"We do not have control of the entire route. You will have to pay for caravan expenses and protection from the Bedouin sheiks of the territory you pass," the king warned.

"We understand that. Three monks wish to cross the desert before the winter sets in. Travel plans of other members of the sect will be made after the winter season," the delegation explained.

"Monks going to India are welcome." The king was pleased with the merchandise from India which brought good profits. "We can get to know of Indian markets from them. There would be caravans leaving Petra towards east with the first winter rains, which you can join too."

The king dismissed the delegation on a positive note.

The desert route was a monopoly of the Nabateans. A week to ten days journey from Petra towards east would lead to the Wadi Sirhan. Till this point, travelers could find some water, even though the wells were owned by various Arab nomads. Wadi Sirhan was a long stretch of dry hills and gorges in the north-south direction, touching the dunes in the south. There was no water to be found further. There were patches of volcanic rocks towards the east. Nabataeans collected rainwater in cisterns cutting these rocks. They made huge underground cisterns and camouflaged them. Winter rains would fill these wells to provide sufficient water for their caravans to reach Basra or Charax Spasinu at the mouth of the river Tigres. No one dared travel this secret waterless route other than the Nabataeans who made huge profit from transporting eastern goods arriving at the head of the Persian Gulf, avoiding tax payments. They reached the Mediterranean coast within a month while other northern routes would take double the time and halt at several cities paying hefty taxes. The nomad sheikhs holding the territory made safe passage at a cost.

Towards the close of the month of October, rains began to fall heralding the seeding season for wheat and barley. These showers would last for a few days. Desert travel also would become tolerable due to the cool weather. Yona and two other monks got ready to take the desert journey as passengers with the Nabataean caravan. The monks were going to the Indian university of Taxila as students of the Vedic religion of India. They were younger than Yona but had already learned a great deal about India from the visiting monks at Qumran monastery and at Alexandria where they had already studied for several years.

Taxila university was visited by Alexander the Great during his campaign against India. He was invited into the city by King Ambi who surrendered his throne to Alexander. During his stay of about three weeks at Taxila Alexander walked around and met many intellectuals and teachers and took part in discussions and debates. He wrote about the intellectual splendor of Taxila to Aristotle and his mother. He was fascinated by the advancement in medical sciences at the university which the accompanying physicians incorporated in their practice too.

Veda means knowledge in general, grouped into four main divisions namely *Rigveda, Samaveda, Yajurveda* and *Atharvaveda.* Each *Veda* has *Samhita* or book of hymns to which Brahmanas or treaties relating to prayer are attached. The philosophical doctrines are contained in *Aranyakas* which forms part of the *Brahmanas* of each Veda. *Aranyaka* provides the allegorical significance of the rites and the mystic meaning of the text of *Samhitas.* Then the *Upanishads* deal with the spiritual topics, the universal soul, the absolute, the individual self, the origin of the world and the mysteries of nature.

The philosophers of the west kept keen interest in the subject, and it was studied in Alexandria, Cyrene, Athens and at Qumran monastery. The monks travelling with the caravan would stay in India for a long time to complete their studies.

●　●　●

Yona and the two other monks in training were taken to the meeting of the council of the caravan leader, the chief sheikh of the caravan.

"These three monks from Qumran wish to travel to Busra as passengers with our caravan." The messenger made the introduction.

"Do we really want a Jew here after all the destruction their king has done to our Gaza port?" A member of the council protested.

"The king approved their travelling with us because they are members of a sect opposing their king's deeds." There was no more hesitation from the council in accepting them as passengers.

"If it rains during the journey, the nights will be very cold. Be prepared for that." The chief sheikh remarked looking at the thin white gowns they were wearing. The sheikh was content with their purpose of journey as they had previously taken India-bound passengers on pilgrimage.

"Once you join the caravan, your loyalty and even life will rest with the chief sheikh. We work as a team to pass the desert. We have friendly tribes all along the route and availability of water will depend on the rains. There has been a loss of men and animals in the past on this route and therefore we keep the numbers small. You can have one camel to carry your goat skins for water and personal effects besides one camel with side bags to carry two passengers and another for the third. You should declare your luggage for valuation and tax payment to the Bedouins chiefs along the route." The caravan leader was a member of the royal family and all the sheikhs and merchants had complete trust in his leadership and had great respect for him.

Fifty camel-mounted guards of the Agail tribe were on fast-moving dromedary camels providing protection for the caravan. They also had a few horses for patrols. The *daleel* or pilot of the caravan was talking to each of them. Piloting is an inherited profession and his position in the caravan was next to the chief sheikh.

"We will march at our best speed till the oasis of Juaf. This will take seven to eight days if we are able to march added hours in the night. At Juaf, we will rest and plan the next part of the journey." The chief sheikh said at the council. "If we get some rain beyond Wadi Sirhan, we will be able to resume and reach Charax in another ten days. Without assured water the second phase would be suicidal. We may have to wait till such assurance either by rain or by the tribes. If the cisterns are also dry, we may have to cut the number of animals too."

The royal blood in the chief sheikh paid off. Till Juaf, they managed twelve hours' travel a day without reaching exertions limits. There was rain, the sky was cloudy most of the days and the night was cool. The only problem was the wet cloths due to the rains making the cold unbearable at night when the wind blew.

Roasted beans of the locust bean tree dipped in honey gave the monks strength. At Jericho, whenever people went out in the wilderness, they carried it. It had all nutrition needed for survival in the desert. Yona and the other monks avoided the lamb and rice dish called *phulaf* made in the evening, which was the only cooked meal of the day, and ate only vegetables. There were watering stations at every halt and the animals also were not tired. The caravan reached Juaf on schedule and pitched camp outside the city.

Many caravan routes to the east passed Juaf, at the southern end of Wadi Sirhan, thus avoiding the big cities of the north and saved on taxes. Most of them turned north from Juaf towards the Euphrates and reached towns like Karbela or still south on the river. The caravan took a direct route to Busra port cutting across waterless paths through the lava stone area. This was also a difficult tract for the camels, and so their load was light. A few rains showers gave the chief sheikh of the caravan enough confidence to start the second phase of the journey.

A couple of days into the journey, there were no wells to be found, but some collected pools of rainwater quenched the thirst of the animals. Several horses and some camels were left with the tribes at Juaf. Men would take the same water, boil it and clean the sediment with alum before filling their goatskins. Times were getting tough for the monks.

The next water source was two days away. The chief sheikh and the guards had gone ahead to find it with Jaleel, the pilot. They discovered a hidden water cistern cut in the volcanic rock like those found in limestone in Petra. It was waterproofed with a type of concrete for which the Nabataeans had expertise. It was completely hidden, and no one would have found it without help. It had collected enough rainwater for the entire caravan. This ingenious method of rainwater harvesting by the Nabataeans in places where there was no ground water was found in three more such locations. It was almost a month from leaving Petra when the caravan reached Charax Spasinu, a Greek town on the mouth of river Tigris.

Charax Spasinu was a port city on the mouth of the river Tigris and was the capital of Characene. The Parthian city of Susa, which was the winter capital of the Parthian kings, used Charax Spasinu as its port. A Greek settlement since the times of Alexander the Great, Charax Spasinu had a Greek quarter called Pella – a namesake of Alexander's native village in Macedonia. The Greek population living on the Tigris was known as Babylonians and those on the Persian

Gulf was called Chaldeans. Jews, Syrians and Persians also lived there mainly for trade purposes.

The caravanserai was already crowded when Yona's caravan reached Charax. Yona befriended a Persian merchant and enquired about asafoetida.

"You are coming from Kurena and asking for asafoetida here?" His big turban and aesthetically trimmed beard gave him the look of a wise man who knew everything. He pointed at Yona and continued. "Are you aware that asafoetida is the same plant you call silphium in Kurena? The conquering Persian king in the past, deported part of the population from the Cyrene city of Barce to Bactria in the east and they brought silphium along with them. The harsh climate of the east yielded inferior resin with a distinctive stench which gave it the name 'devil's dung'. But once you heat it in oil it will start behaving like silphium." He laughed aloud.

"Where can I meet a merchant who can supply asafoetida in large quantities?" enquired Yona.

"You should look for traders from Demetrius of Sind, a port on the Indus river because most of the asafoetida is collected from areas around the port. Their trading vessels hug the ports in Gedrosia and Carmania before reaching Charax. You can meet them at the Buddha Vihara here." His fellow passengers heading for Taxila were also going to the Buddha Vihara and would take the same route to Indus. Yona accompanied them.

Greek traders controlled the traffic of Indian goods from Barygaza, the Indian port on the Sowrashtrene coast. Demetrius of Patala and Kutch were the trade centers in between the Persian Gulf and Barygaza. Inland traffic through the river Indus reached the Demetrius port and those coming from the southern ports of India culminated at Barygaza. The Carmanian side of the Ormuz straits was called Omana. Carmania though never controlled by Indians was called "white India" for its huge market for Indian goods and the Bactrian Greeks who traded here. On the opposite side of the Gulf, on the Arabian side was the port of Oman, the transit center for goods moving towards Punt or the Horn of Africa and beyond.

Fight for political control of the Persian Gulf with the Greeks lasted till the Seleucids had Seistan and Elymais under their control during the rule of Antiochus Epiphanes. After the Greeks lost control, Carmania was neither Greek nor Parthian and thus became a haven for India-bound traders, fortune seekers and freedmen.

Yona met Indranidutta at the Buddha Vihara. It was like a meeting a long-lost family member. The smile on his face reflected his innate happiness; all the years of learning at Cyrene Buddhist monastery in pursuit of happiness had created a mental image of happiness for Yona, and here it was. His clean-shaven head gave him the look of a Buddhist monk, but he was not wearing the saffron robe. The businessmen Yona knew, be it a Roman, Jewish or Nabatean were all serious looking people. But here was a man, Yona thought, with an open-armed welcome and the attitude of a saint.

Indranidutta, a Bactrian Greek citizen of Barygaza delt mainly with teakwood for ship building. Baren deserts and over exploitation of Mediterranean pine made wood a dear commodity for the war-mongering navies and merchant vessels exploring the horizon. His supplies would reach ports till the Red Sea from India but the major market being Oman on the Persian side and Charax Spasinu. Aromatic Indian sandalwood for decorating royal chambers was also his specialty. He would get the wood from south India in the Malabar coast as logs and lug them to Barygaza by the sea where the Greek or Yavana carpenters, as they were called in India, made planks and beams out of the logs, suitable for ship building. Evergreen rainforests of Malabar had an abundant supply of teakwood and sandalwood. Indranidutta made great wealth in trading and donated much of his wealth for the Buddhist cause. The Buddha Vihara at Charax Spasinu was also his contribution.

Indranidutta had knowledge of asafoetida which Yona was seeking. Indian cities of Kandahar and Herat were the major centers of asafoetida trade and the ports of Demetrius Patala and Barygaza had many traders exporting asafoetida to the west. Indranidutta agreed to help Yona in the procuring and shipping of asafoetida to the ports of the Persian Gulf or even further.

6

Aloe Farms of Sukhdara Island

Island abode of bliss, (the present-day Socotra island) was called *Dipa Sukhdara* in Sanskrit. There are several translations of the island's name in different languages, all meaning blissful island. Lying almost two-thousand four-hundred stadia (240 miles) east off the Yemeni coast, it served as a link between India and the west on the Red Sea rim. Indian traders from Kuch used the island as a temporary abode while they awaited favorable wind to head back to India. The island had several long tunnels suitable for such stay. Legend has it that at the opening of the Hoq cave, there was a large Shivalinga which was transported to another center of Indian congregation in the Gulf area when the Greeks took over the island.

The Greeks were brought in at the orders of Alexander the Great. When he found out about the aloe and dragon blood trees growing in Socotra, he sought advice from Aristotle, who suggested to settle

Greeks on the island, and to take control of the production of the aloe juice and dragon blood tree resin. The majority of the Greek families came from Astagira, the native city of Aristotle, trained in making medicine out of the aloe juice and dragon blood tree resin. The island was protected by soldiers of Ptolemy and Seleucus, the governors for Egypt and Syria. Many Syrians (Semitic people from Seleucia) were also brought in as farm workers. As time went by, the Greek population declined, giving way to a mixed population speaking Greek, Aramaic and Arab languages.

Indranidutta and Yona set sail to Quana where the ship would unload the teak planks for reshipping to Red Sea ports. Yona would find a ship going to Socotra from Quana, which was the closest port to Socotra. The ship was loaded to the brim and there were no other merchants or passengers. The cabin next to the captain's was comfortable with hammocks. Yona revisited his past with the like-minded Indranidutta during the days of the voyage.

"You have made the right choice," Indranidutta reassured Yona. "There are already Aramaic speaking people on the island and your people will be at home."

Yona watched the fishermen diving into the water in order to harvest pearls as they sailed past the Bahrain islands. "Yes, I believe so. Moreover, they will not be asylum seekers as we have some place to accommodate them."

"How did the aloe farms come into the hands of the Alexandrian firm?" Indranidutta was curious.

"Actually, the aloe from Socotra was in the hands of Egyptian Greeks from the beginning. The business became sluggish when the Red Sea transport of aloe landed into problems with the Arabs. Our consortium had financed the plantation and trade and later took over the business in redemption of the debts. There was no change in the people involved but only the ownership changed. This is the first time someone from Alexandria is taking up the leadership at Socotra, and that too on my request for such an opportunity," Yona said.

Lofty brown mountains lined the horizon to his right. There was busy fishing activity on the coast. "The next major port is Moska (present day Muscat). Normally, our ships go directly to Moska from Hormuza. This time we had some algum logs (sandalwood) for Charax Spasinu and a long overdue visit to the Buddhist monastery there," said Indranidutta.

"I understand that the monastery building was your gift," Yona said, admiringly.

"This is one of the many Lord helped me to assist. We have many rock-cut Viharas in India where I could perform *Vihaar Daan*," said Indranidutta.

The teachings of the chief monk at the Cyrene Vihara echoed in Yona's ear. "*Vihaar Daan* is considered one of the best forms of *daan*. Buddha had said, 'The Vihar offers protection from heat and cold, wild animals, reptiles, mosquitoes, rains and storms. It is useful for shelter, comfort, meditation and yoga. This is the reason for *Vihaar Daan* being called *Sreshta Daan* (*Agra Daan*). When this is done monks preach Dharma which ends suffering," explained Yona.

Yona sat quietly thinking about the protection he was prophesied to provide to the Essene community.

Days passed sluggishly. Indranidutta spent time meditating. The ship was sailing past Sargos, the port thrusting out into the sea. "Frankincense country starts from here. There is traffic from Sargos to Socotra. But Cana port will be better for you with better ships," said Indranidutta.

"Cana is the port from where frankincense goes to the world. Regardless of religion frankincense is used during prayers, funerals and embalming all over the world. Indian ships also visit Cana and wait for months for favorable wind for their return voyage. There is frequent traffic to Socotra from here. Adramite, a tribe of Sabaeans live here," Indranidutta continued. "The name Hadhramaut is derived from this tribe. The old seat of the Himyarite tribe is also not far from here. It is a well-designed city with black marble high-rise buildings and city walls," Indranidutta added.

As soon as the ship berthed on port, inspection for tax collection was carried out by the port officials and duties were paid. Indranidutta's customers were waiting and quickly enough the offloading of the cargo began. Yona went around the port looking for ships leaving for Socotra.

Yona came across people who looked Jewish selling aloe juice in amphorae ready for loading in the ship's cargo.

A trader spotted Yona and called out to him. "If you have an army, you will need this panacea. It heels the wounds and keep the soldiers healthy." In a low voice he added. "It keeps your maiden beautiful and healthy too." The trader mocked Yona who approached the amphorae of aloe vera juice.

"I know you are getting it from Socotra island. I am looking for a ship going to Socotra. I have friends there," Yona said in Aramaic.

"You can find many dhows going there but for a big vessel you may have to wait. The dhows are faster. If you do not have much cargo,

I can introduce you to a captain." The trader responded in Aramaic with a hint of comradeship.

"I have only my personal effects with me and I am okay with the dhow," replied Yona.

A deal was made with the captain, the trader getting his kickback. Yona bid farewell to Indranidutta after procuring contracts for supply of asafoetida to Socotra. They parted as friends of several lives promising to maintain contact for a lifetime.

Arabian dhows were altogether a different ballgame. Yona had seen them before with their typical triangular sails.

"Hop on the Baghlah." The captain nodded at Yona.

Baghlah means mule in Arabic. Looking at the confused Yona he said, "We call her mule. Look at the beautiful quarter galleries. You can get good rest there. She is the best sailing vessel here and takes a hundred tons with her three lateen sails. You will enjoy your voyage to Socotra. Good value for money."

Yona later realized he had paid three times the normal fare for a passenger berth unwittingly. But he was right, the voyage was comfortable. The ship berthed at the northern port called Hadibo of the island where the market was located. The Greek factory for processing and packing aloe juice and dragon blood tree resin was close to the port.

Message had already reached about Yona at Socotra and men from the aloe farm were waiting to welcome him. Yona rested for a couple of days before he set out to explore the island. The house built in limestone was of Arab style but for the long veranda was reminiscent of Villa Arillii at Kurena.

"Socotra is eight-hundred stadia (80 miles) long and three-hundred stadia (30 miles) wide with limestone mountains rising up to three-thousand three-hundred cubits (5000 ft) in between," explained the men accompanying him in Greek. "The coastal plains are narrow and berthing big ship in ports other than Hadibo is difficult. Indian vessels anchor on the northern end of the island near the Hoq cave but the Arabs prefer Dogub caves where clean water is aplenty on the southern beach. The eastern half of the island has many rivulets, even though seasonal rain provides sufficient water for our farms and people."

"Do we employ Indians and Arabs at the farm?" Yona enquired.

"Indians are traders from Broach and Dimitrius Patala. They come here in December and January and stay four or five months till the wind is favorable for their return. Arabs mainly engage in fishing and sea trade as seamen and ship owners. We employ mostly Syrians, the decedents of the people sent here by Seleucids as workers."

"What about the Greek population now?" enquired Yona.

"It is almost two-hundred years now since Alexander the Great sent the Greeks here. The Ptolemies had control over the island then. The political equation has changed a lot here and we pay taxes to the Hadhramaut kings for the aloe we send to Alexandria now. There is no more influx of Greeks, and the Greek population has dwindled greatly. To be honest, it is a group of Hellenized Syrians now and we speak Aramaic more than Greek here. There is a lease arrangement with the Hadhramaut kings, and our guards protect others from occupying the territory. Once the lease expires, it is assumed the Yemenites will occupy the island."

The picture is grim, Yona thought. He thought about the abundant silphium Cyrene produced when he reached there first, and the complete disappearance of the silphium on his leaving.

"The Roman greed," Yona said aloud as if answering someone. The people around him did not get it but said nothing.

At the factory, large leaves of thorny aloe plants were being cut longitudinally to remove the thorns and the skin was peeled off revealing jelly-like aloe juice. It was scooped up with a knife from the lower skin and the juice came off as jelly which then was packed in amphorae and sealed.

"This is the panacea for all ills." The factory supervisor was eloquent. He also wanted to impress the new boss. "It heals your wounds, cleans your gut and purifies your blood. It is the secret of Cleopatra's glowing skin."

Yona cut him short. "How do you keep the juice fresh during the days of travel to Alexandria and beyond?"

"We ensure the harvested leaves are bruise-free and cut the nearest the stem to prevent exposure to the atmosphere. It is filled in the amphora to the brim without delay and sealed with bee wax. It stays intact for six months," the supervisor explained.

Yona set about exploring the island after a few days of introduction and familiarizing himself with aloe farming. Arabian horses in the farm were versatile animals like the Cyrene horses bred on the Arillus farms. Yona enjoyed their presence and cared for them with a breeder's love to which the animals responded affectionately.

There were many south-flowing seasonal rivulets with wide wadis and the beaches were wide on the south. A great granite wall was situated on the eastern tip. There was a loud roaring sound as the waves broke against the rock-like formations. There were many caves on the island, the longest almost two miles deep was on the northern end called the Hoq cave.

"Indians from Barukaccha and Gujarat once occupied the cave and they had their deity here too," his companion said. "They kept their merchandise safe in the cave. Now they have to move to the mainland after selling their ware at the market in Haribo. Very few sailors live in the southern wadis these days awaiting favorable wind to head back to India."

About three-hundred stadia (30 mile) stretch of wadi on the south was the main aloe farm area. Mule-loads of harvested leaves crossed the mountains to reach the factory. The work was tedious and there was a shortage of work force as Arabs were occupied with fishing and only Syrian settlers were available for farm work.

"I have made arrangements for bringing in some more workers from Syria. The war there is making many leave for safer places," Yona said.

After morning prayers facing the rising sun in the Essene way, Yona climbed down the small hillock of white sand on the shores of Hadibo beach. The boy he confronted on his way to the beach was still there watching the soft rays of the sun. About twenty years back, he thought of another boy who used to stand and watch the morning sun of Alexandria at every opportunity, because his home was eastward. Yona got a sudden urge to speak to the boy.

"I am Ruan, my home is on the other side of the ocean." The boy's accent was different, and his skin tone was darker than the sunburned locals. He looked short for his age, but his eyes were deep and large and were very prominent.

Yona sat down with him on the sand as Ruan told him about the accident that led to his father's death. "That was my first voyage across the sea. My father, uncle and two sailors were on the boat. We carried cinnamon bark and malabatrum (cinnamon leaves). I was sitting at the top mast and saw the big sea roll approaching us and I shouted to Appa. He was struggling to untie the sail and the sailors held on to the rudder firmly, but it was too late. In the first gush itself the mast broke and I was thrown out into the sea holding tightly onto the piece of the mast I was sitting on. The wind took the boat and all of them and they never returned. Later some sailors found the wreck on the African coast. I was rescued and live in the factory ever since."

"I also have lost my parents." Yona consoled him. You can meet me any time you want. I too have to learn about your land and language."

Ruan thus became his personal assistant. Ruan was a native of Taprabane, (Sri Lanka) an island country in the Indian peninsula further south to the tip of India, cape Kumari. Several small islands were a part of Taprabane and Ruan was also the name of the small island in which his family resided. Pearl fishing and cinnamon harvesting were the occupation of the islanders, both the products were in high demand in Socotra. Cinnamon trees grew wild in these islands. Arabs concealed the secret origin of these products from the western buyers, making huge profits. These small boats were not allowed to sail beyond Socotra to keep the secret.

"Tell me about the cinnamon trees." Yona did not remember seeing a cinnamon tree during the voyage with Eudoxes.

"Taprabane is the southernmost part of the Indian peninsula. Emperor Asoka sent his son Mahindra to Taprabane to convert King

Tissa to Buddhism and there are many Buddhists there now." Ruan had learned Yona was with the Buddhist monks at Cyrene.

"It rains most part of the year and there is a large forest area where cinnamon also grows. My native island is small, but we also have many cinnamon trees there. It grows tall to the height of a dragon blood tree with thick branches. The branches are cut down and the bark is peeled off and dried to make the cinnamon quills or rolls we see in the market called Kheneh. The dried leaves are called malabathrum here."

"I know now that the Arabs buy cinnamon from here and sell it as a product of Auxum on the Red Sea, a country known as cinnamon country in Alexandria," Yona intervened.

Ruan loved the sea and had an uncanny sense of direction. He would lie watching the sky at night and could recognize many stars and their movements, a trick boys learn from the elders. Yona was also passionate about astronomy and this hobby strengthened their bond of comradeship. Yona encouraged Ruan to gather boys of his age group and learn the ways of the sky.

"Imagine the earth we live in is encircled by a big round balloon. We call it the horizon. Now imagine the stars we see all fixed in the balloon and the horizon is moving at a set pace. The position of the stars we see is changing even though they are fixed. The position of the stars is fixed in relation to each other but changing in relation to the horizon. How to get direction from the stars in the open sea?" Yona asked the group, all lying on their backs watching the stars.

"Druva star sits in the north and does not move. We can find north by finding the Druva star." Ruan was quick.

"Yes, Dhruva is also called Polaris or the North star. There are other stars too which can be identified to get help in finding directions. Indian monks have identified twenty-seven stars rising and setting at fixed time and days in relation to the moon and repeat the process with every cycle of the moon. With long years of observation, they have documented the rising and setting time of each such star. Here too, changed horizon will give different timings but with experience, we can relate the position of these stars to Polaris and find direction. Once proficient, you will be able to identify the path of each of the stars," Yona explained to the group.

Yona, by imparting the eastern astronomical knowledge to the boys, knowingly or unknowingly, created a fine group of future navigators and pilots for the Eritrean Sea navigation.

Another game the boys played during the day was the stick and shadow method to observe the movement of the sun between the northern and southern hemisphere. Also finding the true east by joining two shadows of equal length no matter which side of the hemisphere the sun is tilted to. Knowledge of the sun rising and setting in different parts of the year was the clue of navigating open sea with the help of sun.

"You will now watch the wind carefully." Yona pleased with the progress the boys made encouraged them to learn more. "You will find that there is a pattern in the wind direction, speed and the moisture it carries. The wind blows in the direction it did in the previous year, and you can expect it to blow in the same direction next year too. You have observed that the Indian dhows head back to their home from here in the months of August to October, and they stay here waiting for the wind to come. The steady wind blowing east from the African coast is the wind they are waiting for, which blows every year at the same period," Yona explained.

The boys were overawed with the knowledge when it was related to the day-to-day life of the island. "There is a wind blowing from India in January which brings the Indian dhows to Socotra. You will become fine navigators, pilots and starboard lookouts one day." Yona said. Ruan could see the bigger picture now.

●　●　●

Indian wares of lower value had a market at Hadibo. Medicinal plants of Indian origin were the main commodity. Indian medical practice had found acceptance among Arabs and even Alexandrians. Buddhists, Essenes and Theraputes of Alexandria practiced this branch of medicine. Most of the supplies came by overland routes but dhows also brought in some medicinal plants. It was at this market Yona met Yishaq.

Dressed in traditional Jewish attire Yishaq had a long list of herbs he wanted to procure at the market. He was surprised to know the new boss at the aloe farm was a Jew and he talked freely in heavily accented Aramaic with a hint of Arabic. He was short and darkish brown like an Indian with a white long beard and payot, the side curls.

"Do you know there was a settlement of Hebrews in southern Arabia from King Solomon's times? This is Queen Sheba's country. The tradition says that our forefathers came here with prophet Jeremiah." Yishaq looked up at Yona and smiled at the quizzical expression on Yona's face.

"I have not heard about it," Yona confessed.

"Our ancestors came to Yemen forty-two years before the destruction of the first temple. Prophet Jeremiah repeated the Lord's words of destruction of the temple and subjugation of the people, but the rulers wanted to kill him. So, he left Jerusalem with seventy-thousand men who believed him and those men are our ancestors," Yishaq said.

Yona was still not convinced. But he nodded.

"The heat of the desert made our skin dark. The Hebrews of the kingdom of Sheba are also dark," Yishaq added.

"Yes, of course", Yona felt guilty that Yishaq had to justify his skin color. "Then why is there no contact with Jerusalem?" he asked.

"Good that you have asked that. We were ostracized from the community by Prophet Ezra," Yishaq explained.

"Another wonderful story." Yona was a bit sarcastic this time.

"Our elders handed down this legend to the generations." Yishaq was serious. "When construction of the second temple at Jerusalem started, we were asked to join in. But our elders held on to the prophecy of Jeremiah and reminded us that the second temple would also be brought down as prophesied. This attitude angered prophet Ezra and he cursed the community to fall into poverty from wealth and to lose its capacity to rule over the tribe; and he excommunicated us never to be buried in Jerusalem. Our elders claimed that we had only reiterated what Jeremiah prophesied, and we did not deserve to be punished in this manner. They told prophet Ezra that the curse could fall back on him and he too would not be buried in Jerusalem which also came true. We do not give the name Ezra to our children even now." Yishaq calmed down as he saw Yona nod in acceptance.

Yona thought about the current happenings in Jerusalem. The Romans were showing more interest in the politics of weakening Ptolemaic and Seleucid dynasties. Would the second temple be destroyed? Elders in Qumran monastery hinted at a destruction. Could it be worse than what the Essene community endured?

To distract himself from unpleasant thoughts Yona asked Yishaq, "Why are you buying these Indian herbs?"

"It is for my daughter, Hanna. She practices medicine. She is skilled by the Greek and the Indian medicine men of Socotra. Many people come to her for treatment of body pains, fractures, inflammation and wounds of many kinds. She has the best cure for cold, fever and chest deceases."

"These herbs grow only in India." Yishaq took out a bundle of thin stems. "Take a bite. It is called *Athimadhuram*, it is very sweet to taste. She makes cough syrup with vasaka and desert honey added to it," he said, holding vasaka leaves in the other hand. "The main ingredient of pain medicine is our aloe juice. This is mixed in heated oil to make the ointment." Hanna was his only daughter, and he was pleased with her popularity as a medical practitioner.

"This is black pepper." He took out a handful of dried black berries which Yona tasted at his insistence.

"Ouch!" Yona was surprised by the hot taste of this tiny berry. "This would indeed make some hot medicine!"

"It is very potent. When added with long pepper and dried ginger to make tea, it is a panacea for many a distress." Yishaq was still smiling at Yona's reaction.

"We use aloe juice in yet another popular medicine," he continued, holding out a bark of the moringa tree, again an exclusive Indian plant which cured sprains, fractures and knee swelling.

"This is great news to me. I would love to meet your daughter someday. We will meet when I come to the mainland next time." Yona was pleased.

"I take it as a promise." Yishaq waved, hurrying to the dock.

● ● ●

Several small batches of Essene peasants arrived at Socotra from Ein-Gedi. More area on the hills was taken for the cultivation of aloe. They had expertise in hill-slope cultivation creating small terraces with limestone protection walls. Godfearing and hard-working the Essene peasants blended well with the farm workers. Aramaic and Greek were the lingua franca, the knowledge of which made them acceptable even more.

The political equation was changing in southern Yemen and Socotra. The Socotra aloe farm was started by Alexander the Great. Two-hundred odd years down the line, there was no control on Socotra either by the Ptolemies or the Seleucids as they themselves were diminishing powers. The frankincense kingdoms of southern Arabia also saw changes in the power fulcrum. The famous Queen Sheba of the Sabaeans ruled from the inland capital of Marib where they had built a mud dam across the wadies to irrigate 250,000 acres of land. They had colonies as far as Ethiopia. Minian kingdom, another southern Arab power, gained strength from the inland caravan routes to the Mediterranean ports they controlled. Then the Hydramaveths controlled the frankincense trade and had allies like Palmyra, Chaldea and India in trading. None of these mainland kingdoms interfered in Socotra and its aloe farms. The Hydramaveths were versatile builders. Their high-rise buildings stood up to nine floors high and had streets full of such buildings in the towns of Shiban and Yishbum.

Then came the Himyarites with the sea connection. Their capital was Bab-el-Mandap at the tip of the Arabian Peninsula in the east. They tied up with the Nabataeans of Petra and moved the frankincense trade by the Red Sea. This changed the equation in the lucrative trade with the west and many Arab tribes dependent of the caravan trade lost business and became hostile to sea trade.

Yona sat outside the factory discussing the political situation with the headman.

"I understand these tribes are the sons of Shem, one of the Noah's sons. Arpachshad, Sheleh and Eber were their descendants. Two sons of Shelah were Peleg and Yoktan. Patriarch Abraham was from the Peleg line and the Southern Arabian kingdoms were from the Yoktan line." Yona recollected the pedigree after the great floods. "Hazarmaveth, Sheba and Ophir were among the thirteen sons of Joktan," he added.

"It is the Himyarite king who demanded lease money for aloe farms of Socotra and now they are collecting tax on every amphora of aloe juice exported from here. The Nabataeans might have given them the idea of weakened Egypt and Seleucid Syria and assured them that no help would come from them as before. It will be only a matter of time that we may lose control of the island of Socotra," said the elder Greek supervisor in the farm.

Even though it was an innocent comment on the current situation, Yona shuddered. Would there be another ordeal in store for his people? Would the weight of the prophecy be heavy on his shoulders once again? The righteous will prevail, Yona consoled himself. He learned it from teachers of various philosophies he came across.

Eight years passed since Yona had come to Socotra. Several batches of Essene villagers had come to Socotra since then, and they were living peacefully and were fully occupied. What satisfied Yona most was the freewill to practice their religion in an alien country. The asafoetida, aloe juice and dragon blood tree resin business had prospered since their arrival. The settled Greeks were happier because they got hard-working people to share the toils of desert farming. The Red Sea navigation came under the ministry of Egypt with a strategos stationed at Coptos near the Red Sea port of Myos Hormos, and transportation became easier under their surveillance.

Eber, the scribe, came from Qumran monastery with a few teachers to Socotra without giving Yona any prior notice. It was a big surprise. The two embraced, meeting after many years.

"Many elders and teachers are leaving the monastery. There has been another quake and the cave monastery suffered some serious damage. But the real reason is King Alexander Jannaeus. People are leaving the country in large numbers, especially the Pharisees. There is fierce civil war between the king and the Pharisees." Eber was truly disappointed.

"Now you are in a peaceful country." Yona assured him.

"I blame the Pharisees too." Eber was assertive. "The king actually wanted to make peace with the Pharisees and asked them why they hated him and what he should do in order to appease them. They replied: 'We will be happy if you kill yourself'. The Pharisees went ahead and invited the Seleucid King Demetrius to lead a civil war against the king."

"Who is this Demetrius?" asked Yona.

"Oh, so much has happened since you left for the east. Dimitrius III Eucarus is his name. He is the son of Antiochus Grypus and Cleopatra IV Selene. You remember the fights between Grypus and Cyzicanus involving the Cleopatra III and her daughters for control of the Seleucid Syria? Anyway, all of them are dead now."

"Yes, I know, Ptolemy Lathyros is on the throne in Egypt now. Tell me about the civil war." Yona was anxious.

"The Pharisees led by the Syrian King Demetrius and the Judean forces of Alexander Jannaeus fought at Shechem in which Demetrius prevailed. Alexander Jannaeus fled to the forest. The unexpected happened again. Many of the Demetrius' forces of Jewish decent changed sides and joined King Alexander Jannaeus which made Demetrius leave the country abandoning the war.

"The worst part was yet to come," Eber continued. "The king captured eight- hundred leaders of the Pharisees and ordered them to be crucified at the city center. He had the throat of their wives and children slit before their eyes. The king witnessed this barbarity while dining with his concubines. This act spread such a scare among the Pharisees that they fled the city and all of Judea that very night.

"The fear rippled against Qumran monastery too. There was constant accusation by the leaders of Qumran against the king. After the mass crucifixion and fleeing of the Pharisees, the leaders advised the masters and the monks to find safer havens. Many have moved to the Mediterranean countries and some of us travelled east. A substantial group migrated to Barygaza and India to continue their studies on Buddhism, Jainism and Vedic religion. As we have a large group of Essenes here, we decided to come here." Eber stopped as if to take a breath.

Yona and all others at the aloe factory were taken aback. And then Yona broke the silence. "You are safe here. I would think you are a godsend. We had no Essene spiritual masters here and we are glad you fulfil the gap. We will now have the right directions in spiritual matters too."

"Amen," said the gathering.

● ● ●

Yona received a message from Arillus to reach Cyrene at the earliest. After the demise of Ptolemy Apion, the ruler of Cyrene, the Roman senate invoked the will of Ptolemy Apion and occupied the cities of Cyrene. There was anarchy in the countryside and the Roman general Lucius Lucullus was drafting a constitution for the country. Arillus had recommended Yona as a neutral representative of the Jews of Cyrene to assist in the process.

After eight years in Socotra, Yona was again on the move.

PART TWO

7

East of the Aegean

The Aegean Sea divides mainland Greece from Anatolia and it is where Europe meets Asia. The Bosporus strait and Hellespont are narrow straits between Thrace in Greece and Anatolia (present day Turkey) in Asia. There were many kingdoms in Anatolia since the time Alexander the Great invaded Asia minor. The northern region included Bethania, Paphlagonia and Pontus bordering the Black Sea, west with Mycia, Lydia, Carnia and in the south were Lycia, Pamphylia and Cilicia. There were inland kingdoms of Phrygia, Cappadocia, Pisidia and Galatia also in Anatolia. After Alexander the Great, the Seleucids controlled most of Anatolia.

Philip, successor of the Antigonid dynasty ruling Macedonia, sided with Hannibal in the Punic war against Rome thereby giving an opening to Rome in the affairs east of the Aegean. Pergamon, a city state of Mycia and the Island state of Rhodes, sided with Rome in the Macedonian war.

Later, the Seleucid King Antiochus III had to concede to Roman terms when he lost the war against Rome for the control of Greece. The peace agreement concluded at Apamea (188 BC) took away the whole of Anatolia west of Taros mountains from the Seleucid empire. He had to surrender his war elephants and most of his ships. A huge levy of 15000 talents over a period was to be paid to Rome as part of the terms which paved the way for the Roman hegemony in the eastern parts of the Aegean Sea. The kingdom of Pergamum and the Republic of Rhodes, Roman allies in war, were granted the former Seleucid lands in Anatolia and called it Asia Minor.

Pontus, an Anatolian kingdom on the shores of the Black Sea rose to strength when King Mithridates VI added Colchis to his kingdom, and invaded Paphlagonia, Cappadocia and Galatia. He allied with the Armenian king, his son-in-law, Tigranes in his extensionist policies. Rome supported the Galatian King Nicomedes when he retaliated and invaded Pontus. But Mithridates won the war and extended his kingdom to the whole of Anatolia, and made the city of Pergamum his new capital, thereby coming in direct opposition with Rome.

There were many Romans now living in Asia Minor as merchants, tax collectors, slave traders, entrepreneurs, shopkeepers and landowners oppressing the community. New settlers had acquired lands which were available for a pittance from bankrupt farmers burdened with war taxes. Many became slaves in the process and fell prey to the slave traders exporting slaves to the plantations in Rome. A large number of prisoners of war also landed in the hands of slave traders. Bitter hatred towards Romans and Italians spread in the east.

Mithridates devised a secret plan to annihilate all the Italians with their families living in Anatolia. He promised the slayers properties of the slain, redemption of debts and other bounties. This was true liberation for the Anatolians, and they did not leave any stone unturned to find a Roman. The plan worked and over eighty-thousand Italians and Roman citizens were wiped out in one single day (88 BC). Rome was shell-shocked and had to take revenge, resulting in the Mithridatic war waged against the most formidable enemy of Rome.

The weakened Seleucid dynasty in Syria and equally weak Ptolemaic dynasty in Egypt gave a free hand to the pirates in the Mediterranean Sea. War-torn and tax-burdened Cilicia became the new pirate hub and Mithridates protected them and provided haven in his empire, literally adding the pirate ships to his already strong navy in the Black Sea.

In Rome, Lucius Cornelius Sulla was elected to consulship and he set out to Greece against Mithridates. His advance guard, and chief of staff, was Lucullus, a newly elected quaestor with proven abilities as a soldier in the civil war he had fought under Sulla. His mastery in Greek and Latin and his training in constitutional and criminal law made him a forensic orator of repute. His fondness was Greek philosophy and poetry and had Antiochus of Ashkelon, the philosopher and Archias the Syrian poet, in constant company.

Lucius Licinius Lucullus, as advance guard or ambassador visited the Greek cities in the east to gain support for the war efforts of general Sulla. The meeting with Roman commander Sura who was already stationed at Greece involved handing over war responsibilities against Mithridates to general Sulla. He restructured the war taxes imposed on the cities by Sura and made efforts to lighten the burden the cities faced in fulfilling war agreements. This made him popular and cities like Chaeronea, Hypata, Synnada in Phrygia and Thyateria erected his statues in the marketplace to express gratitude. Lucullus was successful in his diplomatic mission of turning Grecian cities to the Roman side except for Athens.

Athens with its tyrant ruler Ariston held out against Rome. Piraeus was the port town of Athens which was about ten stadia (5 miles) inland from the shore. Most towns had the walled city away from the shore to ward off the pirates who would be slow and vulnerable inland and easy to catch up with. Sulla arrived and decided to cut off the port from Athens to prevent supplies going there. Then he razed the port town Piraeus to the ground. Sulla borrowed gold and silver from the temples of the Grecian cities and minted coins for the war expenses as the newly elected Roman senate stopped supporting Sulla. The responsibility of minting coins out of the silver and gold collected from the temples for war expenses was entrusted to Lucullus.

The siege of Athens was going strong but at sea Sulla was no match for the pirates and the Mithridatic navy put together. Lucullus was therefore assigned to visit friendly nations with strong navies like Rhodes, Cyrene and Egypt and gather a naval force against the Mithridatic navy.

"This is a dangerous mission, and I am going with you," Antiochus of Ashkelon, a close friend and philosopher who accompanied him from Rome said.

"Pirates are driven away from Piraeus. Also, in the dead of the winter now, very few pirates would be out there. But you are welcome to travel with me for the intellectual company, also because Cyrene and Alexandria are the best spot for the philosopher creed after Athens." Lucullus was always warm towards his close friend Antiochus.

Antiochus of Ashkelon was a student of Philo of Larissa, but his view was different from the master and he studied stoic thoughts and Platonism together in a different path to virtue and happiness, the values Lucullus also adored. "I am happy to revisit my Cyrene friends and those at Alexandria and also spend some time out in the ocean in good company," he replied.

"Then we should have Archias also with us." Lucullus was assertive. The poet friend Archias was patronized by Lucullus for his extempore verses on any given theme. Archias was from Antioch in Syria and had a great following in the Greek and Roman world as a teenage prodigy.

Lucullus could manage a small squadron of three Rhodian biremes and three myoparones from Athens for the voyage. Myoparones were small ships with thirty or so oarsmen. They were fast with their sailing and two-banked rowing power. They were wider, and the hold could accommodate provisions. These galleys were also the favored vessel of the pirates which criss-crossed the Mediterranean. He thought of sailing unnoticed among the plethora of biremes plying the sea. But in contrast, Rhodian biremes were bigger vessels. They had one-hundred-and-twenty rowers. Here too, swiftness was the praiseworthy feature. Being an open galley, the bireme was aggressive and had more manpower to face the pirates in harsh weather.

It was middle of winter with threats of storms. The reluctant sailors were more concerned of the storms than the pirates. Destruction of the port of Piraeus had made the pirates more inimical towards the Roman legions than Mithridate's call for an anti-Roman stand. Storms or undercurrents of war were not to dampen the determination of the young Lucullus to pursue his goal. The party set sail from Piraeus and reached Crete unnoticed. There was no pirate attack up to that point as they were pushed to the Tyhirrian Sea by Sulla and the Rhodian navy.

Lucullus had diplomatic business at Crete. Ironically, Crete was the pirate capital of the Mediterranean till the Silicians took over the credit. The plundering business was lost also due to the resistance of Rhodes with a capable navy. The Silician pirates were, however, in league with Mithridates in the war against Rome. Piracy, sometimes, was a state-sponsored activity. Cities like Pamphylia, Cilicia and eastern Lycia were partners in crime for share in the bounty. The money spinner in the game was the slave trade. And war produced a lot of them by way of prisoners of war and other captives. The conquerors, many a times sold the conquered population as slaves and they landed in the hands of pirates who shipped them to the most lucrative slave markets. Crete was one such slave market.

Cretan cities were in constant battle amongst themselves and had lost the vigor and wealth to stand up against Rome or Mithridates of Pontus. Lucullus called a meeting of the heads of towns and convinced the Roman resolve to destroy Mithridates and take them to his side. They were not able to provide any ship to Lucullus but promised not to take the side of Mithridates in the war.

Lucullus sailed to Lera Petra, the port on the south-east coast of Crete to facilitate the voyage to his next destination Cyrene (present Libya). This port was known as the bride of the Libyan Sea because its position overlooked Libya. A large grain cargo vessel with the Egyptian flag was berthed at the port.

Lucullus was surprised to see that the captain of the cargo vessel and the escorting hemiola vessels greeted him at the port. The toga wearing merchant was introduced as Lucius Marcus Arillus.

"I greatly appreciate your determination and courage to brave the winter and the pirates with such a small squadron," Arillus observed.

"I plan to go back with a full fleet of navy." Lucullus was undisturbed at his predicament. "Is there any shortage of grain here to import from Egypt?" he asked.

"I guess they are stocking the grain for selling at a profit as the war is heating up and the anticipated rise in demand." Arillus did not guess who the ultimate beneficiary would be.

Lucullus liked the Roman businessman heading a shipping consortium in Alexandria with substantial interests in Cyrene. He somehow felt that their paths were similar, though parallel. He invited Arillus to dinner at his place. Antiochus, the philosopher, and Archias, the poet, were also present. Arillus offered an eastern tea from ingredients brought from India to combat colds and sore throat, due to the harsh winter.

"I would prefer hot wine instead," Lucullus objected. "But what are these ingredients?" he enquired.

"My partner Yona, a Jew, in charge of the aloe farm at Socotra island in the Indian sea has sent this and the ingredients are black pepper, long pepper and dried ginger with dried leaves of *vasaka* plant. All these are native of India." Arillus was convinced of its cure.

They all tasted it and found it hot and soothing.

"We heard about this black pepper at the war front in Athens." Antiochus of Ashkelon remembered the incident with the Ariston, the tyrant of Athens.

"Our siege of the city prevented supplies and a sharp famine had set in. Informers reported people boiling shoe straps and leather bags to eat. The priestess of the temple requested twelfth of a bushel (two pounds) of grain and Ariston had sent her equal amounts of black pepper instead."

"Oh, this has reached Athens already?" Lucullus exclaimed.

"I learn this forms part of the medicines Alexander the Great's physicians brought from the east." Theophrastus of Eresos has documented two peppers from India namely the long pepper and the black pepper like our friend Arillus has just mentioned." Antiochus continued.

The discussions turned to the situation in Cyrene and Alexandria which was of utmost interest to Lucullus.

"My ships are also heading for Cyrene and the company can keep the pirates away if we sail together," Arillus suggested.

They rested for a few days before setting sail to Cyrene, in big numbers, unconcerned about pirates.

● ● ●

The grain ship the *Ariola* was a huge four-hundred-ton freight carrier with comfortable cabins for the captain and the merchants. A contingent of archers and catapults were on board for protection. But the escort ships, *Rhodian Hemiolia*, were swift and with an open galley with large and well-trained crew and protected the grain ship from pirates. On voyages under government duty, the Egyptian navy would provide protection and on private freights the hemiolia would be on duty.

The *Ariola* and the escort ships sailed ahead of the Roman fleet. Halfway through the voyage Lucullus and his friends boarded the *Ariola* for a short visit with the intention to know more about Cyrene from Arillus' point of view.

"There are four classes of citizens in Cyrene. The first consists of citizens of Greek origin, the second are the farmers or the natives, the third are the resident aliens including the Romans, Egyptians,

Arabs and the fourth are the Jews. Each group is strong in numbers and wealth. However, the Jewish population has differences with the Greeks, mainly on religious matters," Arillus observed.

"One small thing is the tithe. Every Jewish man was required to give one half shekel (8 grams) weight of silver as mandatory tax to support the temple in Jerusalem. The Greeks objected to taking silver out of the country claiming it was hurting the economy. Several clashes resulted on this issue alone. They have a private militant force called Sicarii among the Jews who instigated the population," Arillus concluded. It was not the best thing post Ptolemy Apion era of Cyrene.

The Ptolemaic regime in Egypt awarded land to Jewish veterans of the armed services in the past and they had legitimate rights over the land. The Greeks settled in Cyrene since a thousand years claimed to be as good as the original settlers. The farmers were the Arabs and the original people of Cyrene. The fourth group was the new settlers and the Romans. After enforcing their claim on Cyrenaica on the strength of the Ptolemy Apion's will, Rome became the master of the country. Rome freed the pentapolis, the five cities, and made Cyrene its capital.

"This is the second visit of a high-ranking official from Rome to Cyrene since the takeover. There is displeasure among all groups and people look forward for a stronger administration from Rome," said Arillus.

After lunch Lucullus went back to his ship.

As the ships were sailing into the port of Apollonia, sails were down, and rowers were engaged in getting the ship enough power to enter the port. Suddenly a few smaller vessels surrounded the myoparon Lucullus was sailing in. Before the rowers could take position for defense with arms, some of the pirates climbed on the deck using short ladders they placed between their ship and the myoparon. They started to set fire to the ship with naphtha they had brought along and attacked the archers with harpoons.

Alarmed at the danger, the hemiola, which was escorting the grain ship quickly came to the rescue. Arillus was also getting ready to embark as the port was close and had moved to the hemiola. The guards of the hemiola quickly made a bridge to the myoparon and helped Lucullus reach to the safety of the hemiola.

Seeing more help was coming the way of the Romans, the pirate ships moved away. The fire was extinguished with great effort but nobody was hurt. They berthed at the port of Apollonia without any further resistance.

The Roman official and the soldiers were welcomed with fanfare and the palace was readied for their stay. When Lucullus arrived the whole of Cyrenaica was in chaos due to the tyrants and their harsh rule. Rome, while taking over Cyrenaica under the will of Ptolemy Apion who bequeathed the country to Rome, had allowed free government of the five main cities and let the rest of the country manage on its own. This resulted in tyranny, wars and bloodshed everywhere. The situation came about when the aristocrats campaigned for honor and glory and the rich non-aristocratic landowners and other groups also exerted political influence. The pirates controlled the sea and in effect life was not safe on land and sea. The population was humbled to the ground.

Delegations of the citizens came one after the other to meet Lucullus with grievances against one another. Everybody agreed on one thing: all wanted a strong constitution and its implementation by the Roman presence. Lucullus with his legal and literary background decided to write a suitable constitution for the Cyrene cities under Roman control. Antiochus, the philosopher, was also a support in the process of preparing the constitution.

● ● ●

Villa Arillii in Cyrene, the official residence of Arillus in Cyrene, was also beaming with activity. It was after many years that Yona, partner of the consortium and the first resident of the villa, visited Cyrene.

"By Jupiter, you have become more of a monk than a businessman!" Arillus greeted Yona. "There is going to be a lot of action for you. A new business opportunity is opening up and Rome's militarily presence would strengthen it." Arillus was excited about his new project.

"God be with you," Yona replied. "I have become a businessman by chance and follow the Buddhist example of using business to reduce the misery of people around us."

"I understand the Buddhist concept but there is so much more to the east of the Aegean than religion. There is great interest in Indian medicines in Rome now. There are elite followers of the book by Theophrastus of Eresos on the medicinal plants from the east. There is mention of over five-hundred such plants to treat various ailments. The medical academy at Taxila is sending trained physicians to Rome and Athens. Their medical concoctions require a steady supply of these medicinal plants and I identify a goldmine there." Arillus could not hide his excitement.

"Yes, there is a steady movement of this stuff through the Parthian route. Every country en route makes huge profits without any sweat. Some spillovers come to Socotra via the Red Sea route. Caravanserais or rest stations for caravans with provisions and protection provided by the Parthians and the Syrians ensure a seamless traffic to which we are silent observers only." Yona was the best judge with his long stay in Socotra – the no-man's land between India and the Red Sea basin.

"It is learned that taxes amount to one-fifth of the value of the goods passing through the Damascus route and it is no wonder that cinnamon is sold in Athens at over ten times the price it is sold in India. Therefore, the Ptolemies always bought cinnamon from Punt, the last point of the Red Sea," Yona continued.

"Yes, the Alexandrian administration understands this. The recent appointment of a minister for the Red Sea trade and the decision to give licenses to shipping companies under the protection of the Ptolemaic government is the outcome of such development. My whole purpose of calling you to Cyrene for this meeting is to discuss the expansion policies of our consortium in the Red Sea. We have obtained licenses to build and operate a port at Myos Hormus, on the Egyptian side of the Red Sea. The canal built from the Nile by earlier kings is usable to some extent with some renovation. The Ptolemaic administration's 'tax points' at Coptos will support us with an escort navy in the Red Sea till Punt." Arillus already had the masterplan drawn up in his head with several touch points where Yona could use his experience.

"What are you suggesting?" Yona could see the bigger picture now.

"You have already guessed it," Arillus said. "Our consortium is planning to build a port at Myos Hormus and build ships there for the Red Sea trade in Indian goods. The only hinderance is the unavailability of wood in the desert and one cannot build a ship with sand. The warmongers of the east and west are busy building ships for their navy. The Roman official Lucullus is here for acquiring a navy for Rome for the war with King Mithridates."

"What is my role in this? I am not a shipwright and have no knowledge of it," Yona protested. "But I know that India can supply quality wood for ship building in large quantity."

"That solves the problem!" Arillus was exited now. "If you make wood available from India, I can provide the engineers and workers and even sailors from the Mediterranean ports."

"I have befriended a Buddhist merchant called Indranidutta dealing in Indian wood. He has regular supplies till the port of Quana on the Eritrean Sea. It will be possible to get wooden planks from India if we can give protection for his ships in the Red Sea. Better still if we move the wooden planks ourselves from Quana. The wood named teakwood, excellent for ship building, is brought from the forests of southern India to Barygaza port in Kutch and hewn to planks by the Greek and Syrian carpenters there for export to Omana." Yona was excited about the project.

Arillus found happily that the pieces were falling into place. "The consortium wants you to take charge of the project at Myos Hormus. We will support you from Coptos on the Nile and you can stretch from Myos Hormus towards Socotra, and most importantly, India."

●　●　●

Arillus returned to Alexandria for drawing up a detailed plan of action and arrange for men and materials for the project. Before leaving, Arillus, hosted a dinner in the honor of the Roman official Lucullus at Villa Arillii. Yona met Antiochus of Ascalon, the philosopher, and Archias, the poet, and Lucullus at the dinner.

While Lucullus was in discussion with Arillus on the situation in Alexandria, Yona and Antiochus talked about the influence of thinkers of the east on Greek scholars.

Antiochus turned to Yona and said, "I will tell you an interesting story. Two Greek philosophers, Pyrrhon of Elis and Anaxarchus were a part of Alexander the Great's expedition to India. There was interaction between the Greeks and the Indians on the spiritual wonders of immortality claimed by the Indian saints or yogis and Alexander wanted to conquer that too. Pyrrhon met the Indian saints or yogis and stayed in the Indian city of Taxila for almost two years to understand eastern thought process. He was amazed at the spiritual maturity of the yogis or gymnosophists as the Greek called naked philosophers. They were tranquil, without any fear of suffering. They had invoked the intelligence within the soul itself by turning inward and had attained the happily serene state of mind. They knew that the human body, like any other in nature, is made up of the five elements, and upon death, the human body dissolves into these five elements of nature, thereby balancing the cycle of nature. The inner self, Indians called *akasha* and the Greeks called ether or void is beyond the senses of smell, taste, sight and touch.

"Pyrrhon, after his return to Greece, taught that meditation was important in order to achieve wisdom and happiness which is the goal of philosophy. All things are made up of atom and void and hence are not what they seem and are not really different from one another," Antiochus explained.

"Buddha also taught how to avoid sorrow to achieve this happy state of mind." Yona recollected the teachings of the Buddhist monks. "Perfection of wisdom or *Prajnaparimita* texts are also known to have propounded the view that nothing really exists," Yona added.

"Pyrrhon is the father of skepticism or inquiry in the Greek world. (This school of thought was later contrasted with academic skepticism.) He had no assertion on the possibility of knowledge and a state of suspended judgment on the truth provided a tranquil form.

To elaborate, he said one can suspend judgement when both sides of the argument are equally compelling but cannot be true. Similarly, when an argument requires justification and the justification requires further justification and so forth, a suspended judgement is the way to tranquility," said Antiochus. He further explained that more than intellectual dissection, as practiced by the western world, a suspended judgement was the answer preferred by the Indian saints.

"Judgement is also not possible when the same situation is experienced by people differently. Judgement can be right for one person and may not be right for another. A suspended judgement gives you peace in such situations."

Antiochus went on to say how he found a middle path between Zeno, Aristotle and Plato stating that for the highest grade of happiness bodily comforts and wealth were necessary as well.

* * *

Lucullus settled the tyrant problem in Cyrene by bringing law and order with a new constitution which he drew out for the Cyrene cities. He was the first official from Rome to visit Cyrene after Caius Claydius Pulchar to preside over the initial administrative incorporation of the kingdom into the Roman Empire in 94 BC. The citizens became meek and subdued by many a tyrant. Different factions of society like the Greeks, Jews, peasants and ethnic Arabs fought amongst each other wasting the freedom given to them by Rome. Lucullus said, quoting Plato, that it was hard to be a lawgiver for the Cyrenaeans when things were going well for them. Now that the tide had turned the time had come, he realized.

This interlude made Lucullus more susceptible to the pirates who gathered strength and waited for his next move. His voyage to Alexandria was disastrous. He lost most of his ships and men in battle against the pirates. Once again, the *Rhodian Hemiolia* sent by Arillus helped to save his life. Arillus had alerted the Egyptian officials about Lucullus' mission and the threat by the pirates on his life. Ptolemy Lathyros realized an attack on a Roman commander in Egyptian seas could be disastrous for his interests and he arranged an open sea reception by the Egyptian navy to Lucullus and the remaining who escaped the pirate attack. Once Lucullus realized that help came from Arillus, he resolved to pay the debt of saving his life twice, at the first opportunity.

King Ptolemy Soter II nicknamed Lathyros gave a splendid welcome to Lucullus. His accommodation was arranged in the king's palace and he dined with the king like family. He showered many presents on Lucullus to please him. The king, however, was torn in choosing between Rome and its enemy Pontus King Mithridates. Ptolemy Alexander I, the previous king of Egypt, in a cunning move, had bequeathed Egypt to Rome in his will which the Romans could enforce. On the other hand, to complicate matters, Ptolemy Alexander's son was in the custody of Mithridates who could claim the throne with the Pontic king's support. Now, Rome had come to his doorstep to ask for naval support which meant Rome was in no advantageous position against Mithridates. The king chose to be neutral and did not give any naval support to Lucullus. Lucullus took none of the presents but a token and spent his time with Ptolemy to champion the Roman position. He spent his spare time at the vast library with the philosophers of Alexandria for company and his friend Antiochus of Ashkelon.

Ptolemy, however, arranged naval escort for Lucullus and his men on their return up to Cyprus which was Rome's ally. Lucullus had collected ships from Cyrene and Syrian ports adding to his fleet. Cretan ships were added to the numbers and Lucullus had amassed a fleet capable of facing the pirates of the Aegean Sea. He reached the Rhodian shore safely and broke the Pontic blockade of the island with his fleet. Lucullus added the powerful Rhodian squadron to his navy and rejoined Sulla with a successful mission. The land and sea attack followed by Sulla and Lucullus forced the Pontic king to come to their terms bringing an end to the first Mithridatic war of Rome.

The Pontic problem for Rome did not end there. A second Mithridatic war was led by Roman general Lucius Licinius Murena (83-81 BCE). Two years of war pushed Mithridates further east but ended inconclusively as Rome ordered a withdrawal after a defeat suffered by the Roman forces and a peace treaty ensued. However, the second peace treaty between Rome and Pontus lasted only for eight years and paved the way for the third and decisive Mithridatic war.

● ● ●

80 BCE saw change in the Ptolemaic kingdom. Son of Ptolemy XI Alexander II with an unknown Greek concubine was crowned as Ptolemy XII nicknamed Auletes, the piper. The will bequeathing the kingdom of Egypt to the Roman people by Ptolemy Alexander II hung like a sword over him as the Roman senate could contest his legitimacy. So, his priority was to please the influential senators of Rome to veto any move against him.

The gold from the treasury was exhausted in bribes and he borrowed from Roman bankers giving out promissory notes for large amounts to satisfy the greed of the policy makers. His friends in the senate saved him every time a resolution to annex Egypt was presented with a veto.

Back home, he increased taxes and cut down government expenditure to overcome the financial crises which resulted in a public outcry against him. He had to look for other means to finance his bribery program. His only option was to capture the market of Indian luxury goods going to Rome and make the Romans pay for the bribe.

Wealthy businessmen were lured by being offered protection of their vessels on the Red Sea and by land to Coptos and further down on the Nile. Caravanserais and water points were built along the desert road which had already existed connecting the mines of the eastern desert of Egypt. The state would tax the goods coming in and those going out of Alexandria, filling its coffers.

Yona moved to Myos Hormus to oversee the building of the private port for the shipping consortium. Materials would be transported by the river Nile and over land to the site. There were ample dead coral rocks onsite which were used as building materials. The wharf, store houses and ship building docks were completed with the help of local workers freed from the mines. A team of Phoenician and Egyptian engineers designed and put in place a facility for building medium-sized ships.

The Ptolemaic administration had built a sea wall long enough to berth vessels bringing elephants from African forests for military use. It was currently abandoned as elephants were no longer used in the Egyptian army. Yona chose a small lagoon close to the port and widened a narrow canal leading to the lagoon. A dry dock and berth for small vessels were built with locally available materials like coral heads and clay from the canal bed. Store houses and accommodation for workers were also arranged. Preparation for ship building at the Myos Hormuz dock was the next challenge. A decision was taken to build an Egyptian kerkoros, a merchant galley at the dock.

The minister for Red Sea trade and traffic of the Ptolemaic administration was stationed at Coptos near the river Nile. Several escort ships of the Egyptian navy, berthed at the Myos Hormus, would ply between Bab-el Mandap and Myos Hormus in protection of the merchant vessels. In the beginning Nabataean dhows tried to block the ships but proved to be no threat to the experienced Egyptian navy.

Trade started picking up for eastern goods to Alexandria bypassing the overland caravan routes. Regular shipments from Socotra improved the profits of Arillus' consortium on eastern trade and there was a demand for more investments in the Red Sea traffic. Yona also was able to visit Socotra more often and a variety of goods of Indian origin was reaching Myos Hormus. Indranidutta sent several shiploads of teak planks making ship building possible in the desert.

● ● ●

Lucullus had stayed on in the east of the Aegean for another four years after the conclusion of the first Mithridatic war as he was assigned with settling the financial matters related to war debts due to Rome. After returning to Rome (80 BCE), he was appointed as governor of African provinces of Rome (76 BCE).

The African province of Rome mainly consisted of present Tunisia. The city of Carthage was built on a promontory with sea inlets on two sides. There were two vast man-made harbors in the city with its large navy and mercantile trade. The densely populated city of Carthage was one of the most affluent cities of the time. Victory in the third Punic war brought Romans as the rulers of Carthage. Rome destroyed Carthage in its rage leaving no stone unturned. (Later, during Julius Caesar's reign Rome rebuilt Carthage.) The Roman governorate was in Utica, a city close to Carthage which sided with Rome in the Punic war against Carthage.

The Carthaginians were Phoenician settlers originating in the Mediterranean coast of Lebanon in the near-east and spoke Canaanite, a Semitic language, and followed a variety of ancient Canaanite religions. They were great ship builders.

Arillus decided to pay his respects to the new governor of Carthage. It was about twelve years since they had met at Cyrene and he was doubtful if the new governor would remember the meeting. The port at Myos Hormuz had not yet reached its potential for want of experienced artisans and sailors. Arillus wanted to use the opportunity to request for artisans and sailors from Carthage.

Lucullus gave a warm welcome to Arillus. "By Jupiter, what a surprise! The grain lord is here!" Called out Lucullus. "He saved my life from pirates at Cyrene." He told the officials attending him. "Give him a fitting reception. Carthage is at peace and the governor has no war to wage here. So, let us celebrate." And days passed before Arillus could present the case of the Red Sea port and the need of artisans, carpenters and sailors.

"Very well. I will give you the best. We have descendants of prisoners of war from the Punic war who will be most appropriate for your needs. They are Phoenicians from Carthage; sturdy and experienced in ship building. Seafaring is in their blood. They make the best carpenters and sailors. But they are freedom loving people and resist undue subjugation even after a total defeat from Rome. The Phoenicians of Utica sided with the Romans in the Punic war and the animosity among these groups remains even after all these years. This attitude has made enemies for them here. Your request is welcome. I will get peace among settlers here and you get the ships and the sailors. They will be useful as good fighters too in any skirmish you may encounter at sea."

"Wonderful!" Arillus was a happy man. "I can take shiploads of them. I can increase the business with the east several fold with their help. They will make profits too from the trade. We are paying large amounts to the Egyptian escort ships for protection during the Red Sea voyage. This can be avoided if we have mercenaries of our own."

"How do you reach Myos Hormuz from here?" asked Lucullus.

"There are two canals connecting the Nile and the Red Sea. One is the Nacho's canal which has some hilly tracts. They have made river locks to overcome this with the help of Greek engineers, and it is navigable for boats. Another is the Coptos route. One must travel up the Nile to Coptos and take a desert route to Myos Hormuz. A navigable canal is dug for some distance there too." Arillus made it sound as a simple feat.

The Phoenicians brought an altogether new direction to the trade. The Carthage connection opened outlets in Europe and investors were easy to find for the consortium. Commodities traded were also diverse now. Red Sea ships would ply between Bab-el-Mandap and Myos Hormus with some exception to Cana, the Hadramout port. Ships coming from India berthed at Cana and waited for favorable wind for return.

Voyage across the Indian Sea was still a far cry. That would need a lot of money, bigger ships, merchants who could deal with traders at the source of procurement, and factories at the Indian ports to collect and store goods awaiting voyage. The consortium was not ready for that yet. But the Phoenician sailors were ready.

In 74 BCE, Lucullus was elected consul and the senate gave him command of the third Mithridatic war. The Pontic King Mithridate was on the run and the Romans captured city after city in Anatolia (modern Turkey) and reached the Armenian boarder. Armenian

King Tigranes the great was married to Mithridates' daughter and gave shelter to the Pontic king who was on the run.

The Armenian kingdom was at its prime, with its new capital city Tigranocerta, built on the banks of the river Tigris. Tigranes' kingdom extended from the Parthian boarder to the Phoenician ports of the Mediterranean Sea. Wracked by civil wars between the dying Seleucid dynasty Seleucid Syria was offered to him on a platter. Judea was untouched by the timely diplomatic intervention of Judean Queen Alexandra, the successor of Alexander Jannaeus, with valuable presents.

Lucullus sent his envoy, none other than his brother-in-law Appius Claudius Pulcher to the Armenian King Tigranes asking him to surrender Mitridates who was hiding in Armenia. Pulcher threatened the king of war with Rome when the king refused to hand over Mitridates.

The Roman invasion of the Armenian kingdom was of great concern to Parthia, the neighboring country, not because they feared an invasion themselves but disruption of their trade monopoly with India. They countered this threat by strengthening the trade route with more caravanserais, cisterns and armed guards patrol for the trading caravans travelling through Parthia up to Seleucia on the Tigris. Trade with India was the money spinner and losing any of it to the Romans would be equal to losing a war.

Eastern kings lived a luxurious life. The gardens, the rivers and the fertile soil made the land rich. Their taste for vast landscaped gardens for entertainments and gourmet food habits were new to Lucullus but slowly the epicurean lifestyle became acceptable to him. The spicy food was new to him, but it was the flavor, smell and color of these exotic Indian spices that won his heart. Smoked meat marinated with spices like black pepper, salt and saffron stayed longer and was tastier than the ration of salted meat supplied to the officers. Lucullus wanted all of Rome to taste it. He realized that control of trade with India was the key to be victorious over the east.

The new capital of Tigranocerta was populated with the forceful migration of Greeks, Jews, Syrians, Phoenicians and Arabs from various wars along with the Armenian population. Art and cultural activities brought in foreigners from various countries to perform at the brand-new amphitheaters. Chefs and culinary experts of east and west catered to the palates of the royal guests. Exquisitely manicured lawns and flower gardens were reminiscent of the hanging gardens of Mesopotamia.

Lucullus' military strategy and the experienced Roman legions subdued the vast but disorganized mercenary army of Tigranes without much difficulty. But the prize slipped out of his hands when King Tigranes and Mithridates, the king of Pontus, both escaped to inner Armenia leaving the war open without conclusion. Lucullus permitted his men to plunder the city, taking the royal treasury of enormous wealth into his own custody. For Lucullus, the best catch were the artists and the valuable objects of art to highlight the victory – every Roman general's dream.

Before destroying the city, Lucullus celebrated his victory with a performance by the captured artists. The feast was produced as a masterpiece of eastern cuisine by the royal chefs. Lucullus asked to document the recipes, again keeping the triumphal feast in mind. One look at the recipes revealed a common ingredient in almost all preparations – the black pepper. The origin of the spice was traced to the southern part of India.

Suddenly, the discussions with Yona, the Jewish monk came to Lucullus' mind and the medicinal drink with black pepper he had tasted at Cyrene. The ship building operations at Red Sea ports by Arillus, the Roman businessman from Alexandria, the Phoenician workers sent from Utica at the request of Arillus flashed in his mind. Introducing this small little seed of black pepper with immense potential to Roman life occurred to him. The thought that it would revolutionize the culinary sphere of the west was a welcome revelation for Lucullus. He sent out an invitation to Arillus and Yona to join a victory celebration at the Syrian city of Antiochus. The philosopher friend of Lucullus, Antiochus of Ashkelon, who had come to Alexandria would also be travelling with Arillus and Yona. Poet Artias, another close associate of Lucullus, was already in Antioch.

Yona was pleased for another opportunity to be in the company of the renowned philosopher and set out to Alexandria. The voyage to Seleucia, the port city of Antioch, was in the best of luxury on the prized ship of the consortium escorted by the Rhodian galleys. Arillus, Antiochus and Yona were the only passengers on board.

"Pleased to meet you, Yona the Essene monk," greeted Antiochus, the philosopher.

"I am happy for this occasion," replied Yona. "It is a great honor that you still remember my name."

"Askalon is not far from Ein-Gedi. I have studied the law of Moses with the zeal like I did with the Platonic teachings and I always found a middle path between these teachings towards leading a virtuous life."

"It is true. I have often wondered about a seminal link among all these teachings. Especially between Judaism and Platonism. Buddhist teachings also gel well with the concept." Yona looked quizzically at the philosopher.

"You can add Stoic teachings too. All these teachings have almost the same baseline of time period and with Alexander the Great opening up the traffic east and west are understood philosophically better than ever before."

"Yes," Yona agreed. "Romans and the west lean more towards Epicurus' teachings while the east is more towards the stoic way of life."

"Actually, it is the other way around. Stoics took more from the eastern way while the Epicureans represented the western way," the philosopher countered.

"It is true that the Essene sect value the teaching of Moses more than the rules framed by the later traditions." Yona was quick to respond. "Pursuing the righteous righteously and the superstitions un-righteously is the key. In other words, holding a balance between the formless spirituality and the un-spirited formalism," he added.

Antiochus of Askelon liked the argument. "Very well the moment man tries to define God's essence in words the problem starts. Plato said that seeing God in all things and all things in God is important."

"We teach at Qumran monastery that to be, as far as possible, in likeness to God is the ultimate solace of the human soul. The father, the word and the holy ghost, the trinity concept we believe in is also seen in Greek teachings." Yona wanted Antiochus to speak more on the soul.

"One of the main arguments of Plato is that the soul brings life to the forms and is unperishable. As body is mortal and subject to physical death, the soul is indestructible," said Antiochus.

"Buddhist teachings on Nirvana or rejoining of the soul with the ultimate spirit hails from the concept of the indestructible soul," Yona added. "They say man's mind is a fragment or particle of the divine universal mind and the knowledge and happiness come from God."

"Yes, you are right." Antiochus expressed it in another way. "There are similarities in the matter of the nature of God, creation of the universe, the role of demons in the management of the universe and the reconciliation of the human soul to the God among religions and philosophical thoughts of the east and the west. 'Know yourself and you will be known' is a key concept from the east and accepted by all of us. The stoic thoughts also have many parallels in Indian philosophy."

The discussions went deeper into the subject of relations between happiness and virtue, criterion of truth and the goal of human life. Yona felt the voyage had ended too soon as they entered the port of Seleucia to a grand reception by Lucullus. The travel to Antioch, a few stadia away, was like a triumphal parade.

Antioch was a beautiful city and the seat of the Syrian kings, founded by Seleucus Nicator after the victory over Antegonus, both generals of Alexander the Great. He founded fourteen cities named Antioch after his father. The port city of Seleucia was fortified with expensive walls. The gates and the road to Antioch were elegant and wide to accommodate the war elephants the king had acquired from India. They rode in majestic chariots into the metropolis through paved streets with open squares serving as commercial and social hubs. Fountains added beauty and brought fresh water from the Orontes river. Within the city, the roads were flanked by colonnaded porches with busy shoppers. They passed elegant royal houses and headed to cross the river and to a small island with palaces and villas. Tigranes had occupied one of the palaces during his fourteen-year rule of Syria and Armenia which he vacated when his new capital Tigranocerta fell to Lucullus. Springs, trees and beautiful gardens and the song of birds created a blissful environment.

Lucullus was waiting for them at the palace. Archias, the poet, was there ready for a recital on the victory of Lucullus over the Aramenian King Tigranes.

"We bridged the Aegean." Lucullus was louder than his usual cool self. All present clapped congratulating him.

"Now we have borders with Parthia. This is the farthest Roman legions have marched till now!" he exclaimed.

Toga wearing Arillus, the philosopher Antiochus in a near-eastern gown and headgear, Yona in a white gown of the Essenes were truly not military fans, but the colorfully dressed poet Archias was ready with a recital on the achievements of Lucullus in the war east of the Aegean.

He recited how Mithridates fled Pontus taking shelter in Armenia ruled by Tigranes, the son-in-law of Mithridates when the Roman army arrived, and Lucullus occupied the whole of Pontus. Archias spoke about the debt relief he gave to the people which made him popular in cities occupied and of the people erecting statues of Lucullus in their squares; how Tigranes refused to deliver Mithridates resulting in war with Armenia; the fall of Tigranocerta and Lucullus bringing all lands from the Mediterranean to the Caspian Sea under Roman occupancy. The poet narrated in detail the murder of Gordyene King Zarbienus and the whole royal family by Tigranes for siding with Lucullus. He described Lucullus performing the funeral rites. His poetry concluded with the misdeeds of Appius Pulcher, incestuous brother of Lucullus' wife Clodia, instigating mutiny in the army out of sheer jealousy. He also subtly mentioned the incestuous relationship Appius was having with his sisters which was a war Lucullus would have to fight without his legions.

He sat down amid great applause and Lucullus stood up spreading his hands as if to hold all his friends in his arms.

"I called you to witness the splendor in which the eastern kings lived!" Lucullus was in good spirits as the guests relaxed and occupied the couches in the grand room.

"Look at the machine they have made to calculate the position of the stars in aid to navigation." Lucullus pointed to the globe-like instrument with so many gears and scales placed on top of the fireplace. "It can predict astronomical positions and eclipses for calendar and astrological purposes decades in advance."

Everyone took a closer look at the machine. "Study of heavenly stars and their influence on humans is very advanced in the east. The positioning of stars at any point of time is calculated using a similar system in India, to the great advantage of open sea voyages," Yona chipped in.

"Not only astronomy, but they have also made great advancements in military techniques with various poison brews for their arrows, the fire throwing javelins with naphtha harvested from the lakes, and training of birds and animals used in warfare. They have documented everything, and these will form part of my triumphal march," said Lucullus.

"Another interesting thing I found is the preservation techniques of meat. We need a lot of meat preserved for the military and it consumes our supply of salt quickly. Here they use black pepper along with salt which improves the taste and keeps the quality. They use this black pepper in all the dishes they make at the palace and I have become a fan of this in such a short time. We need to take it to Rome. My triumphal feast should have this black pepper introduced to Rome. I have also decided to take the 'cherry plant' to Rome for its ethereal sweetness." Lucullus was excited about his triumphal procession.

"I have asked the scribes to document the recipes as narrated by the royal cooks of Antioch and Tigranocerta so that it can be reproduced at Rome. They use a lot of spices of the east, especially those from India. I will require an abundant supply of these items in Rome. The traders of land caravans from India are selling these spices at exorbitant prices. I want these spices sourced directly from India to make it affordable."

"You are asking for a paradigm shift!" Yona protested. "Centuries old trade practices and well established caravan routes are holding monopoly of trade with India. There are several economically and militarily strong nations en route who can create obstructions. Moreover, we do not have any procurement factories in the east to ensure a constant supply. We do not have any access beyond the shores of the Arabian Peninsula or the island of Socotra towards the east. The Indian sea is vast and our ships or the Arabian dhows are not worthy of a month-long voyage to India…"

"This is precisely why I called you here. You have travelled to India with Eudoxes of Cyzicus and you are in the shipping and spice business with the east for the past so many years. I understand that the Egyptian minister for trade in the Red Sea gives you protection from the Nabataeans and the pirates of the Red Sea. The Phoenicians I sent to you when Arillus met me at Utica in Carthage must be helping you in ship building too. I would say that your consortium is best positioned in expanding your activities to India."

"We have a lagoon at Myos Hormus with a dry dock and we build small ships for the Red Sea traffic there. Larger ships for open sea voyage to India can be built there." Arillus suddenly caught up with the business prospects.

"That is like a true Roman." Lucullus was quick to respond. "Romans see things in mega scale. I see it as a bigger business proposition than all the middlemen of Parthia and Nabataea and Arabia ever did. After all, we are the consumers of the goods they carry across nations and if we can avoid middlemen for economic reasons then nothing like it!"

"If it is fine for you, I would like to invest in the business as a silent partner. It is not my intention to make huge profits out of the venture. You saved my life twice when I lacked protection. Your timely assistance helped me to procure ships for consul Sulla during the first Mithridatic war. Now the fruits of the war efforts are harvested, and I sit on the vast riches of the eastern kings. I give you one thousand talents (30 tons) of silver as my investment without any intervention in the trade. You pay me back in Rome with Indian spices at Roman price. If you will require any help in procuring timber from Lebanon, just let me know," said Lucullus.

"Wow, that is a fantastic offer!" Arillus jumped. "We can make large ships worthy for the Indian Sea, the only missing link in bridging India with Rome. We have the men and materials and, more importantly, the presence of the man who made it to India by open sea. I take the offer and I will keep the arrangement a secret among us."

"Very well then, we will party now, and the cooks here will show you what I meant by eastern cuisine," Lucullus concluded.

When the feast moved from course to course, the chef announced: "Pullum Parthicum!" A chicken dish with crushed pepper, wine and silphium presented in earthen pots sprinkled with pepper. The wine mellowed the heat of the pepper and silphium made the smell intoxicating. "Most of the dishes served today have a hint of pepper," he announced.

● ● ●

Antioch was close to Daphne, the city of games and ceremonies. Lucullus was holding a victory procession and some entertainment for his guests there. Along with his friends, Lucullus had invited the present rulers of the cities he had overrun, for the games – king of Commagene and Sopheni and chieftains of the Anatolian cities to name a few. The dancers and the gamers of the captured city of Tigranocerta were to perform at the games.

Yona made a short visit to the Jewish quarter allocated to them by Seleucus Nicator, the founder of the city of Antioch. The synagogue was special to all Jews as five Jewish brothers executed by Syrian King Antiochus Epiphanes for refusing to eat pork, a prohibited food of the religion, were buried. But to his utmost surprise, Yona found many of the teachers from the Qumran monastery living there. Some of the teachers remembered Yona going to Alexandria with the Buddhist monks as a boy.

"How is it that the Essene teachers are here?" Yona could not suppress his excitement.

"After the second earthquake struck the monastery, the chief monk advised the monks to disperse. The villagers had moved to the city of Pella across river Jordan, but many of the teachers preferred Antioch. Rome has not turned against the Jews and we are safe here," one of the elders replied.

"We count the days when God will send the Messiah to save the world," another teacher added. (Almost a century later it was in Antioch that the name Christian was coined to include the community following Jesus the Messiah.)

The next day, they set off to attend the games at Daphne in an open chariot drawn by horses. Well-paved roads by the banks of Orontes river presented enchanting scenic beauty. Orchards and lush gardens flourished on the fertile banks with occasional villas of the super-rich. Away from the rush of the city, further down the road, the vineyards gave a spectacular view. Wineries with rest houses for travelers to rest and enjoy the taste of the grapes of Lebanon was heartwarming.

Lucullus relaxed at the company of Antiochus of Ashkelon, his philosopher friend. "Worries of the world are forgotten with strong friends like you!" he exclaimed looking at the rest of the company. "We can be happy as gods if we live free of anxiety. Pleasure achieved through good friendship and simple living is the beginning and end of a blessed life. I remember the teachings of Epicurus when I think about life. The most terrible evils, death, are nothing for us. As when we exist, death does not exist and when death exists, we do not exist," he continued.

"We have discussed the subject before. I think virtue should be the guiding principle and foundation to the way of life," Antiochus opined. "Teacher Seneca says, 'let virtue lead the way, then every step will be safe.'"

"Qumran monastery also teaches to seek first the kingdom of God and His righteousness and the happiness of life will come automatically," Yona piped in.

Yona was determined in walking away from the Epicurus way. "I would like to join Antiochus in asserting the values of a virtuous living."

"I too value a truly virtuous life. It should be the means to attain life's pleasures. We should never accept a wrong path in our pursuit for pleasure," Lucullus said.

"Living in accordance with nature and agreeing with what happens rather than rebelling against and lamenting what we cannot change is the core of stoic teachings. One can be happy no matter what happens to us in life by understanding that we are never harmed unless we believe we are. Thus, we can avoid suffering and lead a joyful life," Antiochus added.

"Once the war is over, I plan to lead a life of strong friendships and sharing the pleasures of life with my friends. I may also withdraw from public life, staying close to home, to avoid all complex desires and spend a lot of time with close friends and in intellectual pursuits." Lucullus shared his thoughts about his perceived future.

"'A cheerful poverty is an honorable state' to quote teacher Seneca, but I would prefer the Roman way of grabbing every opportunity to be better, bigger and happier," Arillus said.

They stopped at the temple of Apollo, the deity of Daphne, before taking seats at the royal box with the other kings and chieftains to watch the games. The parade displayed Indian ivory and spices in plenty; chariots drawn by elephants got the best applause. The games and dancing went on late into the night.

Antiochus of Ashkelon got sick and had to be put under medical supervision – a sickness from which he did not recover even after the best medical attention. Lucullus was heartbroken.

8

Swans of the Eritrean Sea

Yona went back to Myos Hormuz journeying along the Euphrates to the port of Charax Spasinu with a hope of meeting Indranidutta for the supply of teakwood planks for the new project. He left a message for him at the Buddhist Vihara and met some other dealers in the wood business based out of the Indian port of Barygaza. The deal for more timber was struck to ensure transition from production of small ships to larger merchant ships worthy of the big ocean at Myos Hormuz.

The fall of Tigranocerta released many work forces who thronged Charax Spasinu looking for a safe place for migration and work. The Essene villagers taken by King Tigranes for the construction of the city moved to Edessa, the capital of the semi-independent kingdom of Osroene. Almost a century later, the city of Edessa became an important center of Syriac Christianity where apostle St Thomas converted people to Christianity.

Yona enlisted carpenters and other artisans from the community who were willing to move to Myos Hormuz from Charax Spasinu and headed to Socotra. Life in Socotra was also getting tougher as the Himyarites of the mainland were levying tax for the aloe produced and exported from the island. The Greek control was no longer present and most of the Greeks left for Alexandria thereby leaving the political control of Socotra in the hands of Himyarites.

Yona met Ruan and his team of pilots at Socotra. The lad had grown into a short and sturdy handsome man with black eyes and loosely curled hair. His grip felt like a rock surface due to the constant rope work on the dhows.

"I have big news for you!" We are going to build large ocean-going ships at Myos Hormuz which can take up voyages to India with ease. We will be needing your entire team for the mission in piloting and to gather information about the Indian trade." Yona told him.

"Master, you taught us to admire the stars and now we read them at the palm of our hands. We will be with you as long as you need us," Ruan replied.

"Then join me at Myos Hormuz as we are getting ready for the project." Yona was happy for Ruan and the team of pilots, as they had become experts on the sky and the ocean.

"I have visited Taprobene many times now with the Arabs," Ruan announced proudly. "Unfortunately, I have not yet been successful in finding my native village or anybody who remembers the boy lost at sea."

"You will have many opportunities to find them." Yona knew well how hard it was to leave one's parents at the tender age of twelve.

The elders at Socotra were happy to meet Yona. He told them of meeting people of the Essene sect at Antioch and Edessa during his travels and about the ship-building project.

"As soon as the ships are ready, we will need a group of people who can endure sea voyage to assist in merchandising and procurements." Yona left the elders to find volunteers. He could see a new light of freedom in the eyes of the multitude. The prophecy of the chief monk rang in his ears.

* * *

Coptos on the Nile was a seven-day travel from Myos Hormuz. At one point war elephants captured from Nubian forests along the Red Sea were brought to Alexandria through this route in the past century. Mining for gold and precious stones in the eastern desert had also made the road busy. The road was almost abandoned when the early Ptolemic regime stopped importing elephants and the gold mines dried out. Now there was another reason for brisk activity on the road. The new minister for the Red Sea trade took charge at the custom house in Coptos. An Egyptian army contingent was also posted at Coptos. Caravanserais were built along the road on several locations with water stations. The minister was king's kinsman and trade with India was the last-ditch effort to boost the dwindling Egyptian economy. Unlike the past, Ptolemy encouraged private funding for the Indian trade. The shipping and banking consortium headed by Arillus had connections in both Egyptian and Roman echelons of power helping him to launch the Indian expedition on a bigger scale than Eudoxes of Cyzicus' attempt almost fifty years ago during the reign of Ptolemy Physcon.

The mighty river Nile made a horseshoe bend at Coptos and was the closest point to the Red Sea reaching out to Myos Hormuz. The towns of Kainipolis and Apollonopolis were also developed along this bend. The best thing the new minister implemented was the water stations in between a day's journey along the road. Various taxes were introduced in lieu of water, and protection was provided. Traders found the movement of goods faster than the desert roads crossing the Euphretes. Naval escorts for the Red Sea voyage were an added attraction. Valuable merchandise reaching Alexandria via the Nile increased steadily.

After five days on the road, Yona and Ruan reached Phoeinikon – a day's journey away from Coptos. There were several wells there and the water was sweet. Men and animals quenched their thirsts to their hearts' content, had baths, ate a hearty meal and rested. Men from the quarries of the eastern desert frequented Phoenikon for entertainment making the market come alive with drinking, dancing and gambling.

"The Alexandrian company wishes to sail directly to India from Myos Hormuz. They want to build big vessels worthy of the Indian seas." Yona had not brought up the subject all through the journey.

Ruan looked at him without a change in expression but his mind churned like a highroller of the violent sea.

"There will be war. The Nabateans, the Himyarite's, the Hydermauts, the Parthians and the Indian Greeks will not let this happen!" Ruan looked a bit scared at the news.

"The Romans will support us. They have already reached up to Tigris on the Parthian boarder and have occupied all countries from the Mediterranean to Tigris, and they decide matters in Egypt too. Rome wants the overland trade from India to shift course for a direct sea trade with Rome through the Alexandrian route. Most of the fancy goods reach Rome with a huge price tag while ocean trade can bring down the taxes levied by different countries, thereby reducing the cost to Rome. That is their reason for the support." Yona convinced the wide-eyed Ruan bit by bit.

"Egypt is in great debt to Rome and its senators for keeping the kingdom from falling and they hope to pay off some debt by taxing the trade with India. Egyptians now have a minister at Ptolemais Hermiou, appointed to increase trade with India and we are going to meet him with my friends from Alexandria," Yona continued.

Ruan did not reply. Yona, once a simple monk, was talking big now, he thought.

"Why am I meeting the minister? He broke the silence.

"We are the only two people here with first-hand knowledge about the open sea voyage to India." Yona shared the secret.

Ruan was in deep thought during the rest of the journey and Yona let him ponder over it.

Coptos city was the fulcrum on which the gold mines of the eastern desert, trade with the east and the Nubian elephant imports for centuries ran. Located on the horseshoe curve of the great river Nile, it was at the shortest distance from the Red Sea to the Nile. Coptos was the seat of the god Min, protector of the miners and the caravans. It was the capital of upper Egypt till Ptolemies established Ptolemais Hermiou of Thebaid, not far away from Coptos, as their capital for the province. The Epistrategos, or minister of Thebes, was responsible for overseeing navigation in the Red Sea and the Indian Ocean. He was a close relative of the king and the taxes generated from the eastern trade was important to the king.

Ptolemy XII Auletes was on the throne at Alexandria. His kingdom was not secure because of his questionable lineage as an illegitimate son of Ptolemy IX by an unknown Greek concubine. He, therefore, decided to bribe prominent Roman senators for support to keep his throne.

Though he was weak and a drunkard with sole interest in the flute, which gave him the name Auletes meaning "flutist", he looked towards eastern trade for funds he needed for keeping his throne. He gave many protectionist measures to the Alexandrian banking consortiums which ran on Roman wealth to increase trade with India.

The Arab nation of Nabataea was losing business with these developments and therefore they started pirate attacks on the vessels in the Red Sea. Ptolemy countered this by sending quadrireme war galleys with four rowing decks to sink any pirate boats in the Red Sea. A small petrol fleet was stationed in the Red Sea to guard shipping which gave impetus to the trade with India.

● ● ●

A luxury boat with a wide deck and several cabins owned by the company was docked. Arillus and Hippalos remained in the boat waiting for Yona to arrive. Several rounds of meetings had already been held with Ptolemaic officials in Alexandria. Arillus welcomed Yona and Ruan aboard.

"This is Ruan. He is the native of an island on the southern tip of India called Taprobane. He was shipwrecked while on a dhow going to Socotra island from India. His lost his father and uncle in the mishap and he lives in Socotra now. He and his team of youngsters pilot ships going beyond Socotra and have been to India several times." Yona made the introductions.

The name India made the stranger dressed in captain's uniform turn suddenly towards Yona. "Did you say India?" His voice was louder than expected.

"Oh, I forgot to introduce you. This is Hippalos, shipmaster and captain of our Mediterranean fleet. Native of Corinth but lives in Crete. Hippalos, this is Yona our lone partner from the Middle East. He is strangely a Jewish monk but overseeing the operations of the consortium in the Red Sea and Socotra." Arillus introduced Yona, whose saintly smile was like that of a long-lost friend. They held hands.

"You heard him right. I am still a monk and in the shipping business by happenstance. I was born in an Ionian island and moved to Jericho with my parents as a child. I travelled to India with captain Eudoxes of Cyzicus several years back but my friend Ruan here frequents the Indian seas," said Yona.

Captain Hippalos shook hands with Yona and Ruan with great enthusiasm.

"By Isus!" exclaimed Hippalos. "I am in great luck. I have two Greek speaking gentlemen here with a knowledge of the Indian seas. How many days does it take to reach India?" anxious Hippalos asked.

"One lunar cycle and a few more days depending on the wind speed and the sea, from Socotra. Sometimes the days and nights feel the same with thick dark clouds and heavy rain." Ruan replied matter-of-factly.

"Oh, how do you navigate, then?" Hippalos was concerned.

"The best thing about the voyage towards India is you have very little to navigate. The wind is steady and at a constant speed. You only need to hold your rudder and keep the course. But the return is altogether a different story." Ruan said, smilingly.

"You make it sound very simple." Hippalos protested.

"Yona travelled to India with Eudoxes of Cyzicus years back." Arillus added to Hippalo's surprise.

"Eudoxes is my role model. His book *Descriptions of the Euxine Sea* I copied from the Alexandrian library. I have written about the rims of the Mediterranean myself and plan to write about the Red Sea once we get ahead with our project." Hippalos remembered his role model.

"Hmm, it is not for the book we are putting loads of money into the project. We want you to bring the wealth of India to Alexandria." Arillus was sarcastic.

"With two stalwarts here to show me the way, I can take the ship to any devil's nest!" Hippalos claimed. "Tell me about the stars of the Indian seas." Hippalos directed the question at them both.

"No point narrating the game when you are already in the arena, you have to experience it!" Arillus joked. "We plan to build five merchantman vessels worthy of Indian seas at Myos Hormus. We must be clear as to what we need by way of infrastructure at the port when we meet the minister tomorrow. We must have a plan ready for the stores and inventories with the procurement arrangements." Arillus was a perfectionist when it came to managing business.

"I can arrange some carpenters from Charax Spasinu who were released when Tigranocerta was destroyed by the Romans. They are Jewish carpenters experienced in boat building around the sea of Galilee," said Yona.

"Ocean going vessels are very different to fishing boats of Galilee." Arillus had already engaged the shipwrights of Rhodes to draw up plans on the Mediterranean model. "However, we can hire carpenters locally to work with the Rhodians. Don't we have some Phoenicians from Carthage working there already?"

"My life mission is the settlement of displaced villagers from Jericho who follow the religious brotherhood of which I belong as a monk, if you can call me one." Yona's statement made his position clear.

"Teakwood planks for the new venture hewn at Barygaza will start arriving from Omana shortly." Yona continued. "We are already getting it from India for the Red Sea boats in small quantities. Teakwood is best suited for sea-going vessels because it does not shrink or expand and resists fungus and borers."

"I have not come across this wood. We would need logs for the mast, keel and the frames which need to be procured from Mediterranean countries and transported to Myos Hormuz, which I think is going to be a time-taking task." Hippalos raised his brow.

"We will bring it by the Nile. The wide boats which transport large obelisks from quarries upstream can be used. But transferring it from Coptos to Myos Hormuz on the desert road will be a tough task." Arillus had everything plotted already.

The next day, at Ptolemais Hermiou, the office of the minister overseeing navigation in the Red Sea and the Indian Ocean, the proposal was accepted. The wharf area once used for berthing elephant ships was allotted to the consortium close to the military wharf. Permission to expand the lagoon currently used for building Red Sea vessels was also given. A site for warehouses and tents for men was identified. The minister offered support of the custom and military mechanism available at Coptos and Myos Hormuz for the venture in lieu of which the consortium promised to increase the import of Indian goods tenfold from the present quantity within three years.

Callimachus, the minister was immensely happy. "You are the first Alexandrian shipping company investing in the India-bound trade. We will give military escort with Egyptian biremes up to the harbors on the tip of Arabia and back to Myos Hormuz. On behalf of King Ptolemais Neos Dionysos Philadelphos I (Ptolemy Auletes) I wish you success in the venture." He bid them adieu.

"Ptolemy Auletes is better known as 'flutist', the only thing he cares about other than wine and women is his flute. It is not the love for Roman led consortium that makes his minister say this. The king is deeply in debt to the Roman banks, including ours, and hopes to make some money by way of taxes from our investment." Arillus' thoughts were already in line with the Roman senate who were eager to annex Egypt but for the heavy bribes they were getting to veto the motion from the king.

Back at Coptos from Ptolemais Hermiou, Ruan asked why wood was being imported since he viewed pearls and perfumes as the costliest items from India, and they needed no more space than a dhow to transport a year's production.

"We will need a lot of frankincense, myrrh, cinnamon, malabathrum for the temples of Thebes for burnt offerings for all the gods of the Greek and Roman world and private temples who can afford them. We need it for embalming the rich and famous Egyptians whose tombs run in thousands all along the mountains bordering the Nile, especially in Thebes (old capital of upper Egypt) not far from Coptos. Temples of Phila and Karnak are run by powerful native Nubian priests who can challenge the Alexandrian Greeks if their needs of incense are not met. We need perfumes for our ladies in Egypt and Rome, be it the balsam of Judea or *jadamansi* from the lofty mountains of India or aromatic wood of Ud or sandalwood, medicines of India that Alexander's physicians introduced to the west like aloes and spices. There is a demand for large consignments of black pepper from the Roman military for the processing of meat ration for men, not to forget turquoise, lapis lazuli beads and pearls for the queens and the ladies of all the Mediterranean countries." Arillus was in a good mood and waxed eloquent dreaming of the wealth attached with Indian trade.

"I have seen the markets of India. The spices you mentioned are derived from wild plants and available in limited quantity. Especially black pepper which is used as a medicine and available in small quantity only." Ruan took the winds out of his sail.

"Are you sure?" Arillus exclaimed. "What will happen to the promise we made to Lucullus? By Jupiter, we need to resolve this before we jump into the Indian seas. But there is no going back now." Arillus looked disturbed.

"What does the monk say now? Your love for black pepper brought us to the tip of the diving board. Now only you can solve it. We will take over the ship building activity at Myos Hormuz from you and give it to Hippalos to supervise. Your responsibility will be to ensure enough black pepper for Lucullus' needs at Rome. Otherwise we will be ruined." The buck was passed on to Yona.

Arillus calmed down a bit later. "I did not mean to upset you. We now know India much better than at Eudoxes' times. Rome has almost taken over Egypt now. The Red Sea and maybe India will only be a matter of time if their military success continues. If you can capture the spice business with India, this is the best possible time. The consortium will finance your venture and supplement your financial needs on the go."

Yona kept quiet for a long time. Then discussed the details with Ruan and announced. "I will go to India and find out the truth about the availability of black pepper to fulfil our promise to general Lucullus."

* * *

"Have you seen a pepper plant?" Yona broke the silence while on their way back to Myos Hormuz. There was desperation in his voice as he whispered to Ruan.

"Not really, but I have heard that it is a wild plant growing in the thick forests of southern India, specifically in the land of Ay or Keralaputra, a vassal kingdom of the Pandyan empire." Ruan said meekly, regretful of the mess he had made by announcing the non-availability of pepper in India for large shiploads.

"Who brings it to the market, then? There must be some channel by which it gets to the ports from the forests?" asked Yona.

"The forest tribes bring it to the market in small quantities for barter with salt, dried fish and rice. Pepper is considered a medicine more than a culinary condiment. It is part of many drug combinations of Indian medicine. Since the demand is limited, the supply is able to meet it." Ruan reasoned. Now that we have a demand for unlimited quantity from the Roman army and we have committed the supply, we need a miracle to save our souls," Ruan added.

"Save our souls..." Yona repeated out loud. "This is a God-given opportunity to save the souls of the displaced community – men of the Ein-Gedi." He smiled to himself as if the solution was found. "We will make an effort to increase the supply with their help, but I do not know how."

"We have two to three years' time till the vessels are ready for voyage and that will be our lead time," said Ruan.

Yona grew more confident with the thought. While getting ready for the long voyage a message came from Hippalos. The plan and drawings made by the Rhodean shipwrights were to be finalized after discussions with Yona and Ruan to add specific requirements, if any, for the Indian seas.

Hippalos brought orders from the minister for the allocation of harbor space and land for factory and residence at Myos Hormus. He also had detailed drawings of the ship. He liked the lagoon and the dock where small vessels for the Red Sea were made.

"The seminal deviation from the 'frame first' method which you have adapted here will be the 'hull first' method in our new design," Hippalos said, looking at the boat with the skeleton cage of keel and frames under construction. "We will build the hull first on the keel and then make the frames."

Looking at the twisted brow of disbelief on Yona's face he continued. "These teak planks you got from India are best suited for our design. The mortise hole is made at the end of a plank of wood which is joined to a tenon tongue made at the end of the next piece fitting exactly. The hull will form one big plank with mortise and tenon joints on all four sides of each plank," he explained. "Further strengthening timbers and internal frames will be attached later. Secondly, a cover of lead sheets from bottom will be attached at water level to the hull which will be joined with copper nails. We plan to place a large square sail mid ship and a smaller sail positioned at the prow. This enlarged mainsail at great height will give the speed needed for the long voyage. We plan to use Indian cotton for the sail. We will depend on India for the planks, copper and cotton; an area you can help too," added Hippalos.

Yona and Ruan studied the drawing. "Continuous rain, pirates boarding the ship and shallow ports are the main difficulties for the eastern sea voyage. How are we meeting these issues?" Yona asked.

"Yes, we have provided for these issues. The bulwarks of the hull will be raised, and extra compartments placed on the deck. Extending the hull far above sea level will prevent the deck from getting swamped by tall waves. High bulwarks will also prevent hostile raiders and pirates from boarding the ship. As for the issue of shallow shores, we plan to carry small ship-to-shore vessels when we anchor at the outer sea. We have provided extra cabins and compartments for shelter from rain and to secure valuable cargo," Hippalos explained.

"What is this catapult like design close to the bulwarks on the deck?" Yona could not make out the device.

"It is a catapult. In an emergency ballasts soaked in naphtha can be used against the enemy ship to induce fire. This is a mechanism design provided by the Roman navy at the orders of the general. Naphtha is flammable material harvested from Armenian lakes which has recently come into the possession of Rome." Yona did not understand its use but kept quiet.

"The ornamental swan neck attached to the sternpost is to symbolize the Egyptian goddess Isis. I am a believer of the goddess who protects the sailors. The ship is designed to carry a load of two-hundred tonnes and is eighty cubits long (120 foot)," Hippalos explained.

Phoenician workers at Myos Hormuz did not welcome the idea of the Roman officials taking over the shipbuilding while Yona went to India.

"Take us also to India. We are not keen to work for the Romans," they protested. "Tell us the direction and we will reach there on our own," they said.

"I am going alone to the unknown world and do not want to risk your lives. As for the direction, you can talk to Ruan who has taken many voyages as pilot to India already."

Yona set sail in search of Indranidutta, the Buddhist Indian merchant. From the tip of Arabia, Eudaemon (present day Aden) he got a vessel going to Barbaricon on the Indus river where the Yavana businessmen were settled. The ship took a direct route without coasting ports of Mocha, Omana, the Parthian coast and Demetrias Patala sailing not too close to the coastline but avoiding the unknown mid ocean. From Barbaricon (present day Karachi) Yona travelled to Barygaza on coasting ships and found Indranidutta.

"What a surprise! You are in India?" Indranidutta could not hide his elation. "There must be some serious matter which brought you here. Did the teak planks reach you safely? See here." Indranidutta took him to the hewing yard to show him large logs hewn into planks with large saws. One man was standing on the log elevated on a stand holding one end of the saw while another person crouching beneath the log was holding the other end of the saw, pulling and pushing to hew the planks.

"This is how your planks are hewn." A sweet scent of the teakwood dust permeated the air. Elephants were pulling logs from the harbor to the hewing site.

"We have enough logs here and we are supplying to your needs only at present." Indranidutta comforted Yona. "But the situation has changed a lot since the Greek control of trade moved to the hands of the Sacas." Indranidutta sounded deprived and narrated the story. "After the death of King Asoka, the Mauryan empire declined and the Greek started heading towards India. About one-and-a-half century after Alexander the Great, Demetrius crossed the Hindu

Kush and established the kingdom of Bactria (modern Afghanistan) with boundaries up to Peshawar. He had big plans to capture the Indian trade with the west.

"Then came the conquest of Taxila, the learning seat of northern India. Demetrius sent his kinsman Apollodotus with general Maninder and half of his army towards Pataliputra and led the other half towards Sind. He occupied Patala (Thatta in Pakistan). This march ultimately gave him the coastal provinces of Indus. Rajaputana, Rann of Kutch, Sowrashtra and Kathiawar also came under Greek influence later. Barygaza, on the east coast of gulf of Cambay facing Kathiawar, became a great Greek port of the time. Barygaza was connected to the main inland roads of India. Goods from Pataliputra and the Ganges belt, Kosambi on the Jamna basin, Vidisa (Bhilsa) and Ujjain were all connected by these roads. The road from Deccan with the south Indian wares also met at Barygaza. Greeks were in full control of the Indian trade.

"We the Greek merchants are threatened again by the invasion of the Sacas." Yona listened like a student. The pessimism in Indranidutta's voice made his heart pound harder. How can I present my case when his business itself is threatened by the Sacas? he thought.

"Sacas are Scythians, also called Parsies. The Parthians pushed them towards east and they established Saca rule in Gandhara. They entered India by the Siestan and conquered Patalene and the Greek sea provinces of Kutch and Sowrashtrine coming down the Indus to conquer Kathiawar. In a matter of a decade, the political situation turned tables for the western coast of India. The loss of Patalene and Sowrashtra ended the Greek control of the province but the trade is still in Greek hands because of the strong network of Buddha Vihara and its support to the Greek merchants. This is the political situation we are living in now." Indranidutta sighed with a note of relief when he mentioned the Buddhists.

"What about the business of wooden planks? We are going to need much more of them than the present order." Yona shared his anxiety.

"Every nation and their kings want the business to go on provided they get their taxes. The profits have come down almost to the production cost of the planks. Coasting various ports means more taxes till the consignment reaches the port of Bab-el-Mandab at the mouth of the Red Sea. We need a way to cross the ocean bypassing the Sacas and the various ports on our way," said Indranidutta.

Yona underlined the words open sea crossing in his mind but kept mum.

"I have come to see you with a different problem now," Yona said at last. "I need a lot of black pepper, shiploads of it."

Indranidutta laughed seeing his urgency. "What are you going to do with the black little heat bombs in shiploads? You cannot burn it like frankincense in any alter, lest the gods flee. Moreover, you will not find it in such large quantities."

"That is exactly my problem. We have made a commitment to the Roman general Lucullus to supply black pepper in shiploads for military needs in Rome and have allowed him to finance the venture. We are to build five large ships for the purpose too." Yona sounded a bit shaky.

Indranidutta listened intently. "What do you mean by large ships? How large are you building them?" he asked.

"Each of them will carry two-hundred-and fifty tons." Yona sounded casual.

Indranidutta pondered over the answer for a moment and said, "As far as I know black pepper is the berry of a wild plant found in the forests of Tamil country of southern India, and there never was a demand for any large quantities as it is mostly used as medicine. Spicy Indian food sometimes has it as an ingredient. Tell me, what are you going to do with it?" Indranidutta still did not believe Yona.

"Maybe they want to marinate the meat for drying to be rationed to the soldiers in the war zone. I am not very clear about their end use." Yona tried to convince Indranidutta. "Maybe I can arrange to open a procurement facility there and collect the product throughout the year. I need your help in this."

"We normally do not travel south of Kalliana (present day Mumbai suburbs) for business. The old days of Greek control of the coastline is lost to the Sacas. Moreover, the Andhra kings have a strong navy, and they prevent such travel. But as a Buddhist I have visited the monasteries south of Kalliana."

Suddenly Indranidutta pointing his index finger upwards and continued, "There is a way to reach the Tamil country!"

Yona faintly heard the word Tamil country as he was daydreaming about a large ship with swan heads carved at the sternpost. He envisioned the ship with a high hull well above the sea level protecting it against the hostile pirates and the storms. The tall mast was such a beauty that it surpassed the height of all ships in the harbor. The pennant flags flittering proudly would raise goosebumps on any onlooker. The crow's nest on top of the sternpost gave a feeling of being at the top of the world. The large square mainsail was wings of the great ocean bird no one had seen. It also had a small sail positioned at the prow. The stern side had wooden compartments like a multi-story house with a railed balcony for viewing. The piece de resistance was the goose neck carved as a lovely ornament at the sternpost. It had a lantern attached to it. There was no ship as big or as beautiful in the whole of Indian seas.

"Are you scared of Tamil country?" Indranidutta shook Yona's shoulders with both hands and brought him back to reality of the bullock cart infested Barygaza street overlooking the sea.

9

Dakshinapath - The Highway to Tamil Country

"I have some pending business with the Nasik Vihara. Let us go there, maybe the acharya has a solution for your problem too. We will take a dhow to Kalliana and go to Nasik by road." Indranidutta consoled Yona.

"I remember the monks at Badse cave Vihara praising the elaborate Nasik rock cut Viharas during my voyage to India with captain Eudoxes almost fifty years back." Yona remembered fondly his days at the Badse cave monastery as a twelve-year-old boy.

Inland trade routes or *vanika patha* connected east, west, north and south to Ujjain not far from Barygaza. Greeks or Yavana, as they were called in India, travelled these routes far and wide making trade contracts and shipping goods to ports of the Middle East. Land routes from Ujjain crossed the Himalayan mountain passes and reached the Mediterranean Sea by the Lebanon mountains. The silk route from Tibet and China also converged on this path.

Uttarapatha or the northern grid spread from Manipura (present day Assam) to Taxila and Gandhara (present day Afghanistan) connecting all major cities. *Dakshinapatha* or the southern grid covered Vidisha, Ujjain, Indore, Kallyana, Champavati, Andhra, Tamil Chola, Pandya and Kerala. The trade caravans in these routes with hundreds of bullock carts were called *sartha* drawn by *the sartha vahak*. They travelled during the day and rested around a campfire during the night.

As Indranidutta and Yona's cart approached the shrine, they came across several monks on the road all of whom recognized Indranidutta and gave a welcome namaste with clasped hands and bent head.

Yona looked on surprised when Indranidutta casually mentioned, "I have donated the *vihara* of this shrine and that is why people recognize me here. *Vihara daan* is particularly important for a Buddhist follower."

"I have heard about *vihara daan* done by kings and rich traders. Could you please tell me how a *daan* is done?" Yona was curious.

"*Vihara daan* is a very sacred ritual." Indranidutta said softly. His face glowed with bliss as he explained. *Daan* is considered essential for the donor to start on the path of Nirvana or enlightenment. I have seen *bhikshus* and monks enjoying eternal happiness free from material pursuits and focus on meditation and spiritual practices which is achieved by *daan* alone. One day, I also hope to come out of this pursuit of material things which is immaterial in attaining happiness. As for the *daan*, there are several steps one could perform to achieve perfect *daan* or *daan paramyata* in the path of becoming Buddha and there are ten *paramyata* or perfections, the *daan paramyata* being the first step. The first Bodhisatwa level is achieved when a person is able to give away everything in *daan* including his wealth, prestige, family, and body itself without regret or second thought. He then becomes an 'inverted pitcher' which has been emptied of water. All sages have followed the path of *daan*. The holy books illustrate selfless *daan* with the story of a rabbit who gave up his own body as food for the guest. *Vihara daan, bhiksha, maha daan* and *daan sala* are various types of *daan*.

"The monks here recognize me because I frequent this shrine at Nasik. I had the good fortune to conduct *vihara daan* here which included the construction and dedication of the monastery to the monks. This included a year-long arrangement for provision of food and clothes so that the monks could preach *dharam* or the ways to end suffering to the multitudes without any concern for material needs," he concluded as they climbed the steps to the main prayer hall.

Yona recollected his learnings from his childhood. His father had a thriving family business of spice trade in Ionia which he sold and chose to live a peasants' life in Jericho donating his riches to the monastery. He believed in the Messiah bringing together all the lost tribes of Israel once again showing the multitude the path to eternal enlightenment. The similarity in thought with that of Indranidutta was striking even though they followed different religions.

Yona was amazed at the tranquility prevailing in the cave monastery. It was like a cool morning in the deep desert, alone, entwined with nature.

The main prayer hall was big with stone pillars cut in situ. "The long row of rock-cut rooms on the side are meditation cubicles for the monks. Besides the school rooms and library, this Vihara has dormitories and even a cemetery in the complex," Indranidutta said in a soft voice. No wonder he knows it like the palm of his hand, Yona thought, it was his creation.

The chief monk welcomed Indranidutta and Yona in the main prayer hall. He was old and frail, but his face shone like an angel.

Monks and nuns and lay people present also expressed their love and blessings. The chant *Buddham Saranam Gacchami, Sangham Saranam Gacchami, Dammam Saranam Gacchami* in a slow and stretched rendering produced an ethereal atmosphere.

"The truth you are searching for is here. By going to Buddha and his *dhamma* by establishing the *sangha* or community is where the truth is. Buddha is the one who takes us from darkness to light; *dhamma* is the present and *sangha* is the community. The chant awakens the mind, frees it from suffering and communicates with the divine now." The chief monk explained, and the chant continued for some more time.

Indranidutta introduced Yona to the chief monk and explained about the Essene sect and the Qumran monastery, and that Yona himself was a monk awaiting anointment. He said that the political situation in the country was causing great suffering to the poor people and how Yona rescued hundreds of families providing shelter in Socotra island where he had connections.

"There is war in the countries between the Mediterranean Sea and the river Euphrates. The poor are suffering and are being forced to migrate. Our Viharas at Charax Spasinu have several hundred people uprooted from their homelands." Indranidutta explained.

The chief monk listened intently and at the end of Indranidutta's introduction he called out loud. "Yannai!"

Yona was wonderstruck. Nobody knew his Hebrew name here. Still in a daze, Yona replied. "Rabbi."

"Don't you remember me? I am Somadutta, the monk who took you from Ein-Gedi to Alexandria and then to India in Eudoxes' ship when you were a twelve-year-old boy!" Yona was sixty years old now, agile and healthy.

Yona could not speak as he chocked; he prostrated before the monk and cried in heavy sobs like a lost son reunited with his father after an exceptionally long time. Somadutta held Yona by the shoulder and he got up, still sobbing. The saintly smile and the serene positive energy radiating from the chief monk made Yona regain his composure.

Yona narrated his quest for black pepper in large quantities and his desire to visit the Tamil country to locate the sources.

"We get some black pepper from Tamil country," said the chief monk. "The local king there donated some forest lands as *daan*, and the pepper harvested from those forests is sent here every year for trade by the shrine there. You can go there and find out more about the availability for your needs." Then he turned to Indranidutta. "I have a mission for you in Tamil country too. I will discuss the matter in detail later in the evening."

"I have received your letter at Barygaza, and I am happy to be at your service," Indranidutta replied.

The evening passed and Yona narrated his burden of the prophecy of being expected to be the savior of his community from destruction. He admitted sadly that his efforts had not produced any substantial results other than settling a few families in Socotra and helping some with jobs at Myos Hormus. This was far from the need of a haven to fearlessly practice their religion and live a peaceful life.

They stayed for a few days at the Vihara and made arrangements for the caravan journey to the city of Madurai, the capital of the Tamil country. Bullock cart caravans would start from Nasik on the banks of river Godavari and take the highway called *Dakshinapatha* to Madurai, the seat of the Pandyan kings.

Somadatta presented a direction-finding device to Yona. "This is called *matsyayantra* you have to pour oil in the small vase and the fish shaped pointer will move its head towards north. This is a devise used by royal houses in India to find direction. This will help you in taking right courses in your voyages in seas with dark rain clouds in the day or night." And Yona and Indranidutta both prayed for success in their endeavor.

One of the decorated bullock carts used by the senior monks of the Buddha Vihara and important guests was given to them for the long journey. Yona admired the beautiful cart. It had a hooded top with bright colored cloth and metal wheels which gave it an elegant look. Brass ball-like ornaments fixed along the sides shone in the sun. The yoke made of black ebony wood was polished and at its base there was a wide seat for the driver or the *andavah*. The hooded carts were called *annas* locally. It had space for two people to lie down comfortably under the hood with some added space for luggage. Underneath was a sack for some forage and grains. The *andavah* explained that the cart was called *koodarapandi* in southern India; it was also where they were headed. He kept running his hands on the neck of the young and strong oxen tied to the yoke. Their horns were decorated with flowers, bells and cords made of colorful cotton beads with various kinds of colored stones and glass. Tulsi was the name of the cart driver.

The caravan was preparing for departure on the banks of river Godavari revered as Ganga of the south. The sacred Panchavati shrine would be the starting point where other carts could join the caravan at a cost. When Yona's cart reached the spot, there were about five-hundred bullock carts lined up in preparation. The oxen were given a ritual bath and special nourishment and decorated lavishly. They met the *sarthavahak* or the captain of the caravan. He was like a general of an army heading for action. He called for a meeting of all merchants and other important travelers at a campfire on the edge of the river.

A *sarthavahak* was chosen by the transport corporation or *gomis* as called locally. The corporation would have thousands of draft animals and carts placed along the main highways. Merchants hired them to join the caravans. Maintenance and upkeep of the cart and the oxen, including supply of spare animals or carts when needed, was the responsibility of the *gomis*. Travelers could join their own cart and bullocks or share with other travelers for specific charges for each service they received.

An advance party including road engineers, carpenters, well diggers, bridge workers, laborers and armed mercenaries were already several days ahead of the caravan making arrangements for food and water for men and animals. They would determine the resting places for the caravan and pay for the rent and facilities availed from the villagers.

Everybody invited were seated around the campfire for the first council of the journey. The *sarthavahak* stood on a pedestal to ensure visibility to all. A Vedic brahman conducted a prayer service and flowers and fruits were offered to Lord Indra who is regarded as the benefactor of the *sartha*.

"Lord Indra be our guide, our leader chasing all ill will, wild beasts and highway robbers. Lord, give us riches with your power." He prayed while conducting the ceremony.

Sarthavahak called his assistants and introduced them to the council. The storekeeper, responsible for food, drinking water and shelter was the second in charge. A medicine man also worked with him to provide medical aid to both men and animals.

The head of the loaders was called the *bharavahak*. He assisted the *sarthavahak* in loading and unloading carts and wagons. There was another important person named *karpathika* who was the weatherman whose forecasts influenced the journey.

Thalainiyamika was the name for the land pilot in charge of the traffic control. He would travel ahead of the caravan and watch the directions. He was responsible for taking correct directions for the marching caravan. Then there was the *bhandinayaka* or the supervisor of vehicle engineering who oversaw carts, pack animals and their welfare.

Security of the *sartha* was ensured by the advance party of road engineers. The head of security was called *prapathya* who was the lord of the path. His responsibility included keeping the road in good condition for carts to pass and to drive away robbers and wild animals. One of his team was already days ahead of the caravan on the road.

An emergency council was put in place including all the heads of responsibilities and two representatives of the merchants. Indranidutta and Yona were also added as accomplished Yavana merchants and representatives of the Nasik Vihara.

Once the council members were introduced and their responsibilities fixed, the *sarthavahak* turned to Indranidutta. "We have a few Yavana veteran soldiers on horseback going to Madurai as replenishment for the royal palace guards. They will travel along your cart to keep you company and converse in your language."

Indranidutta gladly accepted the offer and admired the tight hierarchy in which the system worked taking care of every need of the caravan and its men and animals.

The *sarthavahak* dismissed the gathering except for the elected council members. And he continued, "The *sartha* will start at daybreak and will cover about two *yojana* (20 miles) a day according to the terrain. The total distance to Madurai is a little over one hundred *yojana* and we will cover the distance in two months, giving enough rest to the animals and men. There are many Viharas and rest homes on the way and the merchants can use these facilities. However, there will also be several nights when you may have to sleep in tents or under the trees." He paused to feel the mood of the audience, but nobody moved or looked elsewhere.

"The first part of the journey will take us to the Deccan plateau crossing Sahyadri at Bhingar. The road is hilly, and we may take about nine days to cover thirteen *yojana* to reach there. We will rest for a while and collect fresh water and fodder for the next phase. The flat road ahead will be easier, and we can cover eighteen *yojana* in ten to twelve days to reach Bhima river. Rest and rejuvenation of the oxen will be required for the next longer phase of the journey from river Bhima to river Tungabhadra of about twenty-four *yojana*. At the end of this phase, we will reach Kishkinda in Hampi as we enter Karnata Desha or Kunthala Rajya."

The perils of the journey were reflected on the face of the audience, but he continued, "The next segment will be the hardest part of the journey. Travelling from river Tungabhadra crossing the mountains (eastern Ghats) at Krishnagiri, the long stretch of about thirty *yojana* will take us to Kongunadu, which is a part of Tamil country. After some rest, we will cover another twenty *yojana* to reach the river

Kaveri. The last stretch, crossing river Kaveri we will reach the river Vaigai and travel on its bank till we reach the city of Madurai."

He concluded the travel plan. He also told the merchant representatives to arrange for the carts carrying valuable goods to stay near the campfire at night and the other carts were to make several circular formations around it for security reasons. The members of the council clapped in acceptance of the travel plan and other arrangements.

Yona was much impressed about the well-organized *sartha* and the meticulous arrangements the travel corporation had put together for a long-distance journey in India. The caravans plied from country to country without any hindrance despite being governed by different local kings and chieftains, of course, they collected tax for such passing. The camel caravan Yona had experienced was more secretive and the captain was like an autocrat where all the powers concentrated. On the contrary, in this case, the powers were well delegated among many specialized groups without any hindrance.

The five great banyan trees of Panchavati shrine were barely visible in the wee hours of the morning but the banks of the river Godavari had already a festive atmosphere. The merchants, travelers and carters had their dip in the holy waters of Godavari revered as the Ganga of the south. Chanting prayers, the *andavahaks* anointed their oxen with consecrated red sindoor powder on the forehead and hump. The departure prayers were in progress at a temporary alter with holy fire. The prayer chants at the alter and the ringing of bells tied around countless bullocks made celestial music electrifying the atmosphere with piety, anxiousness, and fear of the unknown.

The monks' deep-throated Buddhist chants and the prayers by lay people were also heard from another corner. All prayers were for the success of the journey and so they all blended well.

Drummers at the head of the caravan sounded their drums to mark the start of the journey at the orders of the *sarthavahak*. Drums were repeated at an interwall of every fifty carts till the end of the cavalcade. The *sarthavahak* walked ahead of his cart, moving first, circling the holy fire and the alter. The ladies came to see off their loved ones raised a loud and long ululation, their way of wishing godspeed. The cracking of the metal wheels on the pebbles of the riverbank brought about another rhythm the caravan would follow for days to come. Yona joined Indranidutta in prayers for the success of the journey.

The Greek speaking soldiers on horseback were immediately behind the cart Yona and Indranidutta were traveling in. There were eight of them followed by a bullock cart with their tent and two servants. These soldiers were in great demand at Madurai as the king's palace guards. The horses too were a rarity in southern India.

As the caravan moved out of Panchavati, Indranidutta revealed his mission at Madurai. "Similar to the Alexandrian debates or those in Athens for that matter, Madurai also has a forum for intellectual pursuits patronized by the rulers. The philosophical discourses are mostly in poetic forms. These presentations are argued for and against in front of the king who approves the victorious line of thought with presents and blessings to propagate them. There is a continuing debate about the religions of Buddhism, Jainism and Brahmanism in the court these days and the chief monk at Nasik Vihara desires that I should coordinate to strengthen the presentations of Buddhist thoughts."

"How is the political situation there?" Yona asked.

"At Madurai Pandyan King Nanmaran is ruling and his Chola counterpart is King Kopperum Chezian. The Cheran King Kodunko Vazhiathan is not as powerful as the other two. We have great scholars of Buddhism in Chola country and in the island country of Taprobane; and my mission is to coordinate among these scholars for a successful presentation of Buddhist wisdom at the royal debate," Indranidutta explained.

Yona kept mum but his heart sank at the thought of pursuing black pepper in a politically and religiously charged situation. Indranidutta's mission reminded him of the poet Archias reciting poems on Lucullus' wars at Antioch.

The efficiency of the *sartha*, or the travel corporation, was evident at the first stop itself. The land pilots had arranged the camping site at the foothills of Harichandra ranges. They organized the villagers to run a local market selling fruits and vegetables, fodder, and firewood. A large caravan was big business for the villages.

Yona walked around the makeshift market to look at the wares for sale and to see the people, their dress, their way of life educating himself about a quite different civilization from what he had experienced hitherto. The surrounding green landscape was replete with beautiful trees and he had located wildlife on his way. Tulsi, the cart driver, spoke about chasing leopards and wild boars. White necked storks, herons, ibises were also seen. The birdsong was drowned by the cart's creaking sounds when the caravan moved. Now that the cart was still the songs were loud and clear. After seeing a lot of desert, the green surroundings were invigorating. The caravan resumed its movement after some rest but the landscape continued for many more days.

"The mountains we see on the right are a long chain of peaks running all along the western shore of the country. The sea we call the Eritrean or Indian Sea runs parallel to these mountains. If it were not for the landlocked Madurai, we could have sailed down the sea much faster." Indranidutta felt there was need for speed.

Once they crossed the hills and entered the Deccan plains, the topography completely changed. They were leaving the series of rock cut caves and entering the Satvahana strongholds. They ruled parts of Dekhan (modern Maharashtra and Andhra) and encouraged trade with a chain of caravan rest stations providing grazing lands for animals along Dakhinapatha passing through their kingdom.

Days passed after which they came to the banks of Bhima river – the next long stop at Sholapur. The animals were bathed, fed, and rested for a couple of days. Repair of carts and change of sick animals were tended to by the specialists.

The *talainayak* or the land pilot found a shallow tract to cross the river. A temporary check dam was built to make the crossing easier for the animals and carts through the wet river bottom. Once the caravan had crossed the check dam was opened to restore position. After a few days they reached the mighty river Krishna at Vijayapura. Deciduous forest gave way to rocky plains with boulders of black granite and small hillocks. Like the river Godavari Krishna river was also east flowing and drained into the ocean on the eastern side of the country.

River Krishna flowed quietly but was deep. The *sarthavahak* arranged for the construction of a temporary bridge for crossing. The decision was taken much earlier than their arrival at the riverbank, demonstrated by a nearly completed bridge taking shape under the supervision of the *prapathya* and his road engineers. Rafts made of heavy logs were connected and fixed on the banks to make the road. Loaded carts crossed without difficulty, although the horses were a bit reluctant to step on to the raft and continued neighing till they reached the shore.

Then they came to Kishkinda. It was a pilgrimage center for the Hindu travelers. In the Indian epic Ramayana, Lord Rama set out to rescue Sitadevi and collected the support of Vanara army of King Sugriva from Kishkinda on his way to Lanka to defeat Ravana. The temple at Hampi was reached by crossing Tungabhadra river. The pilgrims had a dip in the river visited the temple and the caravan moved on.

The plains gave way to hilly tracts once again and continued till they reached Chitradurga a few days later. The Chandravalli cave temple located there was built on huge boulders in the shape of a moon, once belonged to the Satvahana kings. Here the western coastal route joined Dakhinapatha. The small hills and plains remained until they reached Thagadoor (Hosur) several days after crossing river Tungabhadra. They were in rich agricultural lands now. Cold breeze from the high mountains of Nilmalai made the journey pleasant as the caravan crossed into the Tamil country at Krishnagiri. Rocky terrain made advance tiresome for the animals and men with aching legs after the long trek from Nasik. But the beginning of the last lap was reached at river Kaveri where they rested for quite a while.

The plateau of Tamil country was traversed to reach Vaigai river which flowed through the great city of Madurai, their destination. Fertile agricultural land boundaries with tall palm trees fed by river Vaigai continued as the caravan kept to the banks of Vaigai river. As they neared the city of Madurai, the Yavana soldiers put on their gear to prove their identity. Their helmet, the round shield, greaves, or the leg protection, and the breastplate were all made of glittery bronze. They also carried a sword.

The king's spies from Madurai had already visited the *sarthavahak* and the Yavana soldiers. Arrangements for appearance before the king were made and the horses were inspected for inclusion in the royal cavalry. Local Buddhist monks were awaiting Indranidutta as the news of their arrival reached Madurai faster than the caravan.

Yona slept well in the guest room at the Buddha Vihara, even though he could not shed off the bumpy ride from his mind. Unconsciously, the sound of the metal wheels cracking against stones and the encouraging shouts of the *andavah* were alive even in his sleep.

It was still dark when Yona rose to the ringing of bells. Day was breaking, and the Vedic temple started the ritual morning puja accompanied by bells, drums and a high-pitched wind instrument called *nadaswaram*. The wake-up call was sounded with a large seashell, long and loud. Yona jumped out of bed as he wanted to witness the activity. Right across the Vihara was the large temple pond where several devotees were already taking their dips. They were loudly chanting praises to the deity, the rhythm of chant mingled with the morning chill made music. As the first rays of the sun emerged, the bathers raised a scoop of water towards the sun, chanting prayers.

"This mode of worship is similar to the Essene morning prayer by the elders back in Ein-Gedi." Yona was taken by surprise at the sight and exclaimed at a Buddhist monk who came to his room.

"They are not Essenes. The morning ritual of Vedic religion includes a dip in the temple pond and sun worship before they enter the temple." The monk answered and introduced himself. "I am Niratha. I am assigned to oversee your wellbeing at the Vihara and to take you around the city of Madurai to familiarize you with the Tamil lifestyle and assist you in communication," he said in fluent Greek. "I have studied Greek at Taxila for almost ten years. There is a good Greek speaking community at the Gurukul there."

"That is wonderful. Thank you for your kind help." Yona was overwhelmed.

"You will find similarity in worship between Essenes and the Vedic saints because righteous people behave in the same way to fellow beings and nature, no matter which religion or which part of the world they belong to. If you are ready to move around, you can witness the fire dance ritual which is another way of prayer and getting closer to the Almighty." There was an invitation in his tone.

"Vedic religion also aims at helping the human spirit to transcend to the creator. Attaining Nirvana is our path and living in likeness to God is what some others practice." He continued as they set out to the temple.

Yona shook his head in agreement as the crux of various religions he came across flashed in his mind.

A solo dancer accompanied by a vocalist and a drummer with his drum suspended from his shoulder was about to perform the prayer dance at the auditorium facing the main door of the sanctorum of the temple.

"The dancer is actually a nun living in the temple complex, learned in the Vedic texts and yoga. She attains the enlightenment by consecrating her body and mind to the supreme spirit through her dance." Niratha looked at the bewildered Yona.

The dancer was adorned with jewels from head to foot. She wore an ornamented headgear at the top of her head where her hair parted.

She also wore a headband with pearls and gems and white jasmine flowers on her hair knot. Her ears and nose were elaboratively ornamented with gems and pearls. She wore bangles and bracelets and an elaborate multistrand necklace which covered her breasts. The gridle she wore had countless rows of beads and pearls which held the sari together from waist to the middle of her thighs. The *ghungroo*, or leg ornament, with rows of small bells sewn to it, made jingling sound as she moved.

"The performance is called fire dance, though there is no fire other than the ritualistic lamp lit around which she performs. It pertains to the element of fire inside, or the godly spirit within is exhibited by the performer. Mystical manifestation of the metaphysical element of fire in the human body is highlighted here with the rhythmic movements. Her poses resemble movements of the dancing flame and fire linking up with the ultimate consciousness. This is like the yogic practice of awakening the kundalini, the energy that lies dormant at the base of the spine through chakras in a process of spiritual perfection."

Listening to Niratha, Yona could see that he had in-depth knowledge of the Vedic form of worship.

Yona watched intently. The dancer's rhythmic measured steps accompanied with meaningful gestures expressed with her hands, her eyes following the hands expressing sublime devotion, her ears listening to the music and connecting the art of body movement to the mind, intellect, and consciousness was sheer exuberance of spirituality. Yona realized her ethereal performance was an act of attainment of her spiritual self, meeting the ultimate consciousness, same as those achieved by sages with constant meditation.

The pace caught momentum and it was truly a homage to fire. Yona could feel its reverberations on his mind and body. Then the rhythm slowed, and the performance ended with signs and gestures of praising God.

"Bharathamuni created the Veda of dance called *Natyaveda* by taking the essence of the four Vedas containing the fundamentals of the Hindu philosophy into this dramatic dance," Niratha explained.

"The rituals in the Vedic religion require long years of practice. For example, the dancer here would have spent decades of study and practice to reach this level of excellence," Niratha said. "We study the Vedic religion so that we can point out how it is different from Buddhist tradition. The rituals require long years of practice also not everyone is attuned to studying them."

"How then, do the common people practice this form of worship?" Yona enquired.

"This is what we are trying to explain at the debate. The religion which allows space for the common man to practice and attain Nirvana or eternal bliss is what we preach. Jainism and Buddhism are thoughts originated by non-Brahmins (Vedic practitioners) who made religion more open to be practiced by all," Niratha explained.

On the way back, Niratha told Yona about the religious and cultural debate called *sangam* conducted at the durbar of the king where religions were discussed and debated.

"*Sangam* or *koottam* means gathering," Niratha explained. "You must be aware that Alexandria, Athens and Rome have similar gatherings of the elite in debate on political and cultural matters. In this country, the Taxila academy and Madurai have the distinction of such gatherings. Here in Madurai, it is held under the supervision of the king who is himself well versed in the matters of art and culture. The king encourages discussions on religion and political thoughts too which in turn help him in taking decisions. This tradition of *sangam* is centuries old."

Yona realized from his words that there was something bothering Niratha but he kept mum and let him continue.

"Jainism and the Vedic religion have many things in common. Jains have branched out of the Vedic system protesting the burden of rituals and its monopoly to one sect of the caste system. They felt seeking ultimate Nirvana should be open for all. Observation of right conduct, right path, and right knowledge is the key to Jainism. The philosophy proclaims *ahimsa* or non-injury, speaking the truth or *satya*, non-stealing and non-adultery are to be adopted by the householder.

"The Tamil poets of Madurai have contributed greatly to the growth of Jainism in the Tamil country. Jains say that all objects, animate or inanimate possess life and feel pain on infliction of injuries, so the greatest emphasis is laid on the doctrine of *ahimsa* or non-injury of any kind on any living being however low may be its state of evolution. The meat-eating communities of south India find it difficult to practice."

"Here we have an opportunity to introduce the doctrine of 'avoidance of sorrow' and attainment of Nirvana as taught by the Buddhist religion. We need such literature with simple stories or short poems to get Buddhist thoughts popular here. The acceptance of the *sangam* is necessary for such a venture. The *sangam* will have to approve our arguments and the treatise before we get permission for evangelizing." Yona remembered Indranidutta mentioning his mission in Madurai.

There was some good news awaiting them when they reached the Vihara. The king of Madurai was to grant an audience to the traders of the caravan the next day. To the nervous Yona, worried about his mission, Indranidutta explained what the king's audience meant.

"The king will receive presents from the traders at the durbar and give permission for the goods to be sold in the country which are already inspected, valued and taxed by the king's men. We must pray for permission to travel to neighboring countries of Chola, Chera and Ay kingdom."

The next day, as appointed, Indranidutta and Yona awaited the arrival of Pandyan King Nanmaran of Madurai at the durbar along with main traders from Panchavati. The ministers, the fan bearers, the poet of the royal court and other philosophers took their seats; Greek bodyguards with their shining armory took their positions. The traders waited at the usher room next to the durbar hall.

The flag bearer appeared announcing loudly, "Long live Deva Poonthanam Ilavanthikai Palli Thungia Nanmaran, our beloved king." All present stood up and repeated, "Long live, long live" till the king arrived and was seated. The king raised his hand, and all sat down.

The chief minister came forward and prostrated in greeting. "Long live the king." He raised himself and submitted. "Lord, a caravan of five-hundred carts has arrived from Panchavati. The goods brought in were inspected, valued and tax collected as per the norms. The traders request your kind permission to show their face to the king in respect. They seek permission to sell their wares in the country."

The king raised his hand again in acceptance. The usher announced each trader and the goods he brought in. The trader presented himself, bowed and submitted his presents to the king. Amphorae of expensive wine, frankincense, myrrh, glass and ceramic wares were among the presents. Indranidutta presented a beautiful shining blue necklace made of lapis lazuli beads.

The king held the necklace in his hand and was pleased. Indranidutta introduced himself and Yona. A letter from Nasik Vihara, introducing them as ambassadors of the Buddhist Vihara and requesting permission to visit the villages donated to the Vihara by the Ay king, a friendly kingdom of Pandyans of Madurai, was submitted which the minister read aloud.

The king thought for a moment and said, "Everything is not well in our neighboring countries of Chera and Chola. Some chieftains have joined forces against us for military action. However, our beloved Prince Nedumchezhian is watching the developments closely. You can travel to Ay country without any difficulty as they are under our protection. You may collect my *ola,* (permission written on a dried palm leaf with a metal pencil) from the minister." The king got up and disbursed the traders by raising his hand allowing permission to sell their wares.

The palace gates were also guarded by Greek soldiers in their shining brass armor. Yona knew they were Indo Greeks and were not from anywhere near Greece. The tall and fair soldiers with their short swords and long spheres contrasted against people of the city. Their horses were big and handsome instilling fear. No wonder they were in high demand in Madurai palace. The soldiers and their horses which had travelled with the caravan were admitted to the palace guards. Yona was told there were five-hundred Yavana palace guards who made up the king's bodyguards.

10

The Ay Country

Decanus, the leader of the Yavana soldiers who was traveling with the caravan was happy to meet Yona again.

"We have joined the group of 'Five-hundred' the contingent of the palace guards." He announced and did not conceal his happiness. "The horses were also sold at a handsome price. How did the meeting with the king go? Will you be here for long?"

"Indranidutta has plans to be here at the Buddha Vihara for some time in connection with the *sangam* debate. He plans to visit Chola country and the island in Taprobane if the political situation permits. As for me, I have plans to go to the Ay country or Aioi as you call it, to look for pepper," said Yona.

"I understand the western end of the pepper country opens to the sea. I found this out from a few soldiers getting discharged and planning to go home." Decanus passed on useful information.

"Yes, it is the same coastline we crossed from Barygaza which goes down south to the pepper country and further south to island Taprobane." Yona could already figure out the topography.

"The Ay country is a vassal nation to the Pandyan kingdom, and my friends will be crossing it to reach the sea. You can travel with them if you like. It will be safe and since they are familiar with the place and the language life will be easier," Decanus offered.

"That would be wonderful." Yona was anxious to get on with his journey. "I have to collect an order from the minister's office to the Ay king to facilitate my mission before I start."

Decanus helped Yona to get the order called *ola*. The order was written on a dried palm leaf with a sharp metal pencil. Aye country was a protectorate of the Madurai kingdom after its subjugation by King Pasum Poon Azhagia Pandyan a couple of centuries ago.

Five veteran soldiers, Niratha, the monk, and Yona started on horseback to Ay country before daybreak the next day. Mud roads were wide and were planted with tamarind trees on both sides which provided good shade from the scorching sun. There were many travelers on the road on bullock carts, riding on donkeys and walking in groups. Horses and horse carts were rare as only the king's men had such luxuries.

By evening they reached halfway and rested in a caravanserai called *satram*. There were several merchants and their bullock carts parked at the *satram*. While the animals grazed in the nearby fields the party rested.

"By tomorrow evening we will reach Aykudy, the capital of Ay kingdom. It is where the mountains start. We will cross through the mountain pass called Aryankav. In another two days from there, we will reach the seashore," Nicanor explained the itinerary. "We hope to get a ship going to Barygaza from some port along the shore, probably at Kollam (Qualum) or Balita (Vizhinjam). We can sell our horses and procure some spices or pearls there too."

"My search is also for large quantities of spice, especially black pepper," declared Yona. "I represent a banking consortium in Alexandria which is contracted to supply large quantities of black pepper to the Roman market."

Suddenly the soldiers looked up interested to know more and Yona continued, "My intention is to establish a procurement center at one of the ports which can collect black pepper and store it for shipment. If you are not keen to reach home urgently, you can also join me in securing storage and collection centers for pepper."

The soldiers did not take the bait but Yona was keen to use their knowledge of the local language and their experience as reputable soldiers at the Pandyan palace who commanded great respect among the locals for the project.

"You will be handsomely paid, not less than what you earned at Madurai. Maybe much more profit can be made by being part of the pepper trade."

The guards still did not answer but they could clearly see a lucrative venture behind the offer.

"The consortium I represent is funded by the Roman general Lucullus. We have ships getting ready at port of Myos Hormus." Yona made the proposal laden with big names and irresistible for the soldiers. He assessed that the veteran guards had no hope of finding an employment in their homeland at this age and would spend away their life savings.

The next day they reached Aykudy. High mountains shadowed the horizon; it was a welcome change against the plains of Madurai with a few scattered hillocks. The guests from Madurai were welcomed auspiciously and provided shelter for the night and their animals were taken care of. The climate in the mountainous country was healthier and pleasant. Yona and the party had a good night's rest and the next morning were ushered to be presented before the king.

Yona noticed there was no pomp around the palace, a two-story building called Nedumpura was the main palace building. An air of humbleness prevailed. King Thithian was on the throne. The *ola* from Madurai was presented. The king looked puzzled seeing the soldiers, and the white-clad monk and the saffron-clad Buddhist monk together in a group.

"Your Highness," Yona said in Greek which the king understood with some difficulty. "I have come to your beautiful country with open arms. Forests of your country produce medicinal spices the fame of which has crossed the seven oceans. Rulers in Alexandria and Rome are keen to have large amounts of black pepper for which they intend to send ships. I am their ambassador seeking your permission to procure it in sufficient quantity. My name is Yona and I belong to a Jewish sect called Essenes. We have close links with the Buddhist monks of Nasik, and I have a letter from the chief monk of the Nasik monastery for your highness. My friend Niratha is ordained as a Buddhist monk attached to the Madurai Vihara. The soldiers are fellow passengers on their journey to the seashore to find a ship going to their homeland."

The king smiled at Yona, read the letter from the monastery and indicated at everyone to sit down. The king spoke in the local dialect and Niratha translated it for Yona.

"Ours is a country of shepherds. Our forefathers came to these parts of India from Sourashtrene area. As you are aware, Buddhist teachings are our guiding force. During the time of our forefather King Ay Andiran, the kingdom was much larger and stronger and his *daan* of his wealth and the country is glorified by poets even today. As he desired, he died a poor man, relieved from the pains as Lord Buddha taught. Level of Bodhisatva is achieved when a person can give away anything in *daan*, including his wealth, prestige, family and body, without regret or second thoughts.

"The coast from Kanyakumari to Thiruvalla and the Ghats were our domain, and the seat is called Pothiyilmala. Now we rule only half of it. The mountain pass Aryankav, where you cross the mountains and travel along the Kallada river takes you to Kollam-Kottarakara area which is our northern boundary now. We have Vizhinjam (Balita) as the administrative capital on the seashore. Kanyakumari remains our southern boundary. With the sea to the west and the mountains to the east, we are well protected and blessed with copious rain and sunshine. The breadth again has the shores with its Neythal lands occupied by the fishermen and the salt makers. Then the wetlands or Maruthva spreads which is the granary of the country where rice, sugarcane and sesame are grown. Then we have the Mullai lands where the shepherd community lives looking after their cattle. They migrate frequently. Finally, the Kurinchy lands is where the forests are. The Kurava community collects forest produce and medicines which you are looking for. All these areas have their own chieftains, and they present the king's share of produce to our palace.

"The villages donated to the Nasik monastery is in the Mullai area where the shepherds practice shifting cultivation. Pepper you are looking for grows in the forests and the chieftains there are the Mala Arayans. I will send my envoy with you to meet the Mala Arayan chief and you can find out for yourself how much pepper you can procure."

King Thithian gave a long speech which clearly explained how helpless he was in matters of running the country and he relied on the king's share provided by the chieftains. The party was then sent to the chieftain of the forests with an escort.

Mala Arayans called themselves Mala Arachans meaning the kings of the forests. They lived deep inside the forests on wooden tree houses for protection against wild animals. Mountains of Ay country was the preferred breeding ground for elephants and the symbol of the country was also the elephant. Tigers and leopards were aplenty, not to talk about other wildlife. No one ventured into the deep, dark rainforests.

Niratha, the monk decided to stay back and head for Madurai, but the soldiers wanted to stay and find out more about the turn of events.

Chathan was the name of the escort sent by the Ay king for Yona. He belonged to the same Arayan tribe. "It is one day's journey on the bullock cart to Aryankav where we can meet our tribal chief. His speech was heavily accented, and the soldiers had to ask for clarification time and again. Aryankav literally meant forest of the Arayans. There were eighteen hills around Aryankav where the tribe lived. Each hill had a chief and the entire tribe was controlled from Aryankav.

"Where are the villages given as *daan* to the Buddhist monks?" Yona enquired through a soldier.

"The villages of monks are further down the hills, in the Mullai lands. The Edayar or the shepherds live there. They do not live at any place permanently. They clear an area, sow some lentils and rice, live there for a few years, and move to a new area. Their animals move where the grass is green, and they follow," Chathan explained. "Our tribe lives in the forests and we do not do any cultivation. The forest gives us enough to survive. When the rains are continuous, we get rice and oil from Aykudy.

"There are monks meditating in the forests also. We protect the monks from wild elephants and tigers. The saintly monks are not attacked by animals normally. They have docile tigers living near their caves sometimes." The narrative stopped suddenly as the horses refused to go further and were snorting and sniffing. "It seems there is a tiger around. We wait for some time. It will go away." He championed their co-existence with wild animals.

It was only then that Yona realized that they were already in the thick forest. Yona had never experienced a tropical rainforest. The thick forest trees stood very tall with dense leaves and the sunlight hardly reached the ground, giving a feeling of dusk even during mid-day. Loud and repeated chirping sounds of the crickets, strange howling noises of the large-beaked rainbirds and the hornbills, accompanied by the sound of the jet-black monkeys jumping from the tall trees as if to scare away strangers scared Yona. The fear of an appearance of a tiger added to his anxiety. When the party reached a small clearing with tree houses, Chathan advised Yona to present the chief with dried tobacco leaves which was customary. Once the ceremony was over, Chathan explained the purpose of their visit and relayed the Ay king's message.

Yona was desperate to see a pepper plant. When he saw one, he was amazed. Like the grapevine, it needed a support to grow and was entwined around the forest tree giving the tree a cylindrical bushy appearance.

Chathan explained. "Pepper grows in the forest where the trees are not so dense and high. The berries are small and cling to a spindle in cluster. Each leaf nod will have a spindle. The Kuruva tribe climb the trees with a ladder made of bamboo for harvesting the berries."

"Why do your people not harvest the pepper?" Yona asked.

"Pepper is found in the forest where the Kuruva people go. They do not cultivate anything. They only harvest when they need rice and salt," Chathan said proudly.

Only if they knew that pepper was sold twice its weight in gold in Rome, they would not be so casual about it. Yona also thought of a counter scenario that the tribes could be following the teachings of Buddha, living free of desires.

"Can I see some young pepper plants? The ones entwined on the tree must be mature plants," Yona said.

"It grows by itself," Chathan explained. "Do you see some vines trailing on the ground? Those vines are called runners and they are looking for new trees to climb on."

Yona picked up some runners. "Yes, these vines have roots already. There are many trailing vines on the base of the tree."

When they all came back to the Arayan chief's residence Yona made a proposal. "I have come here to find a source for more black pepper than that we are already getting. We need to cultivate it like you cultivate rice and sesame. The abandoned clearings available in Mullai area you have mentioned earlier can be used for the experiment. The small trees left out there can be used as climbing standards. There are thirty such villages donated to the Buddhist Vihara by King Ay Andiran. Can you help me to plant the cuttings in those areas?" He asked the chief. "I will give you rice, lentils and salt as reward," he concluded.

Yona was nervous and as he finished his proposal, he watched the chief for a reaction. The chieftain seemed to have liked the idea and was looking at other members of the clan for approval.

"You will get fifty cartloads of rice, lentils and salt for planting pepper vines in all the thirty villages gifted to the Vihara." Yona made his proposal quantitative.

At that point Yona did not know that such an experiment would succeed. He made a calculated guess that the habitat had not changed, and the runners were already rooted, and the risk was worth taking. Moreover, he had no other options available to him to increase the production in this alien country. The grapevine cultivation Yona was familiar with in Jericho and Kurena gave him confidence. Cultivation of the balsam, silphium, asafoetida, aloe vera and now the black pepper reflected as various milestones in his life.

To his great relief the proposal was accepted. Yona arranged for the import of rice, lentils and salt from Madurai in advance to gain the confidence of the tribe. The Mala Arayan tribe was very honest and trustworthy.

A massive plantation program thus started. The process was amazingly simple. The trailing vines were cut, and a few rooted nodes made the planting material. They were planted around all available standing trees of the cleared forest – small and big. More runners were collected from the forest and the planting exercise was completed in all the thirty villages donated to the Vihara.

Yona and the soldiers stayed in the area for a year, constantly caring for the vines which started to grow at a rapid pace climbing on the standards and trees. Yona used the same method as the grapevine cultivation practices he had seen at Ein-Gedi for the pepper vine too. What was good for one would be good for the other.

The summer was hot at Aryankav because the mountain pass brought hot air from the Madurai plains. The pepper vines suffered from the hot spells. Yona arranged irrigation through small channels which brought water from the upper reach of the mountain. He had seen many Roman aqueducts doing it for cities. This was totally new to the locals and they mocked the practice of irrigating the pepper vine.

Mala Arayans who helped Yona to plant pepper vines in the cleared forest refused to work anymore because their community was moving and had much work to do in their new location. As a community, they were averse to working for wage. The mindset of independent people of royal descent was in their psyche. The forest gave them what they needed, and they were happily independent people. Yona tried to woo them with promises for more rice, tobacco and salt but they would not agree. They were free people and freedom for them meant living with nature without any bonds. They had cooperated for the planting operation due to the respect they had for the Ay king.

It worried Yona to see that the weeds were growing faster than the planted pepper vine. Copious rainfall and abundant sunshine, not to talk about the virgin forest soil, had made the weeds grow. Yona needed a better solution than to expect the Arayans to change their minds. Another hill tribe Yona could turn to for help was the Kurava tribe. They lived deep in the forest which was the natural habitat of the wild pepper. They were the harvesters of pepper from the wild, but they never cultivated any land and moved in the forest in groups collecting forest produce and medicinal plants. They would come out of the forest to the plains only to sell or barter. They were free people and not subjected to slavery. The land was fertile, and the kings were kind and liberal. There was no need to amass any wealth except for the king. Abundance of forest produce, ivory and pearls gave the kings enough wealth anyway.

The Edayar community who occupied the Mullai lands were a shifting community with their animals. There was no hope of finding agricultural laborers amongst them. The next source would be the Marutham wetlands which produced paddy and sugarcane. There were agricultural laborers there, but they were attached to the farmlands where they lived and cultivated for the landlords. Neither the landlords nor the laborers would be open to moving out of their comfort zones to the forests. The last group who could be taken as laborers was the fishermen of Neythal lands or the seashore. But the fishermen and salt-makers would find themselves out of their depth in the rigorous forest lands.

Yona had a problem which needed an immediate solution otherwise the efforts taken for the past one year would go in waste. He decided to consult Indranidutta and reached Madurai. Luckily, he was in town having returned from a long stay at the Chola capital Kaverpattinam. He was surprised to know that the available labor force refused to work, and each group of people had their own way of life and mode of livelihood and were averse to any change.

For the tribal people pepper was a forest produce and they believed that the forest would have enough for their needs. But for the greed for profit of the western merchants with new market opportunities for pepper, the sky was the limit for demand and matching supply was somehow to be achieved.

As he always did, the master merchant Indranidutta came up with a solution. "In Chola country, at Kaveripattinam, I have come across thousands of workers without jobs. They were originally captured as prisoners and carried to the mainland from Taprobane by King Karikala Chola who carried twelve-thousand Ceylonese to work for the construction of Kaveri Poom Pattinam, also called Kaveripattinam or Puhar. Once the city was completed, he let them go free, but they became jobless. Many settled near the city and engaged in pearl fishery. They could not go home as generations had already passed since their arrival. Why don't you try and get some of those workers for the pepper garden? I understand that the climate and geography would be suitable to them as it is like their homeland."

"I will go at once to Kaveripattinam," said Yona, eager and quick as hope was building up again for the upkeep of the pepper garden.

Kaveripattinam was altogether an exciting experience for Yona. The city was on the northern bank of the mighty Kaveri river. He remembered crossing it with the caravan on his way to Madurai. The river drained to the sea at Kaveripattinam. The river mouth was deep allowing heavily laden ships to enter the port without slackening their sail.

There were merchants from all lands at Kaveripattinam – Greeks, Syrians, Jews, Phoenicians, Arabs and the Chinese. Yona had not seen such a vast crowd of merchants since he left Barygaza. The port was well designed with separate streets allotted to different products. Artisans also had streets according to their trade. Merchants had warehouses displaying goods for prospective buyers. Greek carpenters were engaged in repairing old ships docked as he had seen at Barygaza. Brisk trade was taking place at the port.

Yona looked for pepper. There was not much available in the market. The trader advised him to try at the ports on the western side of the country.

Suddenly Yona heard someone calling his name. Yona turned around and saw Ruan running towards him.

"Oh, Ruan, how nice to see you here!" Yona welcome him open-armed and they embraced. "We are piloting the Arab ship from Socotra. We are almost done here. When the winds are favorable, we will return to Socotra touching Kanyakumari and Balitha. The merchants with us are buying pearls and therefore the cargo is light. There are pearl divers of my tribe here and we get a better deal. Therefore, the Arab merchants insist that I be a mediator in buying too. Now, tell me how come you are here? How did you come to Kaveripattinam? What are you trading?" Ruan's excitement would not end.

Yona related the pepper story. "I have come here looking for workforce for the plantation. At the meeting in Coptos you were right in raising the doubt about the lack of supply for black pepper for the kind of demand we expect from Rome. For the people here, pepper is only a medicinal herb from the forest and not a cultivated crop like paddy or sesame. My journey is the result of that observation."

"Did you find any work force?" Ruan asked.

"Yes, I have talked to a few people from Taprobane who were forcibly brought to the mainland by the Chola king for the construction of this port city. They are looking for resettlement and are interested. Come and meet some of their leaders. You might be able to convince them better," Yona said.

The communication with the islanders became easier with Ruan's presence as they felt he was one of them. It was not difficult for Yona to find and recruit about a hundred families willing to assist in pepper cultivation. They called themselves the people from the Ezham or the island.

"How are you taking them to the plantation?" asked Ruan. "The nearest port would be Kollam. There are several ships touching Kollam port coasting the ports of western India. The Chinese vessels go up to Muziris. They are large and having offloaded main cargo here will have enough space for people. They take passengers too."

"Yes, I hope to take them in one of the ships going to Kollam." Yona then reminded him about the ship being built at Myos Hormuz.

"I am waiting for the big day. I will catch up with you at Kollam and we will visit the pepper garden if time permits," Ruan said enthusiastically.

The Chinese ships were larger, and they voyaged in clusters. Having emptied most of the cargo at Kaveripattinam there was enough space for travelers. Yona and his recruits consisting of one-hundred families of Ezham people boarded Muziris bound ships. Along with personal luggage, they were carrying coconuts in a sack made from coconut rope.

"Why all of you carrying coconuts?" asked Yona, curiously.

"This is an essential part of our food. When our ancestors came from Taprobane they carried them along. We grow them here and carry the nuts for food. They also serve as a lifebuoy in the sea during emergencies," one of them replied.

"We cook our fish in coconut oil," his wife added.

"Not to talk about the fermented coconut sap or toddy we are fond of," another member of the group said timidly.

The Ezham people were aware that west of Kaveripattinam there was a great mountain all along the shore beyond which was the sea of Kanyakunari. But they never imagined that the other side of the mountain had the same climate and topography of their homeland, Taprobane. They were overjoyed to see the tropical rainforest of the Ay country after a long spell at the dry plains of Chola country.

The arrival of Ezham people brought about a sea of change to the pepper plantation. They cleared the undergrowth, helped the vines to trail the trees by tying it to them. They made small stonewalls on the slopes to prevent the rainwater runoff, though it was Yona's idea to build stone walls along the contours imitating the Jericho vineyards. They planted more pepper vines wherever space was available and supported them with new tree planting. Virgin forest land, regulated shade, the right rainfall, sunshine and drainage made the plants healthy.

Rainwater drained to the numerous whitewater rivers flowing to the west, popularly known as Palaruvi or the milky river. Once the rapids cleared the river was calm and navigable. Kulathupuzha, Chenduruni and Kalathuruthy were the three rivers originating from the hills to join at Parapar at Thenmalai and was called the mighty Kallada river. It was still and joined the Astamudi lake which opened out to the Arabian Sea at Neendakara.

The Ezham people settled in the lower reach of the Kallada river close to Kollam in thatched huts. They would travel to the pepper plantation by the Kallada river. The islanders were divided into five groups of twenty families each under the charge of a soldier. The job was mostly seasonal as de-weeding and training the climbers on to the standards were the only jobs to be done. No fertilization was needed because they grew on rich forest soil and no pest or disease affected the plants. They planted more area, and also planted their staple tree, the coconut from the germinated nuts they carried. Their presence was accepted by the communities as they were peaceful and timid, minding their own business.

Two years later the plantation was well established. Some of the peppervines had already started flowering. Long and slender inflorescence appeared with small mustard like berries. Yona made the soldiers partners to the venture and their share was paid in silver denarii brought from Myos Hormuz which made them happy. The factory at Kollam for procurement and storing of pepper through the last season was full and they were looking forward to the next season.

Yona entrusted the soldiers headed by Nicanor to look after the plantation and to keep buying as much pepper available from the forest tribes.

"I plan to go to Myos Hormuz to find out if the ship will be ready for travel during the next season. I hope there will be a shipload available for the return voyage," said Yona.

"Everything is going fine here, and we will be able to manage the purchases till your return." Nicanor assured him.

A message came from Ruan that they were ready to leave in a couple of weeks when the wind started blowing towards the west by mid-winter. Yona joined the Arab pearl merchants at Kollam to head back to Socotra. Ruan was piloting the ship. He had a hard time convincing the Arab merchants that Yona was his mentor and his presence would be valuable for the voyage. He was travelling up to Socotra island where his people lived. The Arabs feared their secret of the open sea route would be stolen by outsiders. Yona did not mention his ship-building project but told them he was supervising the lands donated to the Buddha Vihara by the Ay kings as a representative of the Nasik monastery.

The Arabs took the open sea route to avoid various ports. Once the tax was paid to the Pandian custom officials they could avoid all the tax points along the western shores of India and the Persian ports.

The pearls were secure, concealed in cloths wrapped around their waists and the ship had no heavy cargo.

"My route plan is simple," Ruan said. "From Kollam we will sail west till the island cluster Lakshadiva is sighted and sail along its coast north bound. And once the island is cleared take a sharp left west and head straight to Socotra reaching in about fifteen to twenty days."

Yona approved of the plan and told him secretly about the *matsyayantra* or the north locating devise presented by the Buddhist monk.

"Keep it to yourself. The Arabs may spill blood for it if they come to know of it." Ruan cautioned Yona.

Ruan had a sack-full of Indian gooseberry brought from Kollam. "In Taprobane, old seamen carry it to relieve fatigue of sea travel. One could find gooseberry trees in the hills of Yemen brought from Malabar for its value to the seafarers," Ruan said, inviting the others to share. The tip was useful and all on board were agile after about a month's voyage to Socotra.

Essene refugees from the mainland kept coming to Socotra island after Yona left for India. While the elders who left Qumran monastery moved to the city of Antioch and Edessa, and other places close to Euphrates. Socotra was the abode for many peasant families of the lay Essenes. Pella across the Jordan river still had some Essene families as well.

There were others too in this bandwagon. Jewish families estranged from mainstream due to broken lineage by marriages from outside the community, members of other Israelite tribes living in the war-torn Syria, Yemeni Jews and black Jews from Ethiopia were there, to name a few. One thing was in common: they all were Essene sympathizers or lay Essenes and were running away from the homeland for some reason or the other. Qumran community always identified themselves from Israel rather than Judea and had many sympathizers outside Judea, hoping someday all the tribes of Israel would unite. A few elders who left Ein-Gedi were also there giving spiritual guidance to the community. The caves of Socotra were used for congregation and prayers.

Without much delay, Yona and Ruan left for Myos Hormuz, eager to see the ship getting ready.

"Get a dhow ready. We are sailing to Myos Hormuz. Load all the amphorae with aloe juice for Alexandria too." Yona told his men.

"Yishaq is sending some frankincense and myrrh with us and therefore we will have a stopover at Bab-el-Mandap. I plan to visit Yishaq… there is a long pending promise to be fulfilled too," he added.

● ● ●

Yishaq was a Yemeni Jew living in the Himyarite capital of Zafar. After the Himayat government encouraged the Red Sea trade voyage to reach the Egyptian and Nabatean market against the camel caravan traffic supported by the rival Hadramout regime, there was enmity between traders taking the caravan route and those taking the Red Sea route. The Himyarite, having subdued the Sabeans and the Hadramout in the recent past, made great riches from the frankincense and myrrh trade. They built multi-story housing complexes reaching up to nine floors with mud bricks. The roof slab was reinforced with wooden logs and plastered with mud. On the outside, they would plaster in mud color or white, making the complex visually attractive too. (These structures are still standing even after two thousand years.)

The Jews residing in this area claimed their origin to the times of King Solomon and followed the rituals of the religion. Men sported plaited sidelocks and wore the prescribed headgear. The community was rich and engaged in trading spices and medicinal plants.

Yishaq was a pioneer among the Jews to transport spices by the Red Sea. He was able to send goods quicker and cheaper to Nabatean and Egyptian markets using ports of Myos Hormuz on the Egyptian side and the port of Aela near Petra for the Nabatean market. The caravan bosses encouraged sea piracy to stop such traffic.

Yona and Yishaq sometimes combined their cargo when space was available after loading the aloe juice amphorae and this strengthened their friendship. Ishaq had only one child, a daughter named Hannah. She was a medical practitioner for women and children in the locality. She evolved a style of treatment combining therapeutic Greek, Essenic and Indian systems of medicine. She had a medicinal garden in her backyard and procured the Indian medicines from the Indian traders of Socotra. Her medical preparation using black pepper, long pepper and dried ginger, all Indian imports, was a sure cure for fever, chest infections and other common ailments. The massage oil she prepared from aloe vera and other herbs and oils was loved by the women patients as a cure for body pain.

"Hanna has gone to collect medicines. Shall I serve you lunch?" asked Yishaq's wife.

"We will wait for Hanna to come. Moreover, it is early for lunch." Yona objected.

"Ok then," she said, bringing some dates. "This year the dates are sweeter due to the good weather," she smiled.

Suddenly, three men rushed into the house holding daggers. Their faces were masked. Without saying a word one of them ran towards Yona and stabbed him in the chest. Yona fell face down. During his fall he unmasked the attacker and recognized him. They had sat face-to-face in the dhow for about twenty days during their voyage from Quilon to Socotra. Another assailant stabbed Yishaq and he fell on top of Yona. The servants heard the cry and ran out of the house crying for help. Yishaq's wife came running and knelt beside him to help him up. The third assailant stabbed her too and ran out of the house.

Hanna came home in the middle of the chaos. She quickly looked for a pulse-rate and found that both her parents were dead. Yona was alive and regained consciousness.

News spread and Yona's men came rushing with medical help. The stab in the chest had not gone past the ribcage. The physician sutured the wound and applied medicine for healing.

Funeral rites of Yishaq and his wife were held and Yona was looked after by Hanna till his recovery. She made medicine from aloe vera, turmeric and snake oil and applied it to the wound several times a day till it was completely healed.

Yona realized that Hanna was alone and had become an orphan because the assailants looking for him had murdered her parents and felt responsible for her. Yona told her about his plans to go to India soon after the ship was ready at Myos Hormuz and invited her to join him. She had knowledge about the medicinal plants of India and an offer to visit the land was irresistible. A group of Yemeni

Jews would accompany her and look for opportunities for trade of medicinal plants as well.

Ruan and his men caught one of the assailants named Muktar and brought him to Yona. He confessed that the Nabateans were behind the killing. Yona realized that the Nabateans must have found out his link to the ship building at Myos Hormuz and the teakwood supply. More importantly, they understood that the secret of the open sea travel to India had been busted and blamed Yona for the same. Yona handed the assailant over to the Himyarite authorities.

A lifetime of learning from all the teachers of various disciplines Yona encountered in the past made him forgive the assailant. The deaths of Yishaq and his wife could not be undone and Yona assumed as his responsibility the wellbeing of Yishaq's daughter Hanna.

Yona and Ruan set sail to Myos Hormuz and this time they had archers on board for protection. Sailing the Red Sea was different from that of the Indian Ocean where the wind was steady in one direction. On the contrary, the Red Sea wind blew from all sides. Maybe the desert on both the shores made the difference, Yona thought.

11

Aramaic Speaking Malabari

Building large ships in the Red Sea port was a big challenge. Thanks to Indranidutta, there was a steady supply of teak planks and beams sawed at Barygaza by the Indo-Greek carpenters to perfect sizes to suit the design. The Egyptian navy, with directions from the Ptolemy's minister for Red Sea transport were on the spot, and therefore, kingdoms on the Arabian side of the Red Sea could not create hindrances other than occasional skirmishes at sea.

Now that the intention of building a new fleet was clear there was no stopping the open sea trade with India. An attempt on Yona's life was a calculated move to break the link established by the Alexandrian traders.

When Yona and Ruan reached Myos Hormuz, Arillus and Hippalos were already there supervising the preparations for the launch of the first ship. Yona could not believe his eyes. One ship as huge as the Mediterranean ships was on the dry dock ready to touch water. And another ship was reaching the advanced stage of hull structure. There was a flurry of activity and the sleepy port of Myos Hormuz where Yona started shipbuilding for the Arillus consortium was now transformed to a place teeming with action.

"Welcome to the game-changer Yona, the monk." Arillus hugged Yona. "What you have achieved with this Indian teakwood is wonderful. It is the best wood I have come across for ship building. It does not shrink and resists borers, fungus and sea water. Getting such wonderful wooden planks sawn to sizes was actually the game-changing breakthrough in this desert port devoid of any timber till the horizon." Yona realized Arillus had never praised his efforts before in such clear words.

"What about your mission in India? How is the political and trading situation there?" Hippalos seemed ready to sail to India.

"We have a large plantation of black pepper in India now, a factory and procuring center at a port and have the support of the local government which will assure a steady supply of black pepper." Yona narrated his saga with black pepper in the Ay kingdom of southern India.

"Attack on your life should be an eye opener. We should report this matter to the stratego and get navy escort for our voyage." Hippalos looked concerned.

"Sure, we will go to Coptos without delay," Arillus assured him. "We have to fix the date of the launch of the ship and invite him to the event to be our chief guest."

"Have we named her already?' Yona asked.

"The minister wanted an Egyptian name, but Roman general Lucullus suggested the name 'Ashkalon' after his philosopher friend Antiochus of Ashkelon. The general has not yet fully recovered from the loss of his friend who died at Antioch. The course of the war also has gone against him. There was a mutiny in the battalion and the forces refused to obey him and Rome replaced the general. The new general Pompey has taken charge of the war with Mithridates and Lucullus has returned to Rome, unsung," Arillus said.

"I know there was enmity kindled by his brother-in-law Pulchar against him. Remember he told us about it during the victory ceremony he held at Antiochus which we all attended?" Yona recollected.

"Pulchar keeps incestual relations with his sisters including the wife of Lucullus. Divorce proceedings are in progress in Rome after he found out the truth of the relationship. He must be really missing his philosopher friend in these times of distress." Hippalos was sympathetic. "Nonetheless we will name the ship 'Ashkelon' as he desired but can we add the name Hermes to it, the deity of great speed and crossing boundaries, maybe 'Hermeskelon'? The deity is the protector of business and wellbeing of all merchants."

Everybody liked the name. The discussion turned to Lucullus, their patron again.

"It seems that his enemies in Rome are getting an edge over him. They have initiated proceedings against his brother Marcus stating irregularities when he held consulship. To add insult to injury, the senate is delaying his rightful triumphal celebrations. I met him at Naples where he is building a villa on the lines of the splendors he witnessed in the east. He took with him the Greek speaking cooks of the palace of Armenian King Tigranes which Lucullus destroyed and is feasting on eastern cuisine already. He reminded me of black pepper which is a major ingredient of most of the dishes, being in short supply in Rome," said Arillus.

"We will fulfil our promise. The first consignment of black pepper our ship *Hermeskelon* brings in will go to Naples." Yona brought smiles all around.

Yona went nearer the ship for a closer look. Hippalos and Ruan came along. Hippalos introduced Kyrillos the Rhodian shipwright to Yona and Ruan. Sixty cubits (100 ft) long with a capacity of seven-thousand-five-hundred talents (220 tons), she was a beauty bigger than the Indian vessels Yona had seen on the Indian seas. Towering rigging would impress anyone, Yona thought and turned to Ruan. "The lookout position on top of the mast with its rope ladder is a delightful sight. What do you think?" he asked.

"I am thinking of the range it can cover with such a tall mast. Half a dozen ropes, each with a function to control the sail for specific action make the rigging visually pleasant along with the towering mast with the pilot's post, the rope ladder and the square sail." This was Ruan's world at the top of the ship and the ship's rigging was his best friend.

The heavy steering ore or the rudder destined to withstand the storms of the Indian sea looked massive. The housing of the steering ore was fitted on the wing-like projections of the side planking, well secured along with the steersman's position.

"Actually, the rudder has a pair on the other side. Connected with a universal joint, the helmsman can operate both simultaneously and each one separately to steer the ship. And look at the bilge keel, it is made in multiple widths to prevent the ship from rolling!" Kyrillos explained.

"See the swan head ornament on the poop deck next to the steersman's position?" Ruan was excited.

"The decorations are Roman, the name a mix of Greek and Phoenician and the rigging Mediterranean; we are taking the western shipwrights art to the Indian seas," Yona said in wonderment.

They climbed the ladder to enter the ship. The planks joined by mortise and tenon joints made a rigid supporting structure. Internal beams were fitted to reinforce the interior of the vessel. A thick planking was attached along the length to reinforce the hull.

"How are the frames secured to the planking?" Ruan asked.

"Each frame is secured to the planking with treenails and then the treenails are transfixed with bronze spikes." The shipwright showed off the workmanship with pride.

Ruan looked closely at the main mast position and admired the seating without the need of any caulking.

Kyrillos showed them the cabins for the merchants, the hold for drinking water and the cargo. The hold was large, and the deck space was enormous compared to the ships in the eastern sea. He showed them the defense mechanism, a catapult fitted in the deck capable of throwing fireball on the enemy ships.

When they came down, the date for the launch ceremony was fixed at the meeting, and invitations for the guests were arranged. Everybody was happy and ready to change the world, which they did literally.

On the day of the launch the shipwright was a tense man. Ship launching imposed stress on the ship not met during normal operations and was a considerable engineering challenge.

A greased slideway sufficiently inclined was built with barricades reaching till deep waters to take the ship to water. The vessel would slide backwards down the slipway greased with tallow and whale oil till it floated by itself.

Prayers and sacrifices were performed in several traditions as the project was truly an international venture. Kyrellos and Hippalos, wreathed with olive branches in Greek style, took the lead of the ceremony. Some poured wine on the ship for luck and Yona poured some water on the ship and prayed. To everyone's delight, the ship *Hermeskelon* touched water in a smooth run, stern first and floated. The big splash made huge waves that rushed to the shore and the lagoons shaking all the nearby boats vigorously, including the one in the dry dock under construction.

● ● ●

"Who are these Essenes and why should we take them to India in our ship?" Hippalos quizzed Yona when he announced that he planned to take about seventy families as passengers in the ship to India, though he knew that the Essenes were a religious sect of which Yona was a member.

"The Essenes as a community are estranged from mainstream Judaism, mainly due to their differences with Jerusalem temple on the issue of animal sacrifice. They believed purity of body and mind was better worship than shedding of blood. Another difference with other sects of Judaism was their choosing poverty as a virtue, shunning all kinds of luxury others crave for. Like everywhere, the wealthy and the influential marginalized the poor by choice leaving them to the vagaries of politics and war and making them flee the country. Many members of the community moved to Antioch and beyond Euphrates; a few of them reached Socotra island tending the aloe farms of the consortium. They will be useful in looking after the pepper plantation in India where we will be heading. I was prophesied decades ago to be a servant in their time of distress when I left for Alexandria with the Buddhist monks." Yona tried to give a civilized answer even though he had much to add.

Hippalos realized that Yona's mind was made up but he lingered on the topic because he wanted to know more about these interesting people. "If it is not for making money, why on earth should they travel halfway around the world for nothing?"

"Can you visualize a community in which the possessions are rightfully equal to each one of them? The possessions are handed over for the common good and there is no humiliation of poverty or superfluity of wealth. Their needs are minimal and, therefore, their worries are also minimal," Yona continued.

"You are talking like a philosopher, Yona," complained Hippalos. "Tell me how does this sect live? Why should they choose such a low living?"

"This is a conceptual difficulty. Your meaning of low living is the opposite for them. They attain spiritual emancipation with the low living. One's journey travels beyond the material world to the spiritual unity with the ultimate truth. Bodies are perishable, but souls are immortal." Yona said eloquently.

"Tell me about a day in the life of an Essene, the ground reality." Hippalos simplified the question.

"Essene wake up before the first rays of the sun and pray facing the sun, thanking God for the brightness of the day and meditate. Bathing in cold water after nature call, they engage in work, mainly agricultural activity or any other craft. They reassemble during mealtime, bathe and purify the body and partake in the common meal and again leave for work. In the evening they reassemble for prayers and meals after purification. Their life is self-disciplined, simple and unpretentious. They condemn sensual desires as sinful and meant for procreation only. Moderation and freedom from passion are considered virtues. The monastic order condemns marriages and upholds celibacy.

"There are no slaves amongst them. White cloths and shoes they adorn are used to the end. The Essenes abstain from meat and wine. They reject animal sacrifices and consider slaughter of animals in general as objectionable. They are believers of providence and credit everything to fate. Next to God, Moses, the lawgiver, is the object of great reverence. They delight in allegorical explanations of dreams and events which make them objects of fearful respect. Revelations and dream visions are seldom faulted."

"By Jupiter, this is diametrically opposite to how we live!" Hippalos had heard more than he could imbibe.

Yona calmed him. "You will find more of such people in India. The Buddhists, the Vedic Brahmans and the Jains of India live even stricter lives. It is not far-fetched to say that the Essenes are influenced by the eastern way of life. On my first day at Madurai itself I witnessed the priestly class called Brahmins doing sun worshipping like the morning prayers of the Essene sect. They had adorned white cloths as we do and had a tuft of hair on the otherwise shaven head like many in our community. The similarity is quite striking."

Hippalos laughed aloud. "You can disguise as one of them but what about me in this Greek costume if things go wrong in India?"

"I have lived there almost two years. The people respect all foreigners and call them Yavana after the Greek palace guards, respectfully feared by the locals. As for me, they think I am a Brahmin too with my vegetarian eating habits and abstention from wine." Yona laughed.

"The Jewish month of Tammuz (June-July) is approaching. We should be ready for the voyage by then so that we can return in the month of Kislev (November-December) which is the best time for continuous wind on each side. I must leave for Socotra to prepare the passengers to be in readiness for travel." Yona reminded Hippalos about the urgency to complete preparations.

The news about the plan for voyage to India spread and the Phoenician shipbuilders brought from Carthage approached Yona.

Their leader shared his concern with Yona. "We have no place here since the Rhodians shipwrights took over the ship building from us. We are sea people, and we assure you to be useful on your voyage to India. We were subdued by the Romans at Carthage and the love of freedom brought us here. We understand that the Romans are taking hold here too. We love our freedom and refuse to be subdued anymore."

Yona smelt revolt. "We may not be able to take you as passengers because arrangements are already made for maximum numbers we can carry. I can discuss with other men in management for an escort ship where you can take able sailors among you to travel with *Hermeskelon*. The ships we use for Red Sea traffic will be the only available vessel though."

Yona expected them to back out and not take the risk of crossing the ocean on a small boat, but they were adamant to take the chance. "We will prepare her for a long voyage. We need only your permission."

Yona convinced other members of the consortium for an escort ship of the Phoenicians to go to India and left for Socotra with Ruan.

● ● ●

Pompey took over the war on Mithridates and made Syria a Roman province which was already conquered by Lucullus. Several groups of people fled the country from Samaria, Galilee and Armenia besides the Essenes of Jericho. Country of Osrhoene, with its capital at Edessa had boarders with Syria, Armenia and Parthia and was a neutral country which attracted many refugees. One thing was common among all the groups, they all spoke Aramaic. When a haven was opened at Socotra they moved in hundreds. When Yona arrived at Socotra, the population there was more Assyrian (regions of modern Iraq and Iran) than Essene.

Yona called a meeting of the Essene congregation at the ground close to the beach. There were some senior monks also at Socotra. Everybody eagerly awaited the news Yona was about to disclose.

As per decorum, the senior-most monk gave the opening prayers and blessings. His words reflected the plight of the community. "I am pained to see the sufferings of the innocent people. You have valued righteous living above wealth and fame and chosen to be poor giving up lucrative professions. To live in likeness to God as far as possible is the guiding force behind the strife you have endured. I am sure a new way will open up for the righteous towards peace and happiness as it always has. "Believe in God, trust our law-giver Moses and follow the Ten Commandments God gave to Israelites personally without any mediator. Beware of excessive desire which brings bodily pleasure which in turn brings about wrongs and violations of the law preventing people in achieving immortality and bliss. It is the mind that violates the law before the body. It is the desire that covets others' property and its unfulfillment brings sorrow. If you triumph over your desire, you can get rid of sorrow. You can avoid sorrow by avoiding extremes of life and following the middle path, the life of moderation and self-control.

"We have had distressing times in the past too. People would migrate to Kurena and other western safe places during such times. The silphium plants would give employment to farmers, traders and workers just as the Judian balsam provided us at Ein-Gedi. The silphium crop is extinct, so is the balsam of Judea. Man's greed devastated nature's gifts. Kurena is in Roman hands now. The Roman general Pompey has already declared Syria as a Roman province after the surrender of King Tigranes of Armenia. Judea can be the next target. Egypt has almost become a puppet in the hands of the Roman senate. Therefore, the only place to look for freedom is the east. East of Euphrates is also not without suffering. Large migration from Nisibis to Mesopotamia has occurred in the recent past due to the capture and selling into slavery of twenty thousand Jews by Roman general Lucullus."

The multitude gathered knew of people who had suffered this fate their hearts filled with sorrow.

The monk continued, "As I said before, the righteous is always looked after by God. Yona has been struggling for decades to find safety for our people. The aloe farms here in Socotra have employed many and given shelter to a community in distress. There is a limit Socotra can sustain and there is need to look for greener pastures. The new hope is the crop which produces black pepper we use in medications. There is a large demand for this product in Rome and the western world now. Yona feels the suppressors will pay for the welfare of the suppressed in the new scenario. He has some wonderful observations about the plant and the country where it grows." He turned to Yona concluding his remarks.

Yona stood up. The sea was silent as if to listen to every word Yona had to say and so was the congregation.

"I want you to imagine a land with steep mountains where tall trees like the oaks of Bashan grow, grasslands similar to those of Gilead where animals flourish, a land with several rivers and sweet water lakes abounding with fish as tasty as the bereme of the Gennesaret and vast navigable marshes like the Mesopotamian marshes." Yona paused for a moment.

"If you have imagined one, believe me, this is the land I have been to. The land gets copious rainfall for several months in a year and is full of vegetation of all kinds." Yona gazed at the arid desert of Socotra as if contrasting it with the land he described.

"There is no harsh winter and prolonged dry season like we have here. They grow rice and sesame like the Mesopotamian lowlands, but the climate is not suitable for wheat, barley or oats. The fruits of the trees are sweet and succulent but most of the fruits grown here are missing. There are no figs or dates or olives. The oil they use is crushed from sesame seeds which is a premium oil here."

The congregation was spellbound. What about the people there? This was the question in the minds of many. However, they waited as it was evident that Yona had more to say.

"It is a land of spices. Priced condiments like cinnamon, ginger, malabatrum, cardamom and pepper are produce of the land, some wild and some cultivated. For centuries, these spices have been brought to the Mediterranean coast by the Nabateans and other trading groups. Many of our brethren from the mainland are also engaged in the trade of spices.

"The people are followers of Buddhism, Jainism and Vedic religion and these religions encourage vegetarian food, but the working class and the soldier class eat fish and flesh which are available in plenty in nature. There are many Buddhist Viharas there and I was able reach the pepper country through a Buddhist monk who had visited Qumran monastery when I was young. The local Ay kingdom is benevolent towards Buddhist monks and has donated rights of harvest of thirty villages to the Buddha Vihara. The neighboring Parambunad kingdom also has donated many villages as alms to the Buddhist Vihara. All these villages fall between two great navigable rivers which drain to the same sea we see here like Euphrates and Tigris drain to the Persian Gulf."

Yona paused again to a pin-drop silence. The sea was getting rough with tide as the evening approached but the crowd did not notice it or hear anything other than Yona's words. Then the buzz erupted, the crowd was assessing the situation. Someone was mentioning the legendary garden of Sennacherib, the Assyrian king, and another compared the land to Mesopotamian (Chaldean) King Murdoch Baladan's garden growing exotic plants of the east. All agreed in unison that here was another Mesopotamia or land between rivers with all its riches.

"My visit to the pepper country was to explore the supply of pepper to meet the increasing demand from Rome as desired by my partners at Alexandria. I was told that pepper grows wild in the forests of Ay country and gathering the produce and its availability in the market was disorganized and therefore inadequate. I was able to convince the local king that black pepper vine could be domesticated like cultivation of grapevine as we do here. The trial was successful, and a large area is already cultivated black pepper crop and controlled by my people there. I have the king's permission to bring more area under pepper cultivation. There is opportunity for some of you to migrate to the pepper country with family on my next voyage to India as soon as the rain clouds start moving east. Are there any volunteers?"

All hands went up at the blink of an eye.

"I cannot take all of you now because the ship can only accommodate up to seventy families as passengers. More ships will be available, hopefully, in the next season as we can sail only with the monsoon wind in the month of Thammuz to India across the ocean. You can select volunteers among yourselves. I will leave for Myos Hormuz and we will sail together from Socotra during the coming Thammuz. You must observe absolute secrecy about the voyage because there are many in the mainland who do not want us to succeed," Yona warned.

The congregation said, "Amen."

While praying before the closing, the Essene elder reminded the congregation of Prophet Jeremiah's words. "'Build homes and settle down. Plant gardens and eat their produce. Marry and beget sons and daughters, in order that you may increase in numbers rather than decrease. Seek the welfare of the country to which I have deported you and pray on its behalf to God and on its welfare your own depends.'"

The congregation again said, "Amen."

● ● ●

Hell broke loose in south India during this time. Nedumchezhian came to power at the Pandyan kingdom of Madurai. He was crown prince when King Nedumaran ruled and fought several successful wars with the neighbors all around. It was only natural for his rivals to form and alliance and challenge him. Chola King Kopperun Chozhan and the Chera King Kudanko Vazhiathan joined hands with the five chieftains of smaller domains against the new Pandyan king. Fierce war took place at Thalaialanganam and the young and swift Pandyan King Nedunchezhian won erasing all opposition in the whole of south India. He brought in Yavana warring techniques and soldiers from Bactria who were serving as palace guards to the war front with formidable force to beat the enemies. He was now ruler of all the three large kingdoms of Pandyan, Cheran and Chozhan and domains of all the five chieftains in between.

It was the trade with the west and the gold they exchanged for the pearls and the spices that caused the trouble. Chola capital was the beautiful port city of Kaveripattinam on the mouth of river Kaveri on the eastern coast of India. It developed into an emporium where the Greek Yavana traders and carpenters had a street of their own to display their wares. Chinese came in with their silk and traded with the western traders at Kaveripattinam. Pearls harvested in Taprobane and spices of the forests in Pandyan country also reached Kaveripattinam depriving the Pandyans of Madurai of the gold by way of customs duty.

Three prominent kings, several chieftains with independent rule, and the tribal lords were responsible for the political tapestry of southern India. The chieftains and the tribal lords were not allowed to wear a crown. The crowned kings were known as *muventhans* or the triumvirate who had lorded over the chieftains and they in turn controlled the tribes. Whenever the balance of power tilted towards anyone war broke out. The kings were of the clan Pandya, Chola and Chera. It is said that they stemmed from a single family and had Korkai as their capital. The Pandyans ruled the south, the Chera in the west and the Chola towards the north.

The chieftains and the kings kept armies relying mostly on the strength of tribal lords' men. Elephants and horses were used in war but skirmishes for capturing territory or livestock were mostly made with the help of archers and lancers. The Pandyan army had an advantage of the fearsome Yavana soldiers attached to the palace guards.

Royalties from the chieftains was the main source of income for the kings and those from the tribes filled the coffers of the chieftains. The trade with the west toppled the cart and muslin, pearls and spices made the kings rich. Korkai produced the best pearls and all the harvest extending to the Lankan coast came to Korkai for trade. Merchants from Yemen and Petra came in small boats during the rains and went back when the wind reversed. The Chola king successfully diverted this lucrative trade to his country by improving the infrastructure of the Chola port of Kaveripattinam with a fine harbor, repair facility for the ships, dry docks and an emporium for selling wares and its security. Slowly the trade shifted to Kaveripattinam port on the mouth of river Kaveri in Chola country. Vessels could sail into the river and berth safely in the well-built wharf against anchoring in the outer sea of other ports. The Chinese silk traders visited Kaveripattinam and then sailed to the western ports controlled by the Chera king skipping Pandyan ports on the east coast, away from its landlocked capital Madurai.

In between the Pandyan and the Cheran ports, the ports of Balitha (Vizhinjam) and Kollam were a part of Ay kingdom who ruled from Aykudy in the hills. Their administrative capital was Vizhinjam. The present Ay King Tithian gave permission to Yona for establishing the pepper plantation. He was a weak king, but he had ancestors like Ay Andiran who had an army capable of defending even a Pandyan assault. Ay Andiran gave away villages, wealth, gold and elephants to anyone who approached him for help. It was during his reign the Buddhist monks of Nasik monastery received *daan* of villages. He was a true believer and died a poor man, a hermit in prayer and isolation rejecting food and water.

The Pandiyan King Nedunchezhians' attempts to reverse the loss of tax on trade made many enemies. The Chola king Ottrumal Vetta Perunarkilli and his Cheran counterpart Yanaikatchel Manthirancheral declared war against Nedunchezhian. Ay King Tithian, Ezhini rular of Thakidur, Erumaiuran of Mysore, Irungkovel and Perunan were the five chieftains who fought against the Pandyan King Nedunchezhian. All of them were killed in the great war at Thalaialanganam except the Chera king who was imprisoned. This victory gave Pandyans unopposed rule of southern India.

Madurai was a landlocked city, and the nearest ports of the western coast were in the domains of Ay chieftains who were no match for the Chola kings in developing trade with the west. The great mountains on the western boarders stood between Madurai and the Western sea. Aryankav pass and Aruvamozhy pass were the natural openings to the western shore for the Pandyans.

The Ay country capital was called Aykudy located in the hills, but Balita remained as the summer capital on the seashore and was developed into a trade center. Locally the port was called Vizhinjam. The new Pandiyan king Nedunchezhian had to capture the trade to survive. The whole of southern India was under his control after the war which killed many a king and chieftain including the Ay king. Control of the port did not increase trade; it was the demand for goods which did the trick.

Reports reached the king about extensive cultivation of black pepper on the cleared forest lands below Aryankav pass in the Ay country. This activity puzzled him because black pepper was not among the most sought-after export goods. But it did not take him much time to know the secret when they nabbed the veteran Yavana soldiers and the people from the Taprobane island who were looking after the plantations.

They revealed the story of Yona who found a demand for black pepper in large quantities and that he was expected to sail to Kollam when the monsoon set in. The king saw a new opportunity for custom tax in the venture and employed spies at Balitha and Kollam to bring Yona to him on his arrival.

● ● ●

Sailing down the Red Sea had many perils. It was the first week of July and the blistering hot sun added to the difficulties. The wind blowing from the desert brought fine sand along, and when mixed with the salty spray of the sea stuck to the body like slime. Yona realized why mariners worked naked on board. Hippalos had his shirt on and Yona in his wraparound monk's garb were the only clothed men on the deck. The archers in their attire, kept low in their hammocks away from the sun.

The supreme commander of the ship was Hippalos and the shipmaster was Kyrillos. Co-pilot position was occupied by Ruan supported by two lookouts from Socotra; the Phoenician ores master was Ahum (his name meant brother of the sea), his two steersmen and a crew of sailors and oarsmen made up the entire crew besides the armed soldiers. Yona assumed the role of owner merchant representing the consortium.

An Egyptian navy vessel was an escort. The Phoenician sailors fitted an aft lateen sail in addition to the square sail to their merchantman twentyer and borrowed two lookouts trained by Ruan from Socotra for direction in the unknown sea. Both smaller ships sailed ahead of the *Hermeskalon.* Wind was blowing west in the north-westerly direction and sailors were fully engaged in adjusting the sail for correcting the course eastward. The dangerous shoals of the Red Sea made the voyage even slower, forcing them to restrict sailing to the daytime and to find anchorage for the night.

Ruan advised them to traverse the open sea during the latter part of the month of August. The shores would be approachable by September when the sea started calming down after the fury of the monsoon. Port Barbera was the last point on the Horn of Africa close to the island of Socotra. The south-westerly wind was strong there too, but the real force came further south. It rained when they set off the African coast.

"A good omen." Ruan smiled.

"A shower of good luck is the best thing we want now!" exclaimed a tense Hippalos, forcing a smile.

Yona was tense too about the Essene members expected to board the ship at Socotra, on whom the future of the project depended. After three days of favorable wind and sea current, the *Hermaskelon* anchored in the open sea along the northern coast of Socotra. Ruan advised against going further near the shore fearful of the whirlwinds.

Passengers started arriving in dhows. They were handpicked young Essene families, arrived as refugees at Socotra island, who could endure the uncertainties of the alien land and the sea. In fact, they included Judean Essenes, the liberated Jewish artisans from Tigranocerta, the fallen Armenian capital, those fleeing the wrath of the Romans from Nisibis where Lucullus had sold twenty-thousand Jews into slavery and some of the Yemeni Jews. They had one thing in common — they were all homeless and eager to start afresh. Hanna, the medicine woman also came aboard and Yona was pleased.

Yona wondered whether descendants of several northern tribes deported by the Assyrians from ancient Israel also would be here.

Yona thanked God for rising him to the expectation of the elders. It was the dream of the Essene fathers to reunite all the tribes of Israel.

The cargo holds were near capacity thanks to ample stocks of wheat, barley, dried fruits, vegetables and olive oil. The wine they carried was mostly for the Indian kings, a present they cherished as red colored and cool unlike the heady rice wine they drank. Brass, lead and glass wares were also loaded for sale. There was enough space for the passengers below the deck too.

Yona noticed that the sailors and the rowers wrapped cloths around their waists once the women passengers boarded. The ladies stayed in the hold areas on temporary hammocks. There was nothing much the men could do on the deck. They helped in the kitchen and other small errands the situation called for.

"The wind direction is more inclined to the north and there is a need to hold the rudder to keep a southern curve." Ruan was demonstrating a wide south bound curve with his hands to Ahum, the ores master.

The large square sail caught the south-westerly strong breeze and at the right spot. The splashing sound of the cutwater felt like music and Hippalos now smiled widely. Slowly, the windspeed caught momentum and the *Hermaskelon* aligned with the wind fully. The aft sail also was full blown.

"This is like a chariot on the desert sands." Kyrillos, the shipmaster shared Hippalos' view.

Yona looked at the wide open sea reaching the horizon all around and realized how similar the ocean was to the desert. The only difference was the sand and the water that filled each one. Waves rising to two men high were like the dunes suddenly forming in the desert with the wind. White caps of foam appearing here and there were small oases for Yona. The spray of water was like the sand forcefully striking the face during a sandstorm. The desert was rightfully called the "sea of sand", Yona realized. Then it rained. Passengers sitting on the deck area descended to the hold.

It kept raining the whole afternoon and continued through the night. There were short breaks, but they were far too little. Visibility was down, the night sky was clouded, and the ores master looked at Ruan for his appraisal of the situation.

Ruan was calm. "This is the weather we are going to face till we reach the Indian coast. My only prayer is that we may face less storms and no hurricane." He added casually, "Hold on to the rudder with all your strength and remember south is to your right." Ruan was the only hope for direction as the sun was hidden under dark rain clouds, the night had no stars visible and the spray of water made visibility to near zero. The air was damp and heavy.

"Their main mast is broken, and they are drifting." The lookout shouted that visibility was low and everyone watched the escort ship, with the Phoenician sailors, drift away into the wilderness of the sea.

"If the wind speed goes beyond a gale, we might opt for a drift." Hippalos was considering options. He directed the oarsmen, who had nothing to do in deep sea, to assist the sailors who were struggling with hauling the sail to adjust position at the captain's orders.

The oars master and the steersmen were exhausted after a week in the high sea with strong wind and rain. Hippalos himself gave them a helping hand during breaks. More oarsmen were deployed at the rudder in turns.

The clouds cleared suddenly one day when the dog star was still rising. Many passengers came out on the deck in a thanksgiving prayer facing the rising sun in the true Essene way. The color of the rising sun on the water gave way to a dull gray and green color of the deep sea. Still, the swelled sea maintained a steady speed towards the east. The prow was plunging down on the waves, sometimes tilting over to one side and getting corrected again. The squealing of the timber and the flutter of the sail made the passengers return to the hold once again.

"We are on the right course!" Ruan announced. "We have crossed halfway, and in a few days we will be approaching a large island group with ridges and shallows and we need to be careful there. There are islands with sweet water here but most of the islands are uninhabited except for a few with unfriendly tribes."

The next few days were sunny and hot with sudden harsh rains which lasted for some time and again cleared as if it had never rained. Navigation was possible with gauging the wind direction, stars and the movement of the sea. Ruan was at home with the situation which was a source of comfort for the others.

Then the lookout cried land. They were approaching the island group called the Lakshadiva islands. The ship's council decided to anchor for water. Hippalos found a safe place to anchor and the lifeboat was lowered to fetch water.

"Dig a well; it is not going to be deep while I pluck some fruits from this tree." Ruan climbed a coconut tree and plucked nuts. There were several trees on the shore and Ruan showed them how to enjoy the sweet coconut water and eat the fleshy mesocarp. "This will drive away all the fatigue of the voyage," he claimed, and they collected as many they could on board along with plenty of sweet water.

Ruan announced at the ship's council meeting about the next crucial part of the voyage. "The mainland is only a few days away. We must cross the island group and sail towards east and then take a sharp turn southwards to reach our port. The wind will blow partly against our direction and it is important not to land in hostile country."

The good news and the coconut water gave new life to the sailors and the passengers alike. The rains were scanty and intermittent. In a couple of days, the closeness of land was felt by the color of the sea and the marine life with the eels, water snakes and dolphins. Birds were also flying close the swan-headed *Hermaskelon* in welcome.

With some difficulty, Ruan located the horn-like projection of the Kollam shore. Hippalos ordered anchor at the outer sea. Country boats with local men raced towards the ship. Yona located Nicanor in one of the boats and waved to board and lowered a ladder. Nicanor came with a whole lot of bad news.

"Kurakkeni Kollam (old name for Kollam) is full of Pandyan soldiers. They are waiting for your arrest at arrival.

"Why me?" Yona was taken aback.

"They came looking for the Chera king who escaped from the Pandyan prison." Then he related the story of the war at Thalaialanganam and the defeat of all the kings and chieftains opposing Pandyan King Nedunchezian. "Ay King Thithian and the Chola King Kopperum Chozhan and five others were killed, and their war drums and flag standards were taken to Madurai announcing full control of their territory. After the war, the whole of south India is under the rule of the Pandyans. Balitha is now Pandyan's port check post for customs duty for the whole of the western shore till the Periyar (big river)."

"Why do they want to arrest me? Yona was puzzled.

"It is about pepper. I think they want to collect tax for the export. We had to explain about the plantation and your mission for exporting large quantities of pepper to Rome." Nicanor tried to ease the tension.

"Alright, I will have to deal with it myself." Yona called the ship's council and announced his desire to meet the Pandyan king. "Let the ship be anchored till I come back. If I fail to make it, you can collect pepper from the factory we have at Kollam and take your own decision for the voyage back. Let the passengers also be on board till I come back."

The Essene elder prayed and blessed Yona before his departure. Yona went ashore with a few men and Nicanor to be presented before the authorities. They were taken to Balitha where King Nedunchezhian was camping on his chase of the king of Chera who had escaped his prison.

Yona was produced before the king. He prostrated himself and offered a beautifully carved vase of silver with three golden citrons crafted in pure gold.

The king seemed pleased and instructed him to stand. "Are you the one who visited my uncle, King Deva Poonthanam Nanmaran at Madurai with the saffron monks?" the king asked.

"Yes, I am, my king." Yona was surprised at the remark and now relaxed a bit and related the story of the pepper plantation and the prospects of its export to Rome. "The people I brought for the upkeep of the plantations are waiting in the ship," he concluded.

The king smiled. "Madurai kingdom now rules Ay, Chera and Chola kingdoms after the great war. The ports on the eastern and the western shores of the kingdom will collect tax for us. If you plant more pepper plantation like those you made around Nilakkal near

Aryankav pass in other parts of my kingdom, will you have enough ships to carry the produce paying the custom tax?" asked the king.

"Yes, my lord, we have five big ships at the other shore of the sea, and we can carry any amount of pepper made available," Yona said confidently.

"You have my permission to set up camp for your people along Kallada river. I want your people to establish plantations along the road to the Chera port of Muchiri from Nilakkal. You can establish camp at Palayur near Muchiri along the Periyar river and plant new pepper gardens. You have my permission also to travel freely on the road or river touching Meenachil, Thalayolaparambu, Chottanikkara, Trikkakara to reach the port of Muchiri. The road to Madurai passing the Mangaladevi temple and that touching the river Achencoil and Thenkasi meet at Nilakkal. This will facilitate inland transport using the rivers."

The king smiled and continued, "We value your souvenir of Yavana gold. If you bring gold, you can take away as much pepper as you want. Nobody other than your people will be allowed to establish pepper gardens and its trade in my domain." The king waved for his minister to produce the order written on palm leaves for signing his approval.

Yona came back to the ship a victor. Kurekeni Kollam was a natural port with breakwater long enough to accommodate large ships. Local pilot boats lead the *Hermaskelon* to a safe anchor. The passengers disembarked. While allotting dwelling sites along the river Kallada, the village headman wanted to know to which caste they belonged to for which they had no answer. He pursued further for an answer.

"Do you eat meat?" No was the prompt answer.

"Do you drink wine?" Was the next query.

The Essene elder explained, "We neither eat meat nor drink wine. We eat only vegetarian food. We do not use any ornaments or perfume our body. We pray three times a day and purify ourselves with cold water several times a day. We believe living close to nature is living close to God. Our guiding rules of living are that 'You shall not kill, You shall not commit adultery, You shall not steal, You shall not bear false witness and You shall not covet others' property, among other rules'."

"Then you should be Brahmins!" exclaimed the village headman. "I suspected this seeing your tuft of hair and the white wraparound dress. Why are you not speaking Sanskrit then?" Was his next question.

"We speak Aramaic and pray to God Almighty," answered the Essene elder.

"Then you cannot be included in the present group of four castes. Let yours be the fifth caste." The confused village headman announced. "You are the favorites of the Pandyan king of whom we are all subjects. We will accept you as 'alien brahmins' for your food habits, purity of living and Godfearing nature." He looked at Yona like a boy who had solved a riddle.

Yona smiled and thanked the headman.

In the meantime, Rome was preparing for another triumphal march, of general Lucullus's victory of the Mithridatic war.

12

The Triumph

The *Hermaskalon* set sail across the open Eritrean Sea once the north-east monsoon was well established in December. Light northerly winds began in October and gained speed during November-December and kept blowing in the north and north-east direction till the end of March. It was a gracious wind, clear and balmy with occasional rains. It was a blessing for the sails providing constant wind speed. Lightning and heavy downpour often accompanied the rains, but it was nothing but an occupational hazard.

The ship was fully loaded with black pepper, collected over the years from forest produce and from the first harvest of the garden established by Yona. It comprised of five thousand talents (150 tons) of black pepper secured in tightly woven coir sacks. The sweet and pungent aroma of the spice was strong in the air and the crew preferred to rest on the dock than on hammocks in the hold. Ruan assisted Yona in procuring pearls from Korkai, cinnamon and malabathrum from his hometown Taprobane island.

The king's men were also happy with the gold they collected as customs duty. The Pandyan king finally was able to provide a source of income with a new product line through ports of the newly captured western shores of his kingdom. The only disheartening thought for Yona was the fate of the Phoenician escort vessel shipwrecked near the Indian coast. One piece of news he gathered was that a group of men who were shipwrecked were now constructing ships for the kingdom of Eli in the north and Yona hoped that they were the shipwrecked Phoenicians, and they were safe. Yona hoped to meet them again.

Twenty days of steady wind brought them to Socotra island. Water, provisions and aloe juice were loaded, and they were ready to sail to the African shore where Egyptian navy vessels would join the voyage. Essene elders in Socotra came to meet Yona.

"By the grace of God Almighty, the voyage was successful, and all our people are safe and were well received by the king's men. House plots were allotted along a sweet water river reminiscent of the mighty Jordan. Many more can travel to Malabar to support the cultivation and the trade of black pepper in the yearly voyages we are planning with more ships." Yona gave a hurried report to the elders and joined the ship heading to Myos Hormus.

No customs duty was paid at any port once they left Malabar and the Egyptian port officials at Myos Hormus took a detailed survey of the merchandise on landing and taxed twenty percent ad valorem.

Everybody was happy. Captain Hippalos had his scroll ready with maps for charting the route to Malabar for subsequent voyages. Arillus came down to Coptos to receive the explorers and the merchandise.

He handed an invitation to Yona from general Lucullus to attend his triumphal victory procession over the eastern kings. The Roman senate had finally approved the triumph after three years of waiting.

"We have a good present for general Lucullus." Arillus gazed at the heap of pepper sacks. "The first payment of dividend on his investment itself is enormous! We will be able to repeat this voyage every year now with multiple ships. We have conquered the eastern trade and fulfilled his dream."

"The best part is that the Pandyan king wants us to repeat the domestication of the pepper vines wherever possible in his kingdom under his protection. Their customs duty is half of what we pay to the Egyptian treasury!" Yona exclaimed.

At Coptos, the merchandise was moved to the transport vessels of the Nile and it was decided to load it to the ship owned by the consortium mid-sea heading for Rome.

The port of Alexandria cleared the goods based on a letter issued by the stratego, the minister for Red Sea operations, posted at Coptos. Lucullus sent a message to Arillus and Yona to wait for him at his villa at Naples before heading to Rome. And the first black pepper ship took to the clear waters of the Mediterranean on a voyage to Naples. The big sea was pirate free, thanks to the iron hand of Pompey destroying pirates on all the shores of the sea before he embarked on the hunt for King Mithridates – an assignment earlier given to Lucullus.

"How did the Indian authorities receive the *Hermaskelon?*" Arillus was impatient to hear the story of the Indian adventure.

"You wouldn't believe it." Yona gazed at the eastern horizon. "They were waiting to arrest me at the orders of the new king! A great war had taken place while I was here, and the political equation changed dramatically. Pandyan king, the new ruler defeated all his opponents and is now the sole ruler of the spice country. The pearls, the silk which they import, the ivory and most of the spices sold here is coming from the ports of southern India. My benefactor king, on whose kingdom the pepper plantations are established, also died in war. I was really in a fix. I asked the passengers and the crew to wait in the ship till I returned and went with the king's soldiers."

"Oh, this is quite an interesting turn of events." Arillus was all ears.

"Here too, Lord Almighty saved me miraculously. The king remembered me visiting the then king, his uncle, several years back along with the Buddhist monks while in search for large quantities of black pepper. He was young then but acknowledged the goodwill that existed between the monks and the monarchy. My present to the king, exquisitely carved golden citrons in an artfully made silver vase, a true piece of art made by Jewish and Persian artisans, was also appreciated. All his wars were aimed at securing the trade supremacy with the western world and my offer to buy unlimited amounts of pepper in lieu of gold was irresistible for him. I had asked for a flower and got a season of flowers in return by way of rights to cultivate pepper in his kingdom including the newly acquired vassal kingdom and monopoly in trade of black pepper."

"How are your people accepted in the community there?" Arillus had never seen Yona excited about any matter before.

"This is again a blessing of providence," Yona continued. "The Indian society is divided into priestly class, warriors, traders and artisans and the laborer class. The living and eating habits are different for each class. Our strict religious practices as members of the Essene community, our vegetarian food habits and abstinence from wine made them identify with us along with the priestly class, accepting us as an alien priestly class. This gave us a lot of advantages in establishing a firm ground in finding settlements and locating vacant lands for pepper cultivation."

"Rome also has this class differentiation." Arillus related the Roman picture. "The patricians, the plebeians, the freedman and the slave classification roughly match your Indian society."

"I am not aware of the class difference in Rome, but for the basics." Yona confessed.

"Now that you will be in Rome for some time, a little education will do you good."

The cool morning air with wind speed large enough to rise a spray now and then together with making water caps of foam in the sea gave the ship a decent speed.

Arillus continued, "Rome was founded by Romulus and he selected one-hundred men to form the Roman senate to govern the newly found city. They are called the founding fathers or 'patres' meaning father and their descendants came to be known as patricians. The political and religious power was wholly controlled by the patricians. They also held most of the landed properties which they rented out or cultivated by employing slaves. The rigid rules were relaxed over time, but the mentality of superiority remains firm in the minds of the patricians.

"Plebeians made up for most of the Roman citizens other than the ruling elite. They too had a council but with limited powers. The plebeians were the fighting class and the ruling class depended on them for their war expeditions. But strict rules and capital punishments forced them to bend to the rules, and the spoils of war also lured them to stay disciplined. The plebeians also included farmers, tradesmen and craftsmen."

"I understand the Arilii family is a part of the ruling class." Yona interrupted with his knowledge about Arillus' ancestry.

"Yes, we do belong to the patrician class. My ancestors were not from the first hundred 'patres' but our progress in shipping and the grain business gave us this elevation.

"A third class of men are the freedmen," Arillus continued. One good thing about the slavery in Rome is that it is not racial. Prisoners of war, fugitives, those captured and sold to slavery by the pirates were the Roman slaves, who belonged to many races and countries. They were freed on many counts. They were freed by owners as rewards for good conduct and sometimes the slaves earned enough money to buy their freedom. Such a way out of the slavery made the slaves more obedient. However, freedmen were often attached to the stigma of slavery even if they were rich.

"The last class in the hierarchy are the slaves. They work in private households, in mines and farms. The building of roads, aqueducts and buildings are completed with the sweat and blood of the slaves." Arillus turned to Yona. "Don't you think the Indian class system has a similarity here?"

"Certainly, the pyramid of the society classes has a similarity everywhere because there are dominant and recessive mindsets created in people. You spoke about the unique options of climbing the hierarchical ladder from slave to freedmen and to the upper class in Roman society. This is something the Indian class system does not permit," Yona observed.

"Another interesting aspect of Rome is the pomerium which makes up the true Rome and the rest are only provinces. There are no walls on its boundaries, but white marker stones are placed for demarcation and this is the weapon-free zone, wisely made so to prevent any military takeover. Legally, Rome existed only within the pomerium. The senate house, the open-air auditorium for public meetings which can hold one-hundred and fifty-thousand people, and the Roman forum, all located here, turn the administrative wheel of the government. The temple of Jupiter Optimus Maximus is the prime place within the pomerium." Arillus loved being a part of the Roman elite.

"Where is the Arillii family house located?" For a moment Yona thought it was an unnecessary question.

"We live on the banks of the Tiber river in the Aventine. Trade and commerce are centered around here and that is where our heart is!" Arillus joked. "The villa at Kurena which you are familiar with is almost a replication of my Aventine house." He paused for a while. "Aventine has people of many races and classes and therefore has law and order problems resulting in gang wars and killings. Slave trade and prostitution is mainly the reason for such uprisings.

"Not only in the Aventine, but the senate also is a cauldron of hatred, jealousy and back-biting, even though they feign not to appear so. Our friend general Lucullus had to wait three long years to get his triumphal march approved by the senate. His old enemy Claudius Pulchar was behind this denial, I heard." Arillus was unhappy over the unjust refusal of a triumph to an extraordinarily successful general.

"At Socotra, I have met people running away from Nisibis where Lucullus had sold twenty-thousand Jews into slavery. They claim his downfall started at Nisibis," Yona recollected. "Anyway, we are partners in giving him a victory over trade with India which will take Rome to even bigger heights. I would like to think that his biggest success is conquering Indian trade bypassing the Parthians and the Nabateans without really conquering them. Yona turned to Arillus, "Have you witnessed a triumphal procession?" Yona inquired.

"There is always a triumphal procession almost every three to four years as Roman legions have reached all shores of the Mediterranean and brought victory and massive wealth as spoils of war. The triumphal procession is approved by the senate on fulfilling strict conditions of victory. Firstly, the general should have conquered a new territory. Secondly, the general be acclaimed an imperator, meaning emperor, by his legions for his military strategy and leadership. Thirdly, he must meet the senate and formally request permission for a triumph. This has a catch. He cannot enter the pomerium, but the senate will meet him outside the pomerium. The senate will take a decision on his request and as the fourth requirement, a list of the general's accomplishments is to be submitted to the senate. The fifth stage is the voting by the senate. Arguments for and against by his friends and foe at the senate will decide the fate of the approval. It will have to go through another hurdle after winning the senatorial vote. This is the approval of the plebian assembly. Many approvals for a triumph ceremony missed to reach this stage in the past," Arillus explained.

"No wonder it took three years for general Lucullus to reach this stage with the number of jealous people in power rallying against him. It is the wealth he amassed from the spoils of war that irked people." Yona could see the bigger picture now.

● ● ●

Neopolis or the new city was so called because it became a Roman city less than fifty years ago. It was a favored port for centuries along with other harbors like Puteoli and Misenum on the west coast of Italy in the Gulf of Neopolis. The voyage from Alexandria was long but was familiar to Arillus because his grain ships to Rome took the same route coasting Kurena and Carthage to enter the Tyrrhenian Sea. Merchantmen vessels and the Roman navy ships constantly plied in the gulf.

"This bay was once a Greek settlement, my ancestors lived here before resettling to Rome." Arillus was nostalgic about the place though he never lived here. "This inlet of the Tyrrhenian Sea positioned the bay at the south-west coast of southern Italy and the city of Neopolis which later came to be known as Napoli. Cape Misenum and the Isle of Ischia to the north and the Isle of Capri to the south help to position the city. The volcanic mountain Vesuvius also flanks the bay. With its natural beauty of the landscape, pleasant climate, medicative sulfuryl springs and clear turquoise waters, it is a bay of luxury for a relaxed living. It is natural for general Lucullus to build a villa here after the hectic eastern wars."

"The easy and luxurious lives of the eastern kings must have influenced Lucullus in contrast to the rigors of the Roman life," Yona murmured.

The general's men in escort boats guided the vessel to berth. After clearing the documentation, the cargo was moved to the warehouses. "The villa is located on the Monte Miseno and you can follow the stairs leading to it," the attendant said, pointing to the elaborate ramp climbing the short hill on the shore.

Yona climbed the ramp and looked around. Mount Vesuvius was in clear sight and the vastness of the turquoise bay along with it was a pleasing panorama. The villa was of a square design with a vast main building, several dining rooms, sleeping chambers and bath houses, separated from the main building with a colonnade. There was a grand pool close to the main building leading to a vast library and banqueting hall. The pool overlooked the bay, feeling like an extension of the bay. The villa had high walls for privacy. The natural sulphur baths were close to the vast garden. A canal was built with sluices letting sea water into a large pond where live fish were stored.

The library was vast and ornate with marble columns capped with Corinthian capitals and floors paved with marble slabs. A long line of shelves along the wall filled with books were placed close to the seats and side tables for the readers facilitated interaction among readers.

More than his private entertainment, he has designed the villa as a medium to transfer a relaxed lifestyle to the Roman elite. War and politics deprived Romans of intellectual entertainment and tasteful cuisine, Yona thought.

The dining rooms were ornate and luxurious. The couches had exquisite gold and silver artwork. Many guests could be entertained in the many dining halls and poolside facility. A walkway led to the pergola at the top of the hill with plush seats and fireplace.

Yona wanted to see the kitchen. Halfway up the ramp from the bay area, there were large warehouses, work area supplying the kitchen with ingredients for specific recipes and further on were the living quarters of the cooks and assistants. They spoke corrupt Greek and some even knew Aramaic being culinary experts from the palace of the Armenian King Tigranes.

"What do you do with the black pepper we brought from India?" Yona asked the chief chef.

"First of all, I have not come across such fresh and aromatic black pepper, not to mention the enormous quantity you brought." He praised the most valuable ingredient of his menu.

"We have fresh meat, fish and aviary kept alive and it is slain only when a guest asks for it. The garden grows fruits and vegetables we need. The exotic ingredients are preserved in various forms. Black pepper was always in short supply but most of our recipes call for it in some form or the other. We use crushed pepper, ground pepper, finely ground pepper, pepper sauce, cook dishes with pepper, boil pepper with broth, moistened pepper rubbed with meat and use whole pepper in dishes. Most of our guests love a sprinkle of black pepper or white pepper on every serving. Now that we have such fresh pepper, our dishes will be loved more." He was thrilled to explain. "We use it right from the appetizer to the dessert," he added.

"Take the case of spiced wine for instance, it is the black pepper which gives it the wild flavor in this starter drink. The chopped meat, fish or sausage that goes as starters all have a generous dash of black pepper as well. Ground pepper goes with all vegetarian dishes along with other eastern spices like clove, ginger and malabathrum. Whole pepper is used in many pot-boiled dishes as a main serving. A fish stew is never perfect without a liberal mix of black pepper also it is medicine when used in legumes with silphium.

"We serve fowl here and have stocked them live here for our masters' other villas too. Meat is also preserved well with a generous amount of black pepper and salt. Ostrich, duck, goose or chicken dishes are never complete without black or white pepper. Pullum Parthicum (Parthian style chicken) is cooked almost every day here and our master loves it. It uses black pepper in various stages of preparation.

"The sumptuous dishes of pork and sheep and beef also take in a good share of black pepper to give it the oriental aroma and taste. Wild species of pepper are exotic and hence our guests like it very much. All those ladies enquiring about the ingredients end the search when it comes to black pepper. It is simply not available in the market and Jewish merchants sell small quantities at cut-throat prices. If black pepper is made cheaper, Rome's elite would gobble a shipload for the magic it adds to a dish." He loved his audience in Yona.

Black pepper is aptly called the black gold, Yona thought.

Lucullus' arrival was delayed by a few more days. Arillus and Yona decided to explore the hot baths of Baiae, a resort town where the elite had their summer villas. The town was in close vicinity to Lucullus' villa and a horse-driven wagon dropped them at the baths. Due to volcanic activity, sulphurated hot water springs were a specialty there. The rich and famous came from Rome and other Roman provinces but only the rulers and the super-rich had villas there. There were many public baths with steps leading to the pool where hot water was circulated artificially. Life-size statues of Venus and Apollo stood at the entrance, and inside, there were many in similar posture in the nude.

"In the bathhouse too, we are trained to see nude bodies only as live statues and therefore nudity is not considered obscene here." Arillus was defending himself against the overclothed easterners.

After an invigorating bath, they walked the colonnaded pathways and the well-paved roads. On the sides of the building, especially those leading to a side road, there were obscene graffiti with names against the characters. Yona looked at one with the name Lucullus.

It depicted Lucullus' wife Claudia in bed with her brother Claudius, the arch enemy of the general.

"The media available to tarnish people in position is the graffiti here. There are many here on almost all walls, some are invitations by prostitutes for sexual orgies. This is obscene and can attract death penalties but in the rat race to fame and power fanning a gossip is one way of gaining power." Arillus was a bit annoyed.

Yona kept quiet. For an Essene monk practicing celibacy and believing that procreation was the only purpose of mating, this was a world upside down. An overemphasized physiological need and the various ways of its gratification was clearly depicted in this graffiti glorifying libido. Men, women, children and animals were the means of achieving it. Graffiti depicted birth control methods, aphrodisiacs, love potions, and various coital acts as an open encyclopedia.

"I have heard about temples in India with thousands of statues displaying acts of lovemaking as part of their religious wisdom." Yona broke the silence.

"Marriages for the rich and powerful is a compromise for enhancing position. Look at the marriages of general Lucullus. He married from one of Rome's oldest and noblest patrician families," Arillus explained. "Clodia Pulchra was the daughter of Consul Appius Claulius Pulchar who died before her marriage. Publius Clodius Pulchar, her brother gave permission for the marriage who was in financial difficulties at the time of her marriage. Lucullus did not even accept the customary dowry for the hand of Clodia who was exceptionally beautiful. But the Clodia family was a problematic lot. Their incestuous, lesbian and multi-dimensional debauchery shamed Lucullus. Brother-in-law Pulchar, serving as a commander was responsible for the mutiny in Lucullus' army at Nisibis. His incestual relationship with all his sisters made Lucullus divorce Clodia. He and Memmius were behind delaying the triumph which Lucullus deserved three years ago. The current marriage is even more problematic. After the divorce from Clodia he married Servilia, half-sister to Cato the Younger of Utica. Lucullus was governor at Utica, the Roman city of Carthage conquered it during Punic war, and Cato's philosophical leanings towards stoic teachings brought them together. Cato was known for his moral integrity and immunity to bribes. This marriage also turned disastrous for Lucullus when he found her unfaithful to him and was discovered in the arms of his enemy Memmius."

"Is the law against adultery weak? Or is it the outlook of society creating this sexual anarchy?" Yona interrupted.

"The law is strong, only it is tilted in favor of men. The sturdy principles of morality on which Rome had her foundations are now diluted. Adulterous women were severely punished in earlier times though men could escape such punishment on the ground that home was the responsibility of women. The moral decadence you see now is the result of success Rome had in her wars. Prisoners of war of both sexes, beautiful slaves from exotic cultures and the adoption of luxurious lifestyles of the conquered countries corrupted Roman society. Divorces made women rich, independent with disregard to the concept of family who turned their attention to money, power and politics. Birth control, use of aphrodisiacs and love potions brought new dimensions to the orgies along with cross-dressing, trans-sexualism and same sex lovers. Buggery, beasts and brothels completes the list." The displeasure of Arillus was evident in his words. "Baiae and Pompei are the fore-runners in Roman debauchery."

"This story is similar to that of Sodom and Gomorrah before its destruction." Yona compared the cites as the wrath of God came down on man's excesses and burned the cities and submerged it in the Dead Sea without a trace as given in the Jewish Bible.

"I only wish Baiae and Pompeii be saved by Jupiter from such an end." Arillus hoped. Both cites were destroyed by natural calamities during later years.

● ● ●

Lucullus came to Napoli to meet Arillus and Yona. "You cannot imagine how happy I am to meet you after your successful voyage to India. You did the impossible and I am dying to hear the details. The vast quantities of black pepper you have brought in cannot have a better timing. I have planned the triumphal feasts to have an eastern menu and the cooks we brought from Armenia cannot cook anything without your wonder spice. Right from the welcome drink to the dessert there is no dish without a dash of black pepper. It is selling at four denarius a pound (12 ounces) and imagine the value of the booty you carried with you. I am really impressed and if the Roman elite embrace it, your wonder spice will value more than gold here!" The victorious general in him was aroused once again long after the conquest of Tigranocerta.

"Our five ships in the Red Sea can make these voyages every year and bring in five times the cargo we carried. The plantations established in India and the goodwill of the local kings secured by Yona can ensure an unlimited supply of black pepper." Arillus was proud that the one-thousand talents Lucullus invested in the business had already provided an equal return on investment.

"Over the past fifty years, I was living with a burden of a prophecy on me. The chief monk of our monastery at Qumran had prophesied while sending me to Alexandria to study that I would be the savior of the Essene community from annihilation. I have successfully settled many of my community members in the pepper plantations already, and if the demand for pepper can reach your estimates, I will be able to settle many more Essenes there." Yona shared the happiness of a successful mission.

Callisthenes, the freedman responsible for the general's culinary matters came in with some cool beverage.

Lucullus urged the guests to partake. "This is a love potion he makes for me to wield away the blues of political setbacks postponing my triumph. Now, blues or red, it keeps my spirits high."

"What is it made of?" enquired Yona.

"It has almonds, pistachio, various other seeds, black pepper, honey and milk. It also has a secret ingredient brought from Himalayan mountains of India called *bhang*." The freedman explained.

"I presume it is Indian hemp, a very potent hallucinating drug. The drink is cool, but I prefer the drink without your secret ingredient." Yona was a bit upset as he had already taken a sip and combined laughter rose at his expense. Yona was laughing easier with the drink taking effect.

Lucullus dismissed the freedman and asked for his favorite Pullum Parthicum for lunch. The monk here was a vegetarian, he was reminded.

"I have invited the elite of Rome for a dinner here for an early celebration of the triumph and propose to serve this love potion as a welcome drink. Among the takeaway, this silver pepper shaker filled with the fresh black pepper is included." Lucullus displayed an exquisitely carved silver shaker. "The Roman elite will see this on every meal and ask for more of your Indian wonder spice." He laughed aloud.

Arillus joined the laughter which sounded like the tinkling of the gold aureus. (One aureus is equal to twenty-five denarii.)

The party turned out to be a splendid event. Many guests came early and visited the sulfur baths of Baiae and Pompeii. Several senators had villas in Napoli and an invitation from Lucullus was more than welcome. Several magisterial incumbents gladly accepted the invitation as the Lucullan triumph was finally approved.

Lucullus paraded the long line of cooks from the palace of the Armenian King Tigranes and the scantily clad serving girls from the east in their traditional dancing dress gave an exotic touch to the evening. Choir groups and flute girls added to the promise of a great evening. The dining halls, the poolside, and the library seating were already full of guests. The Roman elite and friends gathered to felicitate Lucullus' victory over King Mithridates and Armenian King Tigranes. Handsome and celebrated men and exotic beauties filled the villa appreciating every aspect of the sumptuous decor. As the guests settled down on the marvelously carved gilded couches of ivory, welcoming the guests, Lucullus highlighted some curious aspects of eastern living.

"The welcome drink being passed around is made of secret ingredients from the Himalayan mountains of India. It has similarities to the hemp smoked here but is very potent. Most of the dishes being served today, made by the expert hands of the chefs of King Tigranes, have an ingredient called 'black pepper' which comes from southernmost tip of India. My friend Yona of Jericho has procured it with great ingenuity. He will relate the story of his voyage. His exploration was made possible by the experience and support of my friend Arillus, a Roman citizen doing shipping and banking business based out of Alexandria. You already know my friend poet Archias who was with me during the wars I fought against King Mithridates and

King Tigranes and various other eastern kingdoms we conquered. He will recite some poetic creations on the wars. I remember my friend Antiochus of Ascalon, the philosopher who paved the way for a middle platonic path from the school he originated, who sadly lost his life while touring with me in the east.

"We have best wine from Greece, gourmet food from the east, music and dance with an eastern touch, and the great fun of a Roman orgy. Lastly, the dessert is made from sweet cherry fruit of Cerasin originating from the east, unknown to Italy. You can see the trees in fruit in the garden here too."

The welcome drink infused with Himalayan cannabis was already taking effect. People were talking freely, and the class differences were forgotten. The spicy food laced with black pepper suddenly became a hit served as hors d'oeuvres along with the choicest wines.

Poet Aulus Licinius Archias was invited to entertain the audience with a rendition of his poems. He was well known to the Greco-Roman world; he was born in Antioch and came to Rome in his teens as a prodigy in Greek poetry. Lucullus was fascinated by his recitations and became his patron in Rome. Their friendship continued during the Mithridatic wars and he travelled with Lucullus to the east. At the banquet, he recited his poems on all major victories of Lucullus in the east and highlighting the fall of Tigranocerta bringing it down with half the number of soldiers of the Armenians in strength. The applause heightened with the narration of each victory of the Mithridatic war.

Yona recollected similar recitals in the court of Pandyan kings in Madurai. East or west, people think and act the same way once the kernels of cast, creed, color and faith are broken, he thought as he readied himself to recount his tale to the crowd.

The audience listened in rapt attention as Yona related the story of monsoon winds and its reversal which made the travel from Rome to India and back in the same year. The revelation that the open sea voyage reduced travel time and avoided the cost of visiting several ports while travelling along the coastline had great economic value. The taxes such ports charged could be avoided by making the merchandise affordable to the consumer. This affordability could also increase the volume of sales and profit to the trading community. Yona told the gathering that the cost of the produce from India – spices like black pepper and cinnamon, products like pearls and ivory – would be much cheaper for the end consumers by this new open sea voyage. Luxury products like silk and *jadamanasi* or spikenard perfumes would be freely available as the traffic increased. A new era of trade with the east avoiding the land route through Parthia was now possible, Yona concluded.

Arillus spoke about the vast investment opportunity for the wealthy Romans with direct trade with India bypassing the middlemen. He quickly made many new friends during the banquet with the intention to invest in India-bound projects.

Mensae prime, or the main course, was exotic and therefore exciting for the guests. Pheasant, thrush, ostrich, songbird, oysters, lobsters, shellfish, wild boar, peacock, goose and chicken were served. Grilled and roasted meat of various kinds kept the guests busy well past midnight. The food had one ingredient in common – the black pepper Yona brought from India.

Missing dancing girls and occupied anterooms had another story to tell. Ladies shared couches with their lovers, the poolside benches and the pavilion overlooking the sea were in amorous orgy. The discussion in the library was still about the teachings of Antiochus of Ashkelon. Sweet cherry fruits and a silver shaker filled with black pepper was included in the takeaway gifts along with wood carvings of elephants inlaid with ivory.

A few days after the banquet, Arillus and Yona travelled to Tusculum villa, close to Rome in preparation for the triumphal march. Lucullus had already left with the guests.

● ● ●

Tusculum was close to Rome but far enough from the restrictions of the pomerium. It was a hillside resort with a farmland in contrast to the Neopolis coastal villa. Yona thought it had the exotic splendor of the beautiful Armenian hillside and the elegance of the Alexandrian palaces. Many interior dining rooms were exquisitely designed for royal guests with purple silk and gold, large banquet halls and a huge library stocked with the wisdom of the east collected as spoils of war from the two royal palaces of King Mithridates and King Tigranes, made the villa a reflection of the luxurious and laidback lives of the kings of the east in contrast with the fast and furious Roman lives. It excelled the grand library of Alexandria in manuscripts on eastern thought. Leisure and knowledge married here blissfully in the advancement of intellectual pursuits with open-air courtyards and colonnaded seating of black marble imported from Greece.

Another specialty was the grand aviary stocked with various migratory and other exotic birds which made up the fancy menu. At Napoli it was the fish stocked in a protected canal along the sea that added to the vast menu. The villa was large and decorated with rich and rare materials and sculptures.

Artists were working on floats depicting the success stories of the Mithridatic wars Lucullus won which were to be displayed in the triumphal procession. Tableaus consisted of Roman soldiers braving the bears and bees in tunnels while hunting for Mithridates in

Miscyra; depictions of the battle of Cabria and Mithridates fleeing to Armenia; the siege of Amisus and victory and the defection of Mithridates' army; fall of Tigranocerta and fleeing of Tigranes to Artaxata; the attack on Nisibis were all ready for the parade making the story of the war come alive for the public. The city sculptures were freshly painted and decorated.

"Circus Flaminius at the southern end of campus Martius near Tiber river is decorated with a large number of weapons captured during the war. The long battering engines used by the kings to break in forts are also displayed there. Many a triumph I witnessed carried such elaborate weaponry in the procession making it unnecessarily long and tiring, unlike here we have it displayed at one place." Arillus explained.

The tableaus introducing the exotic eastern countries and its conquest were the forerunner in the triumphal parade. Fully armored horsemen led the procession followed by chariots bearing scythes, with their long and glittering blades. Behind were sixty of Mithridates' generals and councilors in chains. Then came the ships. The bronze-beaked ships were one of the favorite weapons of King Mithridates. One-hundred-and-ten ships joined the procession like chariots on wheels. The defeated king was represented by a six-foot gold statue as he could not be captured by Lucullus which remained a blemish in the success story.

King Tigranes' crown and shield set with precious stones followed. One of the purposes of the triumphal processions was to inform the public of the amount of wealth brought into the city of Rome on account of this war and how they benefitted by it. Palanquins of gold and silver beakers set with precious stones carried by men followed leaving onlookers guessing their value. Couches made of gold and silver were then displayed in mule-drawn carts. Fifty-six mules carried ingots of silver. The crowd kept clapping and got tired of clapping when another one-hundred-and-seven mules came bearing silver coins valued at several million denarii. One cart carried a float depicting the bonus paid out of the booty to the soldiers, almost a thousand drachmas to each soldier.

Lucullus, face painted in purple as per the custom, in an all-purple, gold-embroidered triumphal toga appeared in a magnificent golden chariot driven by four majestic white horses. The public thronged behind the barricades along the streets. Multi-colored flags fluttered and the public waved with flowers and olive twigs as Lucullus rode the quadriga wearing all purple reminiscent of the chariot of Jupiter on top of the temple of Capitoline hill. A slave was holding an olive crown over his head.

"Why is the slave holding the olive crown?" Yona whispered to Arillus.

"It is a symbol that the general who triumphs is still a man even though he has achieved a god-like position for the day," Arillus explained.

His soldiers marched behind him gracefully in perfect uniform. Family and friends of Lucullus followed in horse-drawn wagons, Yona and Arillus included.

"It's been almost three years since we have been living in tents here in Campus Martius. What a relief it is to cross the gate in a triumphal procession at last!" exclaimed a soldier.

"Our general has kept us well and paid us a salary without any wars to bother about. At least the family is happy to have us around, I guess," another soldier replied.

"Those cooks from Tigranes' palace changed the way we eat with their eastern spices. But I have no complaints because I feel it was for the good." All were happy by the turn of events.

The procession was now crossing the Porta Triumphalis. It was the arch gate the victorious general on a triumphal march would pass under. During other occasions, they would enter through Porta Carmentalis. Lucullus had provided for temporary seating for the spectators on all available locations. Forum Boarium was the next such location with seating between the hills of Capitoline and Palatine near river Tibor. The procession moved on to Circus Maximus. It was a great stadium between Aventine hills and Palatine which accommodated 150,000 spectators. Receiving cheers and accolades, Lucullus entered the Palatine, the nucleus of the Roman empire. Forum Romanum was next before reaching the destination – the Capitoline hill which was the temple of Jupiter Optimus Maximus. Forum Romanum had all the government buildings, the marketplace where the elections, speeches and criminal trials were held. Even gladiator matches were sometimes held here. This was the most celebrated meeting place of the world and Lucullus remembered the rhetoric and election speeches he had made here during his rise to the most coveted position of counsel of Rome. He was now riding the quadriga to the temple of Jupiter. He had achieved the ultimate a Roman citizen could dream of.

Lucullus remembered his sacrifice at the temple of Jupiter Optimus Maximus on the day of his departure to the east to subdue the venomous opponent of Rome, Mithridates the king of Pontus. Now he was back a victor and as thanksgiving it was custom to sacrifice a bull. The thought that the king was still at large, without giving him the opportunity to finish the game, bothered him while offering the sacrifice to Jupiter at the Capitol.

Lucullus had made a sacrifice at the temple of Hercules at Forum Boarium marking the start of the triumphal procession. He was devoted to Hercules, the god of victory. He dedicated a tenth of his property to the god in thanksgiving. This temple, the Ara Maxima was the biggest temple of Hercules worshipped by soldiers, traders and the cattle breeders. The large ground was also used as a cattle market and as a yard for salt needed for the preservation of meat and cheese production. A herd of fattened oxen was kept ready for the feast there.

Forum Boarium and the grounds of Circus Maximus were converted to festivity arena for citizens once the triumphal procession moved ahead. Tables were set to seat the plebeians of Rome and surrounding villages. The cooks from Armenia rubbed coarsely ground black pepper and salt to the meat marinating it in black pepper sauce with garlic and vinegar, produced an ethereal dish Rome had never tasted. The grilled meat was a favorite among the diners, and they washed it down with one-hundred-thousand jars of choicest Greek wine, each jar containing a quantity equivalent of forty liters.

He also gave the senate a banquet at the Capitol which was customary too. Rows of triclinium couches were spread to serve the senate and the elite. Black pepper was the star there too.

The triumph of Lucullus over King Mithridates coincided with the triumph of black pepper over the palate of the Roman elite, the triumph of eastern thought process on life over the western mindset, and the triumph of Yona in resettling the Essene community in Malabar, also called the Gods own Country.

Yavanapriya, the black pepper from the rainforests of southern India conquered the Roman empire and the hearts and the taste buds of the Romans.

● ● ●

The succeeding centuries saw the Roman gold coins flooding southern Indian kingdoms for trade to the extent that it started hurting the Roman economy. The early Essene settlements later attracted several such migrations from many middle-eastern populations who blended into the society of the present Indian state of Kerala, also known as Malabar. Many thousands of Cochini Jews emigrated to Israel in the 1950s from Kerala. About twenty percent of the population of Kerala state still use Aramaic in their prayers and liturgy and are known as St Thomas Christians. The people of Elam became another strong pillar of the Kerala society. Some scholars claim that the Phoenicians are the predecessors of the Thiya community in northern Kerala populated in the erstwhile kingdom of Eli.

Thank You

Thank You For Reading My Book!

I really appreciate all of your feedback, and I love hearing what you have to say.

I need your input to make the next version of this book and my future books even better.

Please leave me a helpful review on Amazon letting me know what you thought of the book.

Thank you so much!
Easo Varghese

9 7 9 8 7 2 5 5 9 7 6 3 9